Born a Foreigner

Born a Foreigner

A Memoir of the
American Presence in Asia

Charles T. Cross

An ADST-DACOR Diplomats and Diplomacy Book

ROWMAN & LITTLEFIELD PUBLISHERS, INC.
Boulder • Lanham • New York • Oxford

Contents

Foreword

The ADST-DACOR Diplomats and Diplomacy Series

For more than 220 years extraordinary men and women have represented the United States abroad under all kinds of circumstances. What they did and how and why they did it remain little known to their compatriots. In 1995 the Association for Diplomatic Studies and Training (ADST) and Diplomatic and Consular Officers, Retired (DACOR) created a book series to increase public knowledge and appreciation of the involvement of American diplomats in world history. The series seeks to demystify diplomacy by telling the story of those who have conducted our foreign relations, as they saw them and lived them.

Charles T. ("Chuck") Cross spent much of his youth and adult life in China and elsewhere in East Asia, along the way garnering insights he later contributed to the conduct of U.S. diplomacy in the region. Literally "born a foreigner" in Beijing, he and his American missionary family lived under the extraterritorial privileges accorded foreigners before World War II. They also experienced the early Japanese occupation of North China. A decorated United States Marine, Chuck Cross saw World War II combat at the Marshall Islands, Saipan and Tinian in the Marianas, and Iwo Jima. During his thirty-two years as a distinguished Foreign Service officer, he saw the first years of Indonesia's independence and Malaysia's Communist insurgency, participated in the Laos talks with Averell Harriman, served in Vietnam as chief of pacification operations in I Corps, and was ambassador to Singapore (1969–1971) and consul general in Hong Kong (1974–1977). When the United States established diplomatic relations with the People's Republic of China and moved its embassy to Beijing in 1979, Ambassador Cross resigned from the Foreign Service to become the first director of the American Institute in Taiwan. He describes his unique mission in Taipei as two years of action-crammed "real" diplomacy.

In *Born a Foreigner,* Ambassador Cross shares intensely recalled experiences of wars hot and cold. Endowed with extraordinary sensitivity and skills, he pursued his country's political objectives through diplomacy in a life that parallels the story of America's presence in Asia in the twentieth century.

Edward M. Rowell, President, ADST
Kenneth N. Rogers, President, DACOR

Preface

There are many countries in between, but I begin and end with China. In a loose and unsentimental way my story parallels America's experiences with Asia. During the early decades of the twentieth century, the United States was seen by many Chinese as benignly different from the other big powers, and more appealing because of the American missionaries and educators who served China. In the late 1930s U.S. opposition to Japan's seizure of China sparked the Japanese madness at Pearl Harbor. We were China's ally in the Pacific War and drove out the Japanese invaders. Only a few years later the People's Republic of China (PRC) was our big enemy in Korea and forced the permanent division of that country. In Vietnam, the PRC's support for North Vietnam limited United States ground actions to South Vietnam, and Mao Zedong's doctrine of continuous revolution contributed to American policymakers' determination to persist in a failing war.

Even after the Cold War, China entered into American calculations about other countries: our security obligations to Japan, for example; the widespread effect of China's trade practices on our other trading partners; U.S. relations with the former Central Asian possessions of the old Soviet Union and with Russia itself. The Southeast Asian countries all have China connections and influential ethnic Chinese populations. Our relations with China determine the thinking of all these countries about the solidity of United States policies toward them.

My title, *Born a Foreigner*, is also directly relevant to China. The special privileges for foreigners in China before World War II conditioned how Americans lived there and their contacts with Chinese. These extraterritorial rights had been exacted by foreign powers and influenced the Chinese reaction to Americans. The interaction between individuals was subtle, not ordinarily unfriendly, but of a special character that left its marks on both. Significantly, three of the first five American ambassadors to Beijing after the full normalization of relations in 1979 and the first two directors of the American Institute in Taiwan in Taipei came from this background. Being born a "foreigner" in China carries with it a lifetime load of baggage: attitudes, affections, possibly even insights, which I have taken from country to country in Asia. These show up here in subjective snatches of my personal history.

I have a long family connection. My parents and an aunt were involved in the stormy intellectual life of twentieth-century revolutionary China in the 1920s and 1930s as liberal, socially conscious Christian missionaries—members of a distinct, influential element in modern Chinese history. Despite many disappointments, they never wavered in their belief that their message, with its broad visions of education and social justice, could contribute to the modernization of China, always in peaceful ways. Their emphasis, they felt, was essentially American and accounted for our moralistic approach to U.S.-China policy—which they approved, but opened up Chinese affairs to political exploitation, which they disliked—two sides of the same coin still circulating at the end of the twentieth century. Their example is a reason for writing this book.

My parents taught that there are elements of national character that lie behind such things as military might, even victories, economic successes, and technological superiority in so many fields. These intangibles give American strengths meaning and utility in modern international relations. What kind of people others think we are adds to the effectiveness of policies we advocate officially, or defeats their purposes. I was taught these principles in respect to my behavior as a missionary child in China, but as a Foreign Service officer I was skeptical of American idealism and often forgetful of its strength.

A national image of a reliable, stable, forward-looking, imaginative, cooperative, and courageous people goes with our carriers, our airlines, our embassies, our American-supported schools and hospitals, our myriad, constantly increasing companies, our missionaries, our Peace Corps volunteers, our traveling college students, our research scholars, our ubiquitous journalists, our hotels, the millions of our tourists—all making up a total American foreign policy. Because of the simplicity of this idea of an unorganized national way of doing things, it has often been discounted.

Despite the fact that the United States government has only modest influence—to say nothing of control—over the behavior of its private citizens abroad, the Foreign Service tries to set the symbolic style for American dealings with other countries by the way it conducts its regular complex business: in trade negotiations, in issuing visas, in intelligence operations, in advising on investments, by the way Foreign Service families behave toward their host countries, by what individual officers say publicly and privately to foreigners about American policies and domestic developments, and by the accuracy and tone of our reports to Washington.

Even if the Foreign Service performed perfectly in these and so many other ways, rather than just very well, it would be hobbled without the confidence-building strength of the American presence—the Americans, foreigners abroad. That is the theme of this intensely personal story of my lifetime—one worth recording, I believe, as Americans concentrate on the present in foreign affairs. *Born a Foreigner* is essentially one American's account of parts of that American presence in East Asia: missionaries and educators, Marines, and the professional Foreign Service and its families as my family and I have experienced them for over eighty years.

Acknowledgments

We joined the Foreign Service in 1949. It had been my ambition since high-school days, and my wife, Shirley, not only accepted it sight unseen but made it her own as well. Neither of us anticipated how much partnership such a career would entail nor how much pleasure and fatigue would be combined in serving our country in this way. The "needs of the Service"—a phrase in vogue in the State Department from time to time— sent us to eleven posts abroad and gave us several assignments in Washington during our thirty-two years.

Shirley bore the greater burden. This imbalance was in keeping with the times when we started, and I took it for granted far too long. She did all the packing; planned the logistics of our many moves; saw to the children's adjustments to new schools, new cultures, and new friends, and then too soon afterward reconciled them to the wrenching good-byes as we moved on to some other place. Throughout our service she lived by the professional code of the old-fashioned hierarchical Foreign Service system with its close attention to the rank of the husband. She accepted as part of her job the ceaseless official demands on her time—too many of them trivial or foolish—because in common with other Foreign Service wives of that period, she felt that she had a recognized place in representing the United States. This was a special strength of the Foreign Service of our time. She is the first person I thank for helping, advising, and editing *Born a Foreigner* through its several transformations.

Our children, Ann Edmonds, Kathy Leutner, and Richard Cross, their spouses, and our grandchildren put me up to writing a memoir. They saw that my stories were imaginatively improving with age and wished to get definitive versions down before things got out of hand. They laughed, urged speed, installed the personal computer, typed some of the manuscript, mourned cuts, suggested additions, and were supportive throughout. They have been short-changed in the final text but know they are much loved and appreciated.

My parents, Rowland M. Cross and Adelle Tenney Cross, helped inadvertently because they both died before I had even thought of such a project. However, they had kept and turned over to us all my letters from World War II and those about our Foreign Service experiences. They also gave us their journals, diaries, and copies of their letters home from China in the 1920s and 1930s, plus their own oral histories. They had earlier spurred happy, detailed memories of my childhood by long talks after I had grown up. These papers, supplemented by my own journals, have been my chief sources outside those mentioned in the endnotes.

Several friends have read earlier drafts. Robert Dawson and his sister Meg Hellyer; Helen Saunders, a schoolmate at the North China American School in the 1930s; Lucian W. Pye, Ford professor emeritus of International Studies at MIT, my friend from our earliest childhood days in China, who loaned me his versions of some of our joint escapades; and Daniel Chirot, professor of international studies and sociology at the Jackson School of International Studies of the University of Washington, who suggested some vital cuts and a narrowed concentration on Asia.

Others have commented on parts. Roger Hackett, professor emeritus of Japanese history at the University of Michigan, a Carleton classmate, and fellow Marine 1943 graduate of the Navy Japanese Language School at Boulder, Colorado, read the sections on World War II; Ambassador Terry McNamara, a Foreign Service model of courage and responsibility under fire during the last days in Vietnam, looked over the long sections on Vietnam; William J. Duiker, professor emeritus of history at Penn State, advised on the Vietnam and Laos sections; Hildy Shishkin, Averell Harriman's supremely competent assistant, refreshed and straightened out my memories of the famous diplomat; David Dean, a retired Foreign Service officer and the first Washington director of the American Institute in Taiwan, critiqued my coverage of the first years of that unusual unofficial entity.

Ambassador Howard B. Schaffer, a friend from Kuala Lumpur days in the 1950s, read enough of the manuscript to encourage me to contact Margery B. Thompson, publishing director of the Association for Diplomatic Studies and Training (ADST). She has included *Born a Foreigner* in the ADST-DACOR Diplomats and Diplomacy Series and has invariably been a source of encouragement, editorial advice, and sound guidance on the details of book publishing.

Susan McEachern, Executive Editor, and Karen Johnson, Assistant Editor, at Rowman & Littlefield were especially kind and gracious to this amateur.

I owe profound thanks to all the above for their patience, intelligence, and friendship. Suffice to say I have had ample advice.

This acknowledgment allows me to thank some very close colleagues: the Foreign Service secretaries who served with us—all of them brave, good humored, intelligent, skilled, cool in crises. They kept it all together and made things work. We were good friends. We've lost touch with some of them, others have changed their last names, and several have died, so they are listed as we knew them when: Laddie Grimes, Jakarta; Berry Marshall and Mariellen Wilson, Hong Kong I; Inga Tufte, Kuala Lumpur; Pat Saunders and Pearl Hovdet, Alexandria; Millie Stewart and Sonya Foggie, Washington; June Ward, Nicosia; Vivian Gallas, Danang; Sally Smith for nearly six years in Singapore and Hong Kong II; and Dorothy Pascoe, Taipei. They are all in this book but not by name, and their places in our lives must be recognized.

Chapter 1

Born a Foreigner

I told my easily startled, blue-eyed Vermont grandmother that Lenin was the first dead man I had ever seen. We were washing dishes in a pleasant little house in the Walker Missionary home in Auburndale, Massachusetts; I was describing a moist summer day a few months earlier in 1931. I was nine.

My parents and I had stood for three hours in the long silent line in Moscow's Red Square before our turn came to pass the rigid sentries and look quickly into the illuminated glass box at the bearded face of the man who had already become familiar from pictures and statues all across Russia. My father had told me who Lenin was and why the Russians were so unusually orderly and quiet. He had explained that the face, which was really all that we could see, "belonged" to Lenin, but the body and face were no longer the "real" Lenin, which was, of course, his soul. Or, as the Russians were to insist, his memory.

My mother, less tolerant of this worship of the dead and more practical in all things, had, as usual, concentrated on manners. I shouldn't laugh about anything—an inexplicable warning in the light of what was about to happen—and, in what seemed to her the ultimate safeguard against indiscretion, I was to speak only in Chinese. I was frightened, crushed by the heavy solemnity of the slowly shuffling Russians.

The three of us were in a party of American missionaries, professors at Chinese universities, medical doctors and their families, whose every-seventh-year sabbatical, or "furlough," coincided, and who chose the European route "home" to the United States. We had traveled just above the bottom "hard class" from Beijing to Moscow, and we would fervently continue to seek out the cheapest rail fares and lodgings in nine other European countries on the way to New York—a four-month journey.

The passage through Russia began the first big change in my life. I had been used to a world divided into a few "foreigners," like those in our

1

party, who could be addressed in English, and boundless numbers of Chinese, to whom it was even easier to talk. In Beijing, I lived in a mission compound with other missionary families and Chinese Christians. The atmosphere in this enclave, though hectic because of the two famous large high schools for Chinese boys and girls, was warm and kind. Any rudeness or violence I saw was outside the compound gates in the streets and alleys of the huge city. It was always Chinese to Chinese, and so somehow comprehensible. I understood, as much as I understood anything, that Christians and "foreigners" were expected to behave differently.

An unpredictable world appeared suddenly to me in the Russianized city of Harbin, in Manchuria, far to the north. My Manchu amah, Wang Nai Nai, talked and acted as much Chinese as anyone else and had never been out of Beijing. So, although my father had explained how Manchuria was like the American Midwest (which I had never seen) with its wide plains, cornfields, and wheat farms, I didn't expect to see a city full of not quite right "foreigners."

Russians, or, to be more exact, people who had been driven from Russia by the communist revolution and civil war, at that time almost outnumbered Chinese in Harbin, and it was the sight of all these "foreigners" that introduced harsh and disturbing edges into my model of the world. Shouting *droshky* drivers used strange language as they competed for the fare to drive us around the city. (Beijing still had carriages, but we never rode in them because my mother thought the drivers mistreated the horses—which they did.) People were swimming in the muddy river. "Foreigners" not behaving properly. What would the Chinese think? That determining question for a missionary child was unanswerable because there were no Chinese around to ask.

Our departure from Beijing had been sad. There had been the customary large crowd of Chinese friends bearing last-minute inconvenient presents of fruit, but the only person I remember was Wang Nai Nai, who had been with me all my life. My mother's journal mentions her presence at the station almost incidentally, but even after almost seventy years, I can still picture her parting gestures. She didn't cry because she had often said that would be bad luck—an omen she thought I should take seriously. But I was told later that she had been inconsolable for weeks. She patted me on the shoulder and probably said something traditional like, "Be sure to obey your parents." I don't remember crying either, perhaps because I was afraid of being impolite, a worry around Wang Nai Nai.

Otherwise, the trip started well. There were other missionary children in the party, and we were all familiar with the train because we had taken it every year to Beidaihe, now a famous retreat for the highest Chinese officials but then a resort on the Yellow Sea to which foreign families went for the entire summer. Even without the help of my mother's journal, I still remember talking to Chinese soldiers in dirty gray uniforms who were guarding the station at Shanhaiguan, where the Great Wall comes down to the sea from the hills at its eastern end, an everlasting boundary between China proper and Manchuria. I see, too, the Yamato Hotel in Mukden (Shenyang), which my mother described as the best we stayed in between Peking and New York and which was remarkably clean even to my uncritical eye (a characteristic that to this day, and maybe just because of that experience, has set Japan and the Japanese apart for me). I remember playing in the train corridors with a Japanese boy and talking to him in Chinese and, finally, on a hot June morning arriving at Harbin.

There were other jolts at the Russian border. The baggage of "foreigners," always exempt from official attention in China, was piled in a shed and searched by other "foreigners"—the Russians. My mother recorded that the customs officers were polite enough to us but very thorough, and that the process took hours because Russians going back home were taxed on everything they had, even their extra clothing. I was charged with guarding our possessions while the grown-ups went from counter to counter pursuing the formalities. I watched nervously as the guards kept coming back to circle our pile of wicker suitcases, which, meager as they were, represented much more than anything the Russians had. The guards seemed to treat civilian Russians with a casual rudeness I had never seen before.

In 1931, the Trans-Siberian Railroad was still single tracked for hundreds of miles, so there were long stops at stations to let the trains going east pass by. Most of these trains were prison trains bound for Siberia or the Soviet Far East. Although the people staring silently from behind the bars didn't look any worse clothed than the other Russians who crowded the platforms to watch the crossing of the trains, I could sense that my parents were depressed by what they saw. I only understood their emotions after talks with them over the years. Such scenes conditioned their thinking about revolutions for the rest of their lives because they had come to the Soviet Union to study something that wasn't there.

The missionaries of that generation looked on China as a testing ground, and the competition between creeds was a conscious part of their daily lives. The struggle was modern in spirit—no longer just between Christianity and what was labeled Chinese superstition plus Manchu venality as it had been in earlier decades. It was fought on many levels with many weapons, ranging from sermons carefully prepared by my father and checked with his Chinese teacher, to the problem of whether American missionaries should take a public position against extraterritoriality (the right of foreigners to be tried according to their own laws), as my father did, or take advantage of the protection that extraterritoriality provided to conduct missionary activity without the danger of being arrested by warlords. It extended to the organization of kindergartens around the city, which my mother succeeded in doing. It went down to the proper reply to insults on the street and how much to add to the rickshaw fare for bad weather. All were interconnected in their minds; everything, all the time, was involved. At our house I heard "China is changing" as a stirring development about as often as "Let's bow our heads and ask the Lord's blessing" as a thankful routine. By the time I was nine, I even understood a bit about the contending elements in the struggle for the "New China."

Most obvious of these was Chinese nationalism, which I knew about very early from the strikes and demonstrations at the two schools on our compound—usually explained simply as "China being treated unfairly." I'd hear anti-foreign remarks in the streets, which I understood perfectly, so that, although I was well aware of being different from Chinese, I couldn't quite grasp why they would say such things about me, who had been born there and talked like one of them.

I knew nothing about the communists except that my mother said they were very brave. Once I stood with her and watched two trucks taking what she told me years later were "young communists" to the execution grounds outside the city. They were singing and became, perhaps because of something she had said, forever mixed in my mind with the hymn-singing Chinese Christians martyred by the Boxers only three decades before—part of missionary lore.

Then there was Christianity, which in my parents' case was regarded as inseparable from democracy, social and economic justice, racial equality, modern science, and pacifism—all ideals I heard about constantly.

Thus, because they were conscientious in all things, my parents and the other adults in the traveling party simply wished to see in the Soviet Union—carefully and straightforwardly, without prejudgment (even I think hopefully)—what communism could mean to a country they thought was almost as poor and mistreated by its former rulers as China itself.

My father, Rowland McLean Cross, came to China in 1917 fresh from the Oberlin Seminary to do "student work." His advance appointment to a specific job was a small but significant departure from the earlier procedures of the American Board of Commissioners for Foreign Missions, which was by then the century-old missionary organization of the Congregational Church, with its headquarters at 14 Beacon Street in Boston. Before that, intending American Board missionaries usually went through a thorough screening process in the United States that took into account educational background and motivation, character, temperament, and (very important in those days) physical stamina. They were then "offered" to the mission in China, which accepted or rejected them on the basis of its own evaluation of the need for new recruits.

My father went through all this without any recorded trouble. However, in the past the assignments to a particular place and to specific work awaited the even tougher scrutiny of the older missionaries, who watched how the newcomers adapted to life in China, their progress in the language, their compatibility with other missionaries (given the necessity of having to live together at close quarters for years on end), how they behaved with the Chinese, and so on, before settling on their futures. Thus, in effect, the emphasis in the work was established by the veteran missionary leaders and Chinese Christians converted by them. Decades of work in China had attached both Chinese and Americans to favorite activities—mostly evangelistic in nature—and encouraged a noticeable caution about modern ways. The arrival of my father and several other young men and women with specific assignments worked out in advance in Boston signaled the intentions of the American Board to move vigorously in new directions as it seemed China was beginning to do.

In 1919, after two years of language study, my father began his work with the students at Beijing National University. Beida, then and now China's greatest university, was leading the whole country in one of the central intellectual revolutions in Chinese history. Beijing itself, despite the repressions of the warlords who came and went during the first two decades of the Chinese Republic, was flooded with new ideas and slogans. There were study groups, often started by individual teachers for their own students or by other young professionals, doctors and engineers, some of whom had just returned from study abroad. They all sensed for the first time new hopeful possibilities for China and themselves.

None of my father's papers give any real account of how "student work" was actually conducted, how students were drawn to his discussion sessions, or how they became interested in the Bible classes he started. Apparently there weren't very many Christians. (Once, years later in his eighties while comfortably assessing his life's work with me, he guessed that there might have been thirty in a Beida student body of possibly three thousand. But he added thoughtfully, there probably weren't too many committed communists in the university at that time either. Individuals, he maintained, mattered, even in China.)

Debates in these discussion groups centered on the great slogans of the time, led by the most popular, "Save China by Science and Democracy," which had an array of interpreters and interpretations. There was the frightening, never really successful but recurring theme in China, "Do

Away with the Old—All of It," which was to surge again decades later in the Maoist Cultural Revolution, and the one advanced by the outnumbered Chinese Christians, "Save the Country through Christianity." This last tried to make a practical connection between Christian principles—especially the emphasis on individual worth—and remedies for China's social miseries.

Although they were passionately competitive, all the groups were in touch with each other. Chen Duxiu, who became one of the founders of the Chinese Communist Party and an early influence on Mao Zedong, spoke to a discussion group my father had organized. One of my father's good personal friends was Hu Shih, a popular philosophy professor at Beida who had been educated at Cornell and Columbia and who later, during World War II, became the Chinese ambassador to the United States. Hu was one of the leaders in the Baihua (literally "white language") movement, which in a very few years substituted the written versions of the spoken language for the traditional classical style in newspapers and other publications. This opened the paths to literacy for the masses of Chinese, thereby enabling the Communists, Nationalists, and Christians to spread their ideas.

Mixing into these exciting debates, which were followed by students all over China, were some of the world's intellectual elites of that era. My father took tea with Bertrand Russell, the British mathematician/philosopher who visited Peking twice during the early '20s. My father claimed—on uncertain evidence it seems to me—that Russell's advocacy of what was then delightfully called "free love" diluted whatever appeal his pacifism and socialism might have had with his large student audiences. John Dewey, whose ideas on reforming education in the United States had seized the imagination of Chinese educators, delivered a series of lectures in Peking and was a visitor in our house.

One of the fascinating sources of controversial thought in 1920s Beijing was the French Jesuit paleontologist Pierre Teilhard de Chardin, who, differing from Catholic doctrine of that time on the origins of mankind, was formulating an almost mystical connection between evolutionary theory and religion. His complex ideas might never have won much general interest except that Teilhard was a colleague of the Canadian anatomist Davidson Black, another friend of my father's. Black, while digging for fossils near Beijing, found a single tooth and, a couple of years later, the top of the skull of the Peking Man, who had lived 500,000 years earlier. This was a major anthropological discovery of the young century and ignited debate among Christians everywhere over interpretations of the Bible's accounts of the Creation. My father said the subject occupied the minds of the younger missionaries because of the difficulty of coming to any sort of agreement among themselves, to say nothing of explaining the arguments to the Chinese. My father heretofore had not been a convinced evolutionist and many years later, in giving me Teilhard's major work, *The Phenomenon of Man*, suggested that Teilhard had been influential in changing his mind.

All of this happened before I was born, or when I was very young, and was not really a part of my own life. However, a distinct stage in my father's career affected me because it had to do with behavior. From 1926 until we went to the United States in 1931, he was the General Secretary of the American Board Mission in North China. He shared his administrative and overseeing duties for seven mission stations, five hospitals, eight large high schools, and dozens of churches, both large and very small, with a Chinese counterpart. The two of them had adjoining desks in a tiny office in the basement of the duplex we lived in. I remember Pastor Zhang as being exceptionally kind—even for a Chinese to a child. Even so, I was carefully coached by my parents and Wang Nai Nai on what to say and do when I met him. Bowing politely and asking permission to come into the office were meant to show special courtesy. I didn't grasp it then but Pastor Zhang was a symbol of equality between Chinese and Americans in mission enterprises in which the American Board proudly thought of itself as a leader.

Although the ostensible purpose of missionary efforts from the beginning had been to establish a Chinese church, there were Chinese and American reasons why the Chinese had not been given—or had not taken—control before. Chinese Christians were always a minute minority in the country and had been regularly persecuted. It was not easy for them to stand up publicly as leaders of a foreign-inspired movement, especially as what little protection they had from their fellow Chinese came about from treaties and obligations imposed on China by foreign armies. At the same time, older American missionaries, particularly, often felt that Chinese Christians, although typically good at personal relations, lacked experience, perhaps even ability, in running things (especially, as my father noted, in running some of the Americans).

Forward-looking missionaries, a majority in the American Board, understood that change would inevitably be brought about by the sensitivities of the modern Chinese nationalism sweeping through the great cities of China, allying the intellectuals with soldiers—rare in Chinese history—and even bringing the Kuomintang (the Nationalist Party) superficially together with the newly formed Communist Party for a short period during the mid-'20s. The calm, exclusive sense of cultural superiority and proper order that had bolstered Chinese leaders over the centuries had been battered by the irresistible lure of advanced science, often expressed in terms of Western military power, while at the same time the vast ill-equipped armies of the warlords, sometimes supported by foreign powers, were looting the country. Visible to everyone were the symbols of China's weakness: the foreign concessions in the major cities and the special rights of extraterritoriality allowing foreigners everywhere in China to disregard Chinese laws if they chose.

The concessions were metropolitan enclaves controlled by foreign powers ranging in size from small cities in themselves, as in Shanghai or Tianjin, to a few blocks of riverfront in Hankou on the Yangsi. They were usually grouped together in the Treaty Ports, so called because they were designated as trading places for foreigners by treaties signed by China with one power or another. By 1927 there were almost fifty of these. Each concession displayed its own national characteristics by its garrison forces, its police (the British commonly used Sikhs imported from India; the French often used Eurasians from Indo-China), its architecture, businesses, churches, schools, and, central to its social life, its clubs. The concessions were the most modern, the cleanest, and—because they were isolated from China's internal wars by foreign troops and warships—the safest places in China. The Chinese flocked to them in times of trouble. It could even be argued that except for the all-important psychological aspects, the concessions were a net gain for China because they were centers for modernization amid China's turmoil. Most Chinese did not see it that way, or if they did, other Chinese would not accept their saying so.

The United States did not have concessions of its own, but Americans took advantage of those of others—principally Great Britain—under a "most-favored nation" treaty signed with the Qing Dynasty in 1844. As in modern trade agreements, rights given to any other country accrued to us as well. The United States was a lesser but important participant in the system and my father opposed it.

From his first day in China, my father had been uncomfortable with the privileges the foreigners had extracted from the Chinese. Right after landing at the port of Dagu, near Tianjin, he had seen an American businessman kick a Chinese. The powerlessness of the victim and the unfairness of the American's immunity affected him all his life. The Beida students put the feelings of all Chinese into words for him, and he became an active advocate of the United States renouncing its special position. In 1925, he was one of the drafters of an open letter to the United States government, signed by most of the American Board missionaries then in China, that urged the United States to take immediate steps to withdraw from the privileges of extraterritoriality. He believed that for Christian missions and missionaries to work under special treaty rights and privileges did not accord with Christian principles.

The Japanese invasions of the '30s caused the missionaries to make some practical adjustments of their stand on extraterritorial rights in order to provide some protection of the missions, but my father never faltered in his belief that these privileges were basically wrong. He always listed this document—which had no effect on American policy—as among the most important things he ever did. My mother was never entirely sure, having heard from the older missionary survivors of the siege of the Peking Legations in 1900 that they and hundreds of Chinese Christians owed their lives to the American Marines and other foreign soldiers who had defended them.

In 1927, the Nationalist forces led by the young Chiang Kai-shek had begun a major drive to the north aimed at neutralizing the warlords in Central and Northern China and eventually unifying the country. There were anti-foreign overtones to Kuomintang propaganda; some foreigners had been killed and, in retaliation, many Chinese, especially in the bombardment of Nanjing by British and American gunboats. The American consuls all over China began urging American missionaries to clear out as tensions increased. Many missionaries went to Korea or Japan, leaving the Chinese to run things by themselves. (My mother refused to go, thus putting my father in a rather difficult position as he was advising other families to evacuate, but she made up her own mind about things; and nothing happened to us, just as she had foretold.) In a final move toward "devolution" as it was called, the Chinese Congregationalists were given control of the American Board properties throughout North China, although the board still retained title to them. My father and Pastor Zhang smoothed out the innumerable administrative details of this significant change. Thus, very early on, ideals of equality and of genuine cooperation between Americans and Chinese were impressed upon me.

My mother, Adelle Tenney, came to China in 1915, two years ahead of my father. Like him, a Carleton College graduate, she had gone to Oberlin and Wooster in Ohio, which were also prime sources for recruiting missionaries. She studied music and received training as a kindergarten and elementary school teacher. I have always been unsure why she chose to be a missionary. Her parents, unlike my father's, though conventionally religious in the American small town way of those days, were not ministers or religious workers; and if there had been some stunning religious experience she never stressed it to her son. In fact, she found piety boring and was inclined to suspect hypocrisy when religious fervor became too obvious in someone.

I think my mother went to China for adventure, to do something spectacularly different from the rest of her family. She also may have been challenged by the high academic standards applied to single women missionaries in the American Board, the wider scope for their talents, and the heavier responsibilities of working in China than they would ordinarily have had at home. Her opportunity to lead in a big enterprise came immediately after the required two-year intensive language study (she was very good at Chinese and had a better accent than my father did) when she organized a kindergarten teachers' training school—the first of its kind in the city. She set an example of devolution by helping one of her students receive advanced training in the United States and then serving for several years as a teacher under this young woman in the Education Department at Yanjing University, the American-established liberal arts institution located just outside the city.

My mother didn't seem to get as much fun out of life as my father did. He was a person of impossible good cheer, full of "rise and shine!" in the morning, equipped with a vast collection of corny Minnesota dialect jokes where supposedly dumb Norwegians outsmarted stuck-up city folk or—in Chinese—crafty landlord-types lost out to the village loafer—laughing much louder and longer at his own stories than they deserved. He admired many things about the ordinary—which meant poor—Chinese, but most of all their patience and good humor amidst their endless calamities. Above all he never seemed to worry about himself. Undoubting in his faith, comfortable in his quiet, prayerful methods of deciding right from wrong, he enjoyed the present, sure of the future.

Often my mother found this sustained optimism contrary to objective fact and hard to live with. She was inclined to overestimate the hazards of day-to-day life in China. Brave in facing the dangers from Chinese bandits and Japanese soldiers, she warred ferociously on flies and garlic breath, uncooked vegetables and unwashed hands, on the "singing through your nose" of dozens of choirs, and on Chinese attitudes. The worst in her mind was *"cha bu duo"*–ism, literally "lacks not much" meaning "almost all right" or "good enough," to which she regularly traced all of China's ills. She struck against the unfairness and cruelty she saw around her, once physically stopping an astonished carter in midblow from beating his exhausted donkey. Once she led a hesitant Beijing policeman to a courtyard, where the cries of a young girl betrayed that her family was defying the law by binding her feet—a vicious national crime still being committed even in the 1920s by some middle-class Chinese families and accepted by their neighbors. She lost that one and almost all her other battles, China being China, and was not consoled. She never gave up, but there was more sadness and resignation in her voice when she talked about her work to my father and me as I got older and could understand. Yet she made her mark, perhaps only an infinitesimal scratch on the immensity of China.

In 1986, my wife, Shirley, and I went out from modern downtown Beijing to Tongxian on the old Tianjin Road. Tongxian had been a walled city, a county capital fifteen miles from Peking; now it is part of Beijing City and indistinguishable amidst the mess of ramshackle apartments and factories. We were looking for Luhe Academy, called Tongxian Number One Middle School. Formerly a top-flight Chinese boys high school founded by Americans in 1866, my mother had taught music and English there for seven years. Fortunately, as the car cruised aimlessly through crowded alleys, I spotted the crenelated roofs of the Luhe buildings. After much roundabout maneuvering we were able to find an entrance.

Although we had arrived without notice, we were greeted warmly by the gateman and the assistant principal, who came up on his bicycle and showed us around. While we were being served tea, the gateman reverentially brought out the 1934 Luhe yearbook from deep in a cupboard. Among the faculty was a passport-style picture of my mother—bobbed hair, gazing shyly across the five decades since it had been taken. The Chinese inscription said that she taught music to both the junior and senior high-school classes. The assistant principal, really too young to know, kindly said that she was remembered. Later I received a letter from a former student of hers, then well over seventy, who said the same thing— comforting and reassuring. I reflected with pride that a couple of generations of Luhe teachers had protected this evidence of American service to China through the Japanese Occupation, after the Communist takeover in 1949, and, most dangerously, the ten years of the Cultural Revolution.

My parents met in 1917 at a dinner on my father's first day in China. They were married in 1919 after a courtship carefully circumscribed by the American missionary elders, who insisted that the two never be alone together in the sight of Chinese. (Apparently it was unthinkable that they could be alone together, seen by no one at all.) The special privileges for foreigners helped them out because they managed to go separately to the foreigners' enclave in Peking, called the Legation Quarter, and walk on the city wall from which all Chinese were banned. I was born on May 4, 1922, in the Peking Union Medical College, built with Rockefeller money in the heart of the city a few blocks from the Forbidden City. It was also not far from the American Board Compound where we lived until the journey that began this story. The PUMC is still a major Beijing hospital under a different name.

I thank my parents in my late evening thoughts for many things, but, for the purposes of this account, I thank them especially for the China experience—not only for the excitement of living there but for their deep-seated appreciation of the Chinese. As the years passed, my studies and my professional work made me more knowledgeable about China in some respects than my parents could be. The sweep of the Chinese I dealt with in many places and for different reasons was far broader. The frustrations and irritations I felt toward some Chinese individuals were possibly sharper than theirs would have been, but by example my father and mother taught me an awareness of Chinese reactions and sensitivities— especially to the words and behavior of foreigners. They had acquired it; I absorbed it without trying, as did my childhood American friends. It was not a skill. It had little application to high foreign policy but some to carrying it out. It came from being brought up as an American "foreigner" in China.

Chapter 2

Growing Up in Peking

Juliet Bredon, an American resident of Peking,[1] began her loving description of the city where I was born:

> Cities, like people, have their personalities. Some are commonplace and soon forgotten, others make a striking impression on even the passing stranger. Although what pleases one often fails to interest another, the majority of travelers agree that Peking has the richest and most attractive personality of any city in the world, not excepting Moscow or Constantinople. Indeed there must be something lacking in the nature to which the place makes no appeal, for its charm is one of infinite variety.

Her book, *Peking*, published in 1920, was regarded by foreigners who lived there as the most comprehensive guide to the ancient city. Even though she denies that any Westerner could have "the thorough knowledge of China's past, an infinite sympathy with the Chinese character and religion, an intimate familiarity with the proverbs and household phrases of the poor, the songs of the streets, the speech of the workshop, no less than the mentality of the *literati* and the motives of the rulers" for a proper appreciation of Peking, she came closer than any other, in the estimation of my parents, to capturing in words my childhood home. And it was as a usually happy, well-watched little boy, before I was aware of any other city, that I came closest to being a Peking child—not a Chinese Peking child but a real one nevertheless; one who knew well for his age how the poor talked and the differences between their ways and those of my parents' Chinese friends; one who absorbed the sights of the tumultuous streets and learned the reasons for the festivals; one who, without understanding why, was proud of his place in the dusty, decaying capital.

My parents traced back my earliest memory of anything at all to a moment when I was three. Heavy rains had flooded the back courtyard

12

of our Western-style house and my mother had complained that Wang Nai Nai, my amah, "will need a boat" to get from her one-room house to the kitchen. I knew about boats from rides we had taken on the Bei Hai, a lake in one of the Imperial parks in the city, so I ran to the back door only to see Wang Nai Nai calmly stepping along the row of bricks the cook had thoughtfully put down for her through the puddles—an early disillusionment.

We shared a large three-story Western-style house with a most senior missionary who had "given my mother away" at her wedding. I don't remember him at all but my parents described him as kindly, even to picking me up occasionally. Because of his scholarly achievements in Chinese and a supremely dignified presence, he was awesome to adult Americans and Chinese alike. My mother maintained that with his white beard he "looked the way God ought to look."

My most enduring early memories are of the Chinese adults closest to me—the three servants in our household.

WANG NAI NAI

It isn't true that Lenin was the first dead person I had seen. During the 1920s no Peking boy living outside the Legation Quarter, a foreigner's area where deaths weren't allowed to happen in public, could have been shielded from the grim end of some of the city's poor. Even before I went to school and could see the bodies over the heads of the throng from the compound rickshaw, I had been taken for walks by my amah, gripped firmly by the wrist for control, along Dengshikou (Lamp Market), the street that ran in front of the American Board Compound. Traffic was not controlled in those days, and the behavior of cars and even bicycles was not well understood. Pedestrian casualties were enormous, and some were fatal. Wang Nai Nai always pushed our way to the inner circle of the crowd surrounding any accident victim we came across; like other Chinese, we would stare silently until she had seen enough.

My parents didn't like her showing me such sights because they felt she lacked sympathy for anyone outside the family—which was true—and that I could get hardened, or fascinated, or both—which may have happened. They were concerned that what looked like Chinese unresponsiveness to the miseries of others would seem natural to me and the right way to react. After I had described some gory scene and confirmed their suspicion that nothing had been done for the victim, they would dutifully explain why Chinese were unable to help others, because "in the Chinese custom" they would become responsible for the future of the individual.

Wang Nai Nai regarded it differently. Besides, she never missed a training opportunity. When I asked about some battered sufferer, I was sternly told, "Oh, he didn't bow nicely to the principal," or, "She didn't come when she was called," or, most often, "He was *taoqi* (mischievous)," a generic sin.

Wang Nai Nai had been hired shortly after I was born. She was a Manchu whose normal-sized feet set her apart from most Chinese women her age. Her family must have been well-off and enlightened because she could read. She came to us because her family had been dispossessed by the 1911 Revolution, which displaced the Manchus, and couldn't make a good marriage for her. Pictures of her show a serene young woman, immaculate in white, solemnly proud of her baby charge—I love her still.

My mother's relationship with Wang Nai Nai seems quite modern in its requirements. Mother worked in several fields at once. She gave piano lessons to individual students from the girls and boys high schools, using her own beloved piano, filling our house from mid-morning to late afternoon with stumbling renditions of Western classical music. She was also the choir director for the Chinese church on the compound, recruiting members from all over the city—not all Christians by any means—but enthusiasts who could read music and were willing to practice for the regular concerts they gave. She ran a training school for kindergarten teachers, which she had deliberately designed to be led by Chinese, helping to meet the growing demand for teachers of the very young. She taught similar courses three times a week at Yanjing University, then an hour's ride by rickshaw and bus from our compound to its glistening new green-roofed campus outside the city walls. (Yanjing disappeared after 1949 when the communist regime came in, and its buildings became the main campus of Beida.) My mother assisted my father in his work at Beida by befriending some of the few women students, suggesting discussion topics and leading some of the discussions until he became more relaxed and fluent in Chinese. My parents were members of several book and current events discussion groups that, along with the nearly compulsory weekly compound prayer meeting, took up most evenings. In short, I was at the heart of a two-career family problem; and Wang Nai Nai was the solution.

The situation was complicated because Wang Nai Nai was not just a passive baby-sitter as were most other amahs, hoping to pass the days without tears or tantrums from their foreign charges. She favored firm limits on free-flow activity and self-expression, while my mother felt that the habits of upper-class Chinese society were too restrictive for American boys. Experimentation and undirected play could avoid the defects of "being brought up by an amah."

I learned all this in retrospect, but from my earliest days I was conscious of a gap in my life that set me apart. I was an only child and a boy besides. Among Chinese in general, a boy was supposed to be a precious commodity and had certain privileges denied his sisters. This did not appear to be the case among the Christian Chinese families of our compound, who tended to favor the theory that girls were better behaved—especially the Back Gateman's Youngest Daughter, who was held up as a paragon of smiling rectitude. She was even younger than I at that. Unless everyone was careful, boys, especially only sons, could become spoiled. It all amounted to being the center of close attention, which, even though I was technically not allowed to be spoiled even by the stiff standards of the American Board Compound, gave me a strong sense of self-importance—or so I have been told.

The other servants lived at home, somewhere else in the city, but Wang Nai Nai had her own one-room house with a small courtyard behind our big house. She would invite me to sit on the *kang,* or brick bed, while she read me a story. The plots were almost incomprehensible because they concerned adult goings-on, which she wouldn't explain, and involved too many ghosts and villains. I was aware of the privilege, however, and I always listened politely, pretending to follow better than I did. Sometimes she would tell me of the home of her childhood with its many courtyards, when she had an amah of her own to take care of her. So she said, but this may have been to provide examples of the proper relationship of child to amah—a constant subject of her concern.

MA ERH

Ma Erh (Ma Number Two Son) did all the housecleaning, washing of clothes, waiting on the table, and delivering messages in lieu of a telephone. He was called "The Boy" in China Coast English, but my parents despised the term so we used only his name. Ma Erh was a Moslem—referred to as a Mohammedan in those days—and consequently, with only one God, was regarded as being somewhat nearer a Christian than Wang Nai Nai or the cook. This didn't confer any advantages on him that I can recall and he remained at the bottom of the hierarchy. He was enormously important to me in the matter of pigeons.

On a trip back to Peking in 1986, I was happy to see that people were raising pigeons again, because I had seen almost none on a visit in 1975. Hobbies such as pigeon-raising for other than eating were frowned upon during the Great Leap Forward in the latter part of the '50s as being wasteful, and then as decadent during the Cultural Revolution of the '60s. In 1986 pigeon coops appeared on the roofs and balconies of the new apartment buildings, and here and there flocks were circling in the old disciplined way.

Almost sixty years earlier I had become a fanatic on the subject, when, in memory, the skies were the purest ice-cold northern blue. I would stand in our backyard shivering with excitement, watching my flock meld with others from the neighborhood into a huge gathering, maybe fifty birds in all. Few of the pigeons were the plain gray of the American and European breeds, and it was easy to pick out my own all whites and mixed browns. Usually, several of the bigger ones had ingenious, delicate gourd whistles attached to their tails. Their high clear chords rose and fell with the birds and entertained everyone in our part of the city. Ma Erh would stand beside me giving tactical advice about when to start signaling our flock down—too early and they would not all come because they seemed to like amiably flying around; too late and they would get hungry and follow another group to its home. Captured pigeons were never returned.

Despite his claims to expertise, Ma Erh and I lost lots of pigeons before we were able to keep a flock going. At least three times he took me on my father's bicycle to the Longfusi Market, a huge dirty complex of temples, stalls, and small shops, where we spent hours choosing and bargaining for enough birds to make up a new flock. Then, whether we had let them fly too soon or the tough compound cat (all outside Peking cats had to be tough) scared them, or they didn't like the mates we chose for them, they would fly up nicely to join the big flock on the first day we let them out, and then somehow never came back.

On our third try we were more careful. All six pairs had their wing feathers sewed so they couldn't fly. Plenty of chicken wire and attacks with scalding water kept the cat away. Later, when we started to let the birds out, we held one of each couple as a hostage. We stopped losing pigeons and even captured two or three from other flocks. After a stranger was inside the coop and claiming its reward of *gaoliang* (sorghum) for its defection from our neighbor, we would grab it, sew up its wings until we could find or entice a mate for it. Unless it redefected, it was ours.

One afternoon the front gateman informed Ma Erh that a Chinese older person had come to call and that the purpose of this odd visit was to announce his common interest in pigeons. Obviously, he had lost one of his to us and was taking this opportunity to check up on it. Since it would have been bad manners to indicate that a boy had accomplished this feat, or even a servant, my father was summoned from his office in the basement of our house and played the role of flock owner. We sat in the living room and were served tea by Ma Erh and established a very pleasant relationship with the gentleman, who actually lived only a few courtyards away. We didn't show him our pigeon establishment and he never did get his bird back, but I suspect that he earlier had won most of ours.

THE COOK

Our cook's surname was Xu. I don't know the rest of his name because we called him Da Shi-fu, which means "big expert," or Xu Shi-fu. He was tall and thin, not much of a smiler, but without any temper that I ever saw. He had stature on the compound and was well known by the teachers in the school and the shopkeepers in the neighborhood, which is rather surprising because he came from Shandong Province and never lost his country accent. Nevertheless, he achieved fame as the great mediator in a notorious row between the gateman and janitors of the girls school that neither the American missionaries nor the Chinese principals of the schools could resolve.

Xu Shi-fu began working for my father in 1917 and stayed with our family until we left China in 1940. Like Ma Erh and Wang Nai Nai, he had never thought of becoming a servant, or even a cook, and had never seen a foreigner until he got to Peking. When he was sixteen or seventeen, he had been seized by a warlord's press gang while he was working in the family fields. He had been a soldier for several months when one day his officer took his rifle away and put him on a freight train with hundreds of others, eventually ending up in Peking. No one seemed to be in charge of the group, so he and a friend simply walked into the city, found jobs at a restaurant run by someone from their county in Shandong, and was introduced to my father, who was studying Chinese at the time and needed a part-time houseboy. He stayed on after my parents were married, and my mother started him on Western cooking. He became very good at it.

Some time before I was born, Da Shi-fu had managed to find a wife from his own village, a smiling, good-natured peasant woman with courage and brains. They had a boy and a girl somewhat older than I whom I only saw a few times but whose progress in the schools my parents paid for was mentioned as an object lesson in hard work. When we moved to Tongzhou after returning to China in 1933, the Xu family came with us but lived inside the city walls sharing a small courtyard with one of the male nurses at the mission hospital and his family. Before the Japanese Occupation, this joint dwelling had won a prize for cleanliness from the New Life Movement established by the Kuomintang and Madame Chiang Kai-shek. Life must have seemed very happy and prosperous with much to look forward to when, suddenly early one spring, both the then teen-aged children died from scarlet fever. Unbearably, both the elder Xus were unusually kind to me from then on but, confused in my own mind, I found no natural way to respond. I saw Da Shi-fu in Peking at the end of the war in an unforgettable way, but he never was the same.

Both Ma Erh and Xu Shi-fu were good for a little bending of my mother's rules. She sternly forbade candy bought from outside the compound gates—in warm weather because of flies, and in winter because of dust from the streets. These were serious practical sanitary regulations, but Xu Shi-fu often slipped me some anyway, especially *tang hulers* (candied breadfruit on a stick), after washing them off first with our boiled drinking water. Nothing happened to me, but I had to be careful not to comment on the treat to my parents. My mother was strict about my health.

Ma Erh, for his part, was supposed to go directly from our compound to another mission and to come straight back when he was delivering notes for my mother (the compound telephone was in the gatehouse and was only used for emergencies, because the other party also had to walk outside to the phone). But when he took me along we often managed to go into the covered Dongan Shichang (until 1994 the huge market for everything), a few blocks from the compound. That was forbidden territory except with my ever-alert parents because of crowds, coughs, and spitting, and thus irresistible to me. The malleable Ma Erh usually gave in to my pleas to check the place out if I promised not to stray. We never had any money and always moved quickly to the toy area to look at the clay toy soldiers in the uniforms of the warlord armies that I ached for but was not allowed to own on the theory they would glamorize war. On the way home we occasionally stopped to watch a bloodless—indeed blowless—shouting street fight, which my parents and Wang Nai Nai never did, being embarrassed by the repetitive, fascinating, bad language used to express the extreme emotions of the participants.

The two men never reported my own slip-ups except to Wang Nai Nai, who chose which ones to pass on to higher authority. Chief among these was climbing on the roofs and courtyard walls of the Chinese houses ringing the compound, which I did a couple of times with a Chinese friend my age—eight or nine. Wang Nai Nai had strong objections to this form of amusement. Although she regarded anything more than three feet off the ground as unsafe for me, the roofs of the small one-story houses were loosely tiled over straw and plaster, the ridge poles sagged, and the ten-foot-high walls between the houses were studded with broken glass. They were dangerous. Besides, we used her own roof as a starting point when she wasn't watching.

The Chinese neighbors retaliated against her by throwing pieces of brick and burnt-up coal balls (coal dust mixed with clay into small balls used for heating and cooking—very hot when properly lit) into her court-yard. She described the situation to my father who, despite the enormous loss of face involved in having such a son, took me to each of the houses and had me apologize flatly and without any of the excuses I had devised, to the slightly opened big doors. My companion did not go along, nor did he have to apologize, it being generally understood that no Chinese boy, unled, would get into such unheard-of mischief. Needless to say, his father insisted that we cease our collaboration. This turned out to be a solid career move for him. After an interval of several decades, John Fei taught economics at Yale and became an honored advisor on economic development to the government on Taiwan. He reminded me of these events fifty years later.

Servants, on whom our comfortable daily life depended, and the large Western-style houses in which we lived were anomalies for American Board missionaries, who mostly came from ordinary New England and Midwest families. Even during the Depression they were among the poorest paid professional-class Americans. This didn't matter in China because the seminary-to-grave support system in the mission provided housing, education for the children when they were old enough to go to a missionary-supported boarding school, medical care by skilled mission doctors, and transportation every seven years from China to the United States on "furlough." Missionary men and women, roughly equal in pay and perks, lived energetically according to simple principles—"to each according to his needs and from each according to his abilities"—Christian concepts (Acts 4–35) arrived at long before Karl Marx and unreachable, I learned, in the wide world outside the compound. But servants required explaining to friends and relatives in America. The large mission houses, some of them built with funds extracted as indemnities from the Chinese government for the cruelties of the Boxers, set the missionaries apart from their Chinese neighbors.

Being born in China never did seem surprising to me. I briefly minded being called "Chinky Cross, the Chinaman" by some of my less-polished classmates in the fourth grade at the Williams School in Auburndale, Massachusetts, where we settled for a year after our European trip. But this was not because I had been ridiculously confused with a real Chinese. After all, some real Chinese had yelled "little foreign devil" at me back home in Peking; Wang Nai Nai had ordered me not to answer back with some of the awful swear words like "turtle's egg" (indicating misbehavior by one's mother) or even worse that I had heard on the streets. A couple of my new American friends introduced a saying of the day to me beginning "Chink, Chink Chinaman, sitting on the fence," and ending reasonably enough for the depths of the Depression in 1931, "trying to make a dollar out of ninety-eight cents." "China Man" was what Chinese called themselves in Chinese, but I fully understood that "Chinaman" and "Chink" were among those words like "Wop" or "Nigger," which were totally unacceptable because they hurt feelings. Thus, in this silly, childish way, I, a certified American by passport, felt just this slightest touch of prejudice in my own country, but I remembered it always.

However, this was never, even momentarily, something to brood over. In Auburndale, I quickly began to exploit my China background—a process I've continued to this day. I took advantage of my cousins' parentally enforced polite interest in China to talk about the street sights, funerals, soldiers, and palaces of Peking, even—one told me later—giving authoritative nine-year-old explanations of the concepts of "face" and respect for elders in Chinese society.

I was able to smooth out my presentations by the time we moved to Oberlin, Ohio, the next year. There I found support in Lucian Pye, my own age, also an American Board missionaries' son whom I had first met in Peking when we were both four. Because we are only sons, we have acted as brothers all our lives. Lucian was large for his age and, with red hair and a firmly confident manner, was able without doing or saying much of anything to turn our China births from a disadvantage into, possibly, a PR plus. The trick was to look faintly exotic (in my own eyes anyway) while hopefully always appearing indisputably a true blue American.

For a missionary child this was hard. In the first place, I already felt somewhat out of the American mainstream because "preachers' kids" were expected to behave in uncomfortably polite and upright ways; for example, in speech, which for me included impossibly high standards of accuracy. Somehow I got the idea that it wasn't exactly that one had to be so good, but that one had to look that way. Nothing could have been farther from my parents' teachings, and they would have been depressed if I had ever expressed that thought. I suppose everyone learns the uses of hypocrisy at an early age.

The trouble was that while I felt that I was not thoroughly American in America, I was not—and could not be—really acceptable as a Chinese in China. True, when I was little, I spoke upper-class Mandarin, knew the proper Chinese manners appropriate for my age, and had mostly Chinese playmates. As I grew older though, I inevitably became a special kind of American—a "foreigner" in China.

TONGZHOU

Our family came back to China in 1933 and lived in a large house in the campus-like American Board Compound outside the walled town of Tongzhou (a.k.a. Tongxian) fourteen miles east of Beijing.

Tongzhou had a history. In imperial times it had been the storage place for the emperors' tribute rice, which was shipped up the Grand Canal from all parts of China and its dominions. The long, low sheds that held the grain had been dismantled after the fall of the Manchu Dynasty in 1911, accounting for the wide fields within the walls and giving Tongzhou an empty atmosphere—different from other rural towns near Beijing. A nationally known, classic thirteen-story pagoda surrounded by twisted old pines dominated the northern section of the town and was solemnly countered by the dull brown and red brick of the Congregational Church, just inside the southern walls from the compound.

One corner of the city wall across the moat behind the compound had been rounded, giving it a medieval European cast. The story was that Tongzhou had taken the punishment of another town for parricide—the ancient rule being that for each murder of both parents, a town had to build a round corner on its wall. Four parricides and the town would be closed. The other town already had three so Tongzhou was being nice. That's the Tongzhou version. But no one had ever heard of a three-rounded-wall town anywhere, so it was possible, but unacceptable to Tongzhouites, that we could have had a parricide of our own expunged from the records centuries later. The walls were torn down in the 1950s, and our dingy, loved town is now a nondescript district of Beijing, pretty much defeating memory.

The North China American School (NCAS), which became my life for seven years, was one of three boarding schools on the compound. We separated the Chinese girls school, Bridgeman Academy (named for a famous nineteenth-century American missionary but called Fuyi in Chinese), and the school for Chinese boys, Jefferson Academy (named for an American president and known in Chinese as Luhe).

NCAS was a small school, grades 7 through 12—never more than fifty boys and girls—supported by several Protestant denominations whose families were stationed in the North China interior. Significantly, while there were also nonmissionary American children plus White Russians from Harbin in Manchuria, Germans from Qingdao in Shandong Province to the south and east, and assorted Austrian, British, Australian, Danish, Italian, French, and Greek boys and girls from Tianjin, there were no Chinese. Some American-educated Chinese had inquired about places for their children but had been quietly discouraged. Again, I think, like so many contradictions in our lives, this had to do with the special privileges of foreigners. The presence of Chinese in an otherwise all-foreign boarding school would dilute a very special right and might encourage official Chinese—and in the late '30s possibly Japanese—interference. We students and our teachers were free to build a school culture of our own—in China but not at all Chinese—casually cosmopolitan but firmly based on an idealized America.

Our mostly young teachers—recent graduates from Ohio State, Yale, Smith, and Haverford, to name those most prominent in my mind— struggled with nearly total success to provide us with the kind of instruction that would get us into an American college. They also tried to pass on American social skills, keeping a tolerant eye on our fairly restricted dating practices—conscious that more was going on than the mission boards would have thought proper, but less than what they knew was possible in high schools in America. They couldn't watch everything. We lived the semi-secret, intense, ingrown life of a boarding school, where among the boys, for example, cruel bullying was common during my first three years. I was consecutively a minor victim (I lived at home), a vicious perpetrator, and, finally, a genuinely repentant reformer—behavior intruding on my memories ever afterward.

We were foreigners living in China, and our contacts with Chinese had little to do with our studies or the inside life of our school. Because this book is about my feelings—especially those about China—I describe a couple of my teenage brushes with Chinese and their lives that have stayed with me.

ICE HOCKEY

NCAS had a full schedule of sports involving Luhe and Fuyi—tennis and basketball for boys and girls, baseball and ice hockey for the boys. These were mostly successful Sino-American encounters, although occasionally we found Chinese refereeing erratic and unfair. That some of the worst officials were known Christians was especially disappointing.

We had the most varied competition in ice hockey. Our school team at times was good enough to play older Chinese teams like the Furen Catholic University, freshmen who were coached by French Canadian Brothers. We could even occasionally compete with the Legation Guard Marines.

We also had a pick-up team with one or two boys from Luhe that played some senior league games in Peking. The team was supported in train tickets and dinners in town by Wang Baoquan, a large man in his early thirties who was a money lender and landlord from the neighboring village of Fuxingzhuang. Wang was wealthy enough to support this community effort and to equip himself with a special unbreakable hockey stick that he used like a golf club, taking wide frightening swings to swat away others' sticks wherever he saw them and batting the puck along the ice as he lumbered after it. He never passed to others and he didn't much accept the rules of hockey. Since he paid for everything we tried to let him play for awhile in each game, but only if we got ahead, barring him when it was close by not leaving the ice so he couldn't come stumbling on. He vocally resented this even during the games, but we were his only chance to play at all and he floated us during each season.

Peking hockey at our level was not a North American contact sport, but at its best featured fast skating, quick stick work, and smart passing. Bao-quan's pugnacious approach did embroil us in mostly verbal altercations, as well as some tripping and pushing when the single referee couldn't see. This happened most often with a team of Chinese high-school stars known as the Black Cats. The memory seems to have stuck with both teams.

In 1961, while I was in Geneva with the American Delegation to the Fourteen Nation Conference on Laos, I was attracted by the clear Peking tones of George Lee, the chief Chinese/English interpreter supplied by the United Nations. We established our connections immediately after the first plenary session. George had lived less than a quarter mile from the American Board Compound, had gone to Yuying, the elite American Board boys high school, and then to Yanjing. George told me that he liked all sports, even indoor tennis in New York, but his favorite in high school had been ice hockey. He had, in fact, played against a mixed team of Chinese and Americans when he was on a team called the Black Cats. The games had been marred by the dirty play of the American Chinese "gang" from Tongzhou. Had I played hockey? I replied cautiously that I usually played right wing on that very team. "What position did you play, George?" His eyes misted at the thought of our twenty-five-year-old encounters. "I played left wing!" (thus opposite me). We enthusiastically shook hands and became good friends.

RICKSHAWS AND TB

One of our thoughtless and conspicuous young foreigners' games when we went into Peking was to race rickshaws through the crowded streets. Usually, we would pull the rickshaws ourselves, giving the rickshaw men a ride. Sometimes we would offer a bonus to the rickshaw men who raced, plus a bigger prize for the winner—infinitesimal sums, in any case, but significant, nevertheless, to those poorest of the poor. Bargaining was friendly, and the races were never long. It was hard for us to see this as exploitation, as my parents contended. "But we pay more," "They have a good time, too" arguments were countered with the observation that Chinese, no matter how rich, never did such things. And, anyway, it was wrong to make light of someone's toil, especially in public where it would be taken for arrogance. My mother hated the whole concept of rickshaws and would seldom ask the puller to do more than trot slowly. "Please don't go too fast," she would say quietly, letting the rickshaw man rest a bit and saving his face. The rickshaw men's harsh lives were always with us.

One day we had just started a race to the railroad station when my puller slowed suddenly and began to cough, bending over and spitting heavily to one side. For no other reasons than the realities of life in China and being a constant worrier about my own excellent health, I knew instantly from the flashes of red in the dust that the man was in the final stages of tuberculosis. I told him to walk slowly, which he did for a few more paces, and then fell face down between the shafts. I jumped out of the rickshaw, lifted him carefully, and had him sit on the footrest. He tried to apologize, begging me to let him rest for a minute before going on, evidently assuming I wouldn't pay him for such a short ride. Horrified at my small role in his misery, I gave him all my money, much more than he could earn in a healthy week, keeping only my return train ticket. "Go to the hospital." (The Peking Union Medical College—then and still Peking's major hospital—was only a quarter mile off.) "They'll give you some medicine," I said, and walked away, ashamed that all I had was money and knowing that it wouldn't help; that except for me, for a few moments, there was no one nearby—perhaps no one at all—who cared what happened to him.

THE JAPANESE COME

Life changed for Chinese and Americans in Tongzhou when the Japanese began the war. They had been openly insinuating their way south of the Great Wall into Hebei Province for several years after their capture of Manchuria in 1931, using small puppet governments headed by Chinese traitors and enforced by lightly armed Chinese troops recruited from Manzhuguo (their wholly owned state in Manchuria). In 1935 they had capped this unopposed movement by declaring an East Hebei Autonomous Region composed of twenty-two counties of northeastern Hebei. The capital of this arrangement was established at Tongzhou, so we had a taste of what was to come. By the fall of 1936, a small garrison of hard-bitten infantry plus the already feared *Kempeitai*, the military police (with black neck patches on their tunics), Korean heroin dealers, prostitutes, and simple thugs (called *ronin* by the Japanese after the roving warriors of Japanese history), and a few Japanese civilians (shopkeepers and school teachers) had come into town. They were the advance elements of the East Asian Co-prosperity Sphere—shouldering aside those Chinese officials who didn't join them.

The first few months of the Japanese Occupation of Tongzhou were mild because the Japanese ineptly were trying to show that the East

Hebei Autonomous Region resulted from the spontaneous wish of the Chinese there to be separated from the rest of China. Several hundred regular Chinese army troops of the Twenty-ninth Route Army were even permitted to remain camped in three large temples south of the walls near the American Board Compound. Nevertheless, it was obvious the Japanese planned to stay, and that sooner or later they would take another much larger bite of North China. The American missionaries—in a hesitant and pragmatic reassertion of extraterritoriality and an agreed temporary reversal of devolution—quietly began to reassume the titles of leadership, which they had given up as part of mission policy years before, appearing on lists as the principals, deans, treasurers, and so forth, in an effort to protect their Chinese colleagues.

Everyone despaired that the central government in Nanking, floundering in endless "anti-bandit" campaigns against the Communists, would ever try to resist. Sullenly, the Chinese at Tongzhou were making the inevitable adjustments to their new rulers by filling in the proper new documents, quietly removing flags and other symbols of loyalty to the Republic of China. Outside the city walls at Luhe, and less noticeably at the girls school, the students talked of going south, away from the Japanese, to join the Nationalist forces or, more commonly, to pursue their educations—the age-old response of Chinese intellectuals to trouble.

However, in December 1936 a flash of hope and a new mood came from Xian several hundred miles to the west. After their quick defeat by the Japanese in 1931, the "Young Marshal" Zhang Xueliang, former warlord of Manchuria, had moved his forces within the Great Wall into China proper in Shaanxi Province. There he had established contact with the Chinese Communists headquartered in Yanan, also in Shaanxi, at the end of their 5,000-mile Long March. The two forces collaborated in kidnapping Chiang Kai-shek, the leader of the Republic of China. The purpose of this drama of ancient Chinese caliber was to force Chiang's agreement to a united front against the Japanese.

News of Chiang's release on December 24 came to us in Tongzhou by radio. Although local comment was cautious, it was accepted by the missionaries and Chinese on the compound that China was, at last, formally united against Japan. On that clear North China Christmas Eve, Luhe students carrying torches paraded past our house to the girls school, and then the joint group marched back singing and shouting anti-Japanese slogans, "Dadao Rihben Kuomintang" ("Beat Japan Kuomintang") to the tune of "Frère Jacques, dormez vous?" The cook reported that armed Japanese soldiers were standing on the city wall overlooking the compound. I rushed down from our porch and joined the students in this satisfying, provocative gesture of defiance. No one knew what those Japanese thought and they didn't react openly. My father guessed that they must have realized, if they hadn't before, that because of the aroused patriotic feelings against Japan displayed by such demonstrations all over China, Japan would have to move soon on the rest of China before it became too strong. Crazily exhilarated, I thought only of the impression of solidarity I was making on the students. But I can see now that World War II began for me then.

THE TONGZHOU FIGHTING

My mother and I were in Beidaihe for our regular summer holiday and my father was due to arrive for his when, on July 7, 1937, the Japanese began their long-expected outright invasion of China proper with a staged pretext at Lukouqiao, known to foreigners as Marco Polo Bridge, near Beijing.

A few days after the Marco Polo Bridge Incident, the Japanese began clearing operations along the road from Beijing to Tianjin, which, at Tongzhou, ran between the mission compound and the three-temple complex still manned by Chinese regulars. The young Chinese commander had alerted the missionaries the night before to expect fighting on the compound grounds and many casualties, because the Japanese had given him an ultimatum to withdraw by 5:30 the next morning, and he proudly said he was going to resist. During the night, the hospital was prepared to receive casualties and American flags were raised above the gatehouses at the compound entrances. What happened the next day became known as the Tongzhou Massacre, actually several massacres by both sides running over a week.

The Japanese attacked an hour before their ultimatum expired and by mid-morning had driven the Chinese from their positions around the temples, including a machine gun nest near the skating pond in the compound itself. In the process, they destroyed the gatehouse and dropped a bomb on one of the Luhe school buildings. (The bomb didn't explode and lay beside a path for several weeks before the Japanese came and disarmed it. The building was patched up, but the scars were still there fifty years later. The Chinese were fascinated when I pointed these out on a visit to Luhe in 1986.)

The Tongzhou Massacre began when the main body of Japanese chased the remnant of the Chinese Twenty-ninth Army units into the countryside to the south, leaving their puppet Chinese forces in possession of the city. Many of these promptly turned into patriotic Chinese, seized the Chinese figurehead of the East Hebei Autonomous Region, whom they took to Beijing, thinking it was in Chinese hands. They were all captured and the traitor freed when the group of puppets arrived at the Peking gates and ran into Japanese troops who had taken the city earlier. Other puppets stayed in Tongzhou and began shooting and hacking to death Chinese collaborators, Koreans, and Japanese civilians—perhaps one hundred in all were killed. A few, horribly mutilated, escaped to the mission hospital, where they were treated side-by-side with some wounded Chinese soldiers brought in by nearby farmers. A handful of Japanese civilians, including several children, first took refuge in the church, which was inside the city walls, and then came into the compound itself. The missionaries, insisting that the mission was American property and therefore neutral, kept out the ex-puppets and rampaging mobs.

This was just as well because the Japanese Army came back in the early afternoon, having wiped out the ill-equipped Chinese regulars, and began slaughtering Chinese in their turn. The first to be caught and executed on the spot were the ex-puppets still in uniform. Ironically, many of these were passively loyal to the Japanese in that they had not joined their comrades in looting and killing, but had simply sat down in small formations and waited to see how things came out. The ex-puppets who had been involved changed their uniforms for peasant clothes when they could, leading the Japanese to shoot any young male they came across. Almost immediately the people of Tongzhou began swarming through the compound gates. By nightfall, there were some 20,000 Chinese, or half the population of Tongzhou, mostly foodless, waterless, and beddingless, crowding into the school buildings and houses. Over 200 used our house and yard alone.

These refugees stayed for days, some even for months. There was enough pure water from an underground spring near the moat at the edge of the compound, and food and cooking fuel were brought in from nearby villages and sold at exorbitant prices; but sanitation collapsed immediately. The cesspools overran, and outdoor latrines were dug into vegetable gardens, which quickly filled up and had to be redug. Jim Hunter, an inspiring agricultural missionary, and my father inexpertly assisted the small hospital staff in giving hundreds of typhoid inoculations in an effort to head off an epidemic.

More danger, however, came from the Japanese. They could be seen on the city wall looking at the compound through binoculars, and for the first few days, their firing squads operated ceaselessly. Everyone knew that mixed in with the thousands of ordinary Chinese hiding in the compound were many of the ex-puppets the Japanese were searching for. Japanese pressure had started right away in the hospital when the *Kempei*, accompanying the Japanese doctors who came to pick up the Japanese survivors of the first massacre, requested that the Chinese military wounded be turned over to them. This was refused on the grounds that as the neutral role of the hospital had benefited the Japanese most of all, it was ungrateful of them to change it. The *Kempei* gave in on that but followed up with demands to conduct searches for puppet deserters among the refugees. The missionaries were able to stymie this in time by appealing to the American consulate general in Peking, which sent a consul to insist on the inviolability of American property. Meanwhile, the puppet deserters escaped to the countryside, often leaving their families behind, some of the millions upon millions of separations of the war.

My mother and I, sitting on the beaches of Beidaihe, knew very little about what was happening in Tongzhou. It was a hard time for her because we didn't hear anything from my father for several weeks, while the endless Japanese troop trains rumbling south from Manchuria just confirmed her fears that he was in danger. My own morale was high because I believed all the rumors of magnificent Chinese victories passed on to me by Xu Shi-fu, who was with us for the summer in Beidaihe and who, thinking of his own family in Tongzhou, naturally put the best light on things. It wasn't until I got back to Tongzhou in late October 1937, my school having stayed in Peking until the buildings and grounds could be cleaned up, that I began to feel a little of what the war really was going to mean to the Chinese. Even then, my reaction was one of excitement and adventure. Only later, when I was more directly in the same war myself—on islands thousands of miles from Peking—did I understand how callous I had been as a fifteen year old.

It was easy to see the course of battle. The Japanese had erected wooden markers precisely on the spots where each of their soldiers had been killed. These and the Chinese positions that had been captured were untouched. We didn't realize it then, but we gave ourselves—those of us who were to be soldiers later—our first lesson in infantry tactics. The Japanese attack had started on the southeastern corner of the compound near the Luhe pond and the gatehouse, where three of them were killed. They then assaulted a small hill where the Chinese had placed a machine gun. They swept from there over a large soccer field across the Beijing-Tianjin main motor road and up an open slope to the first of the three temples. Two more Japanese were killed along the fence line of the compound by the road, and then just below the red temple walls several more markers were clustered, indicating some close-in combat. The local Chinese claimed that the Chinese soldiers, who were equipped with broadswords, had charged out of the temple at the Japanese and decapitated several of them.

The temple was not totally destroyed, as it probably would have been in an American operation, but it had been mortared. Most of the roofs were gone, the idols were chipped and shattered, but one or two were still standing. The ancient spreading cedar trees were broken, and everywhere lay the solid waste of war—ammunition clips, cartridge cases, pieces of uniform, bloody bandages, half a rifle, canteens, and a surprising amount of paper—letters and official papers, I suppose.

We grabbed souvenirs. I took a gray Chinese Army cap with the blue and white Kuomintang insignia of the twelve-pointed sun and a metallic object with small brass-like fittings, which I identified as a radio part. This was to show that the Chinese had radios, a point I thought worth making at the time. I occasionally wore the cap in walks outside the compound as a gesture of defiance, causing the Chinese who noticed it to shy away but stirring no Japanese reaction at all—possibly because the Chinese forces had been driven from the Tongzhou area months before and the Japanese garrison troops had never seen the real thing. I took my "radio part" home and put it on the mantelpiece where it stayed until the cook, who had once been a soldier, cast doubts on its real function. I stealthily threw it in the moat behind the house. A few years later, during my training as a Marine officer, we were being shown some Japanese weapons, and I felt the back of my neck begin to crawl when the instructor, holding up a small metallic object with brass-like fittings, said, "This here is a Jap rifle grenade."

Mr. Sun, who taught us Chinese at the school, lived inside the city walls. One day, in describing the events of the summer, he mentioned unemotionally that "many" suspected puppet soldiers had been executed in the little field behind the courtyard of his house. There had been much firing, and in a few days, a "bad smell." He gave this as a reason why his classes were not being invited to his house for his annual, not very good, Chinese dinner. He also probably thought the Japanese, who had appropriated the Chinese Normal School next to his house, might become suspicious of him if foreigners appeared too near to them as his guests. Naturally, several of us immediately planned to go into Tongzhou and see.

Trips into the city had to be applied for to the teachers, and permission was not automatic. Reasons had to be found that fit the season and the school's strict health rules. In the spring when there were too many flies in the shop we could not ask to go to buy sticks of white malt candy—a famous Tongzhou specialty—nor could we watch the Chinese opera on stilts—another Tongzhou pride—when there was no special, relatively uncrowded place to stand. Because the students knew more about Tongzhou than the teacher, a recent Haverford College graduate who trusted us more than we deserved, it wasn't hard to find a reason. I don't know what excuse we used for our gruesome visit, but of course, after the near disasters of our battlefield explorations, anything like what we eventually did was firmly forbidden.

I believe we took some notice of Mr. Sun's concerns and went up a different alley from the one leading to his house. We came to an open field with the wall of the Normal School behind it. Perhaps Mr. Sun had been wrong. Perhaps the puppets had not been executed but had been attacking a few Japanese holed up in the Normal School at the time of the Tongzhou Massacre. Perhaps also the roving dogs, part of any Chinese town, had gotten at the bodies. Anyway, dozens of skeletons in rotting khaki were scattered everywhere.

I think, and now hope, that initially we were horrified. But something perverse took over, and we went back to these killing grounds several times with cameras. The general scene seemed too uninteresting, so we moved bones around and made a neat pile of skulls. Two old Chinese gentlemen who turned up each time noncommittally watched us young, macabre foreigners commit these deeds and even, for a small payment, posed—each holding a skull. What did they think?

We brought back a couple of skulls for our biology classes, which alerted the teachers, and we had to stop our visits. It was probably belated shame over the crass, unfeeling awfulness of our behavior and a need to do something for the dead Chinese that caused Lucian Pye and me to send copies of our photographs to *Life* magazine. Fearing that the editors wouldn't get the point, we provided our own captions, "Skulls piled up by playful Japs." The Japanese could easily have traced the source but *Life* showed no interest.

As far as I know, my parents and the other missionaries in Tongzhou had no connection with any organized resistance to the Japanese in the sense of actively assisting it. This was mission policy and carefully adhered to, but there was no hands-off as to individuals in trouble with the invaders. Several times late in the evening after the servants had gone back to their quarters, there was a knock on the door. Someone would come in and wordlessly be ushered by my father into a room where we had a ping-pong table. The hard, high table served them quite well as a Chinese-style bed. The Chinese were gone before dawn, having carefully replaced the net on the table, and I never saw them. My father would only say that they had to leave their homes because they were in danger of being arrested, and I doubt if he knew what eventually happened to them.

After these occasions, which were very tense for my parents, my mother would again urge my father to find some way to hide our guests if the Japanese or their Chinese collaborators, who might be following them, wanted to search the house. The various closets and even the large attic and cellar were too far away from the ping-pong room to be reached quickly. We spent much time discussing various procedures, but none of them seemed to be feasible until I remembered that there was a small unused closet under the stairs, entered by pushing a single wooden panel. I had discovered this when we first moved into the house, but as I grew out of the urge for secret places of my own, I had forgotten it. My mother left a blanket there and a bottle of water for anyone who had to be concealed. She changed the water regularly herself, but we never had an occasion to use the hiding place.

In the fall of 1945, Lucian and I, by this time Marine officers, wangled a trip out to Tongzhou shortly after we had arrived in North China. Our truck was greeted by a Japanese soldier bearing a sign printed in English that said something like, "Please be patient, Japanese Army is preparing houses for American forces." I tried to tell the soldier in Japanese that the two of us were not anxious to move into any houses but that we wanted to look them over, especially because we had lived in some of them. He thought this was nervously laughable, and in an affected, bored way, he agreed to take us around.

All of the school buildings and the seven homes of the missionaries were in bad shape—windows missing and gardens destroyed. The Japanese had actually used our house as a stable, standing their horses out on the stone porch and breaking the large windows so that the horses could put their heads over the window sills and eat in what had been the living room. Some straw was still stored in neat piles. Chinese from Fuxingzhuang had pulled out all the electric wiring. The plaster had been scraped or had fallen from the interior walls, and the front steps had been made into a ramp for the horses. It was no longer a real house.

We made a thorough tour, the soldier giggling dubiously as I sternly pointed out, "This is my parents' room; this is my room; this is the guest room." Then I remembered the hiding place under the stairs, and in a final proof of ownership, I walked over to the stairwell and pushed on the panel. Sure enough, it swung open; in the little cubby hole was a moldy blanket and an empty water bottle. The Japanese soldier stopped smiling then, "Ma-a-a-a," Japanese for "wow!"

By September 1939, when my senior year at NCAS began, we had become used to the Japanese Occupation of North China because the areas they held were pretty well established and stayed that way for the rest of the war. When they could spare the troops, the Japanese would concentrate their forces and push into communist areas. The communist guerrillas of the Eighth Route Army then followed Mao's dictum— "When the enemy advances, we retreat; the enemy camps, we harass; the enemy tires, we attack; the enemy retreats, we pursue"—and would pull away from the villages, leaving them undefended. Casualties among the armed men on both sides were light but were enormous among the peasants as the Japanese raped, burned, and slaughtered in these ruthless punitive campaigns. I think there was something about the dull brown and gray of the flat countryside, especially in winter, and the immensity of North China compared to their own islands, that created a sort of madness in the Japanese. Cruelty only compounded their problems, because the rougher they got, the stronger and more active the resistance became. They could destroy but not really conquer.

Tongzhou was only fourteen miles from Beijing, which was firmly in Japanese hands, but we could occasionally hear heavy firing and see smoke jump up as the Japanese burned another village. Once during the 1938 Christmas period, on a cracklingly winter night, three small villages only five miles away were destroyed. We thought we saw the flames from our upstairs porch. My father had been in the area only a few days before and knew some of the villagers. Later on he was told that they had been killed.

The position of the American missionaries was again ambivalent because the United States government insisted that, despite the Japanese Occupation, Americans still retained extraterritorial rights. Flying the American flag over mission property afforded some protection from the Japanese for the missionaries themselves, but little for the Chinese in charge of the schools and hospitals, and none if the Americans were not physically present. This meant that if the missionary institutions were to continue to operate, they had to appear to be nonpolitical and neutral in the war. Because of their own undisguised sympathies and those of the Chinese they ministered to, this was almost impossible. The missionaries, like most of the Chinese themselves, usually tried to observe the forms of subservience without being seen to side publicly with the Japanese.

Nice distinctions abounded and were debated at home and at school. Was it right, aside from the obvious danger, not to bow to the Japanese sentries as they often demanded of the Americans and always of the Chinese? Would the Chinese interpret our getting away with not bowing as a sign we were above the Chinese? Never mind that the Japanese civilians also bowed to Japanese soldiers. In fact, the Japanese bowed all the time. Broad parodies by tough, Peking street-types amused the expressionless Chinese onlookers and often softened the required obeisance. But what about giving in and bowing when it wasn't sure that one absolutely had to? Would that mean to the Chinese that the Americans had accepted what was happening?

Most of the high school students—under Lucian's leadership—and stubborn adults like my mother were all for making points and took big chances in trying to avoid bowing, especially when our foreign peers were around to watch. But others, like my father, thought an unpracticed American-style friendly nod and smile were neither humble nor recalcitrant. He was quite wrong; there was no noticeable interest in friendly gestures, and he was occasionally growled at. Most of us didn't try to test our bowing theories and followed the Chinese practice of walking out of our way to avoid the sentries whenever we could. Lucian maintains we never bowed—I fear I probably did.

I have some tragic memories of receiving treatment different from the Chinese. During the Christmas vacation of 1939, Lucian and I carried a large sum of money sewed into our winter underwear from Beijing to Fenzhou in Shanxi Province and delivered it to some Chinese in the unoccupied area near that town. Twice the train stopped suddenly on the way out, and we and the Chinese passengers, deliberately incurious, watched the Japanese guards unhesitatingly charge out into the frozen hills. They were followed along the aisle by the Chinese conductor, who walked through the car with his thumb and forefinger spread in the hand sign of the Chinese character for eight to indicate to the passengers that the Communist Eighth Route Army had again blown the track. Not a person changed expression.

After New Year's, we headed back to Tongzhou. The tracks were again blown twice. After the second time, we spent the night in a silent, dark train waiting for them to be fixed. Lucian and I were pulled into the station *Kempei* office at the rail junction of Shijiazhuang, where we had been mildly interrogated on the way out. We were ashamed to be treated politely with smiles because there were two Chinese prisoners of the Japanese, arms trussed tightly behind their backs, squatting on the floor like prisoners throughout Asia. Both had been beaten, and their eyes had dull, exhausted, hopeless expressions. We knew that they would soon be killed and, while we didn't want to appear to be friendly with their captors, we knew we couldn't help and would only hurt them if we tried to talk to them. We acted as cold and unfriendly to the Japanese as we could, surely without any effect, but those few moments in the Shijiazhuang *kempei* office irrevocably hardened me against the Japanese for my later part in the war and affected me for a lifetime.

Thus, and in many other such incidents, my high school days became burdened with a searing hatred of the Japanese. We learned pride in the stubbornly enduring Chinese people, sometimes courageous but mostly ineffectual in their resistance, and learned to appreciate the fine lines they had to walk between dangerously uncooperative acceptance of Japanese rules and toadying compliance. Slowly we grew mature enough to feel embarrassment that, as foreigners with our special rights, we were mostly onlookers to misery that we did not often have to share.

Emotions such as these combined with what would have been my own high-school problems anyway, primarily serious attention to the erratic behavior of girls of several nationalities, too sharp a focus on sports, too modest efforts in studies, followed by distress over grades. Taken together they filled three tumultuous years. At last, apprehensive and wrenchingly sad at leaving the familiar, war and all, I graduated from the North China American School Class of 1940—the next-to-last class, after which the school was closed forever. On July 4th of that year I left China on a small Japanese coastal vessel for Kobe, Japan, accompanied by Lucian Pye; thence by the SS *President Coolidge* for the United States. Our destination was Carleton College in Northfield, Minnesota, our fathers' alma mater and the college of choice of almost all known relatives on my father's side of the family.

CARLETON

Carleton was only an interlude between two parts of the same war for me. In the beginning, still a foreigner, I resented the casual uninterested way some of my fellow students treated the fighting in Europe and Japan's rampages in China, in my fervor not crediting the sincerity of their midwestern isolationism. Within days after we arrived at Carleton, my roommate, a well-off lawyer's son from Chicago, had demanded "Forget all that crap about the Nazis—it's not about us—and I'm not interested." He was killed by the Germans in 1944, an infantry private in a war he had not thought about. Later I realized that the prevailing Carleton attitude was maturely practical: since no one could tell about the future, nor do anything about it, why fuss nervously—why not prepare for the future one really wanted? For me that meant searching out courses in history, international relations, and English on an instructor's excellent advice that they would be useful for a diplomatic career.

Academically, I did quite well, but it seems to me now that I concentrated my efforts unnecessarily on becoming one of the boys. Chameleon-like in sweaters and dirty corduroys, wearing the freshman's required silly beanie, I tried to fit in. I played on the hockey team and also got a letter in track. I participated in what were called "college pranks," but were usually mild vandalism, and in one spectacular "scavenger hunt"— really outright robbery—which got me and, among others, a future secretary of defense arrested in St. Paul, where we experienced an American big-time jail for the first and last time (so far) in our lives.

Like many Carleton students, I earned part of my tuition by waiting on tables, cultivating pseudo-suave professionalism as I competed for tips in the Carleton Tea Room. In the summer of 1941 I stayed on campus, building small dams and clearing paths through the college arboretum with Lucian Pye during ten-hour days, six-day weeks. I hitchhiked everywhere, usually with him—long trips to Chicago and Cleveland—less dangerous than now certainly, but exciting enough. It was entirely different from my life in China.

Happiest of all events in my life then, or ever, was meeting Shirley Foss on Christmas Day 1940 at my uncle's house in nearby Faribault, Minnesota. It was uphill: Shirley was already starring in the University of

Minnesota Theater and was serious about a teaching career. She was surrounded by a group of outstanding "jocks" including a later Heisman Trophy winner—all good Catholics as she was and is. I did have superb luck in that my cousin Janet was Shirley's best friend and I supplemented her efforts on my behalf with unconstrained, because uncheckable, boasting about my adventures in China. By the summer of 1941 we were almost "going steady," and by the time I left for the war in June 1942, we had reached an "agreement" about a life together.

Pearl Harbor was not especially a shock to me. China had made me feel that Japanese treachery was to be expected. I heard the news in the kitchen of the Carleton Tea Room, and I was surprised only that one of my customers didn't know where Pearl Harbor was. I sensed also that my quick surge of enthusiasm for a war with my personally hated Japan would be misunderstood if I expressed it too early and might even require some spectacular backing up. Carleton was not strong on gestures, and real patriotism, I knew, was private.

Almost immediately though, a decision was required as to how I was to spend the war. Navy and Marine recruiters were already on campus with schemes that allowed one to finish college on an accelerated program and then become officers. I was told I was too lightweight and looked too short to become a Navy or Marine officer, but because I was otherwise splendidly healthy, I could certainly enlist. I was in the process of cautiously checking out the Marines when I learned from a classmate, Roger Hackett, who had been raised in Japan, that the Navy was looking for people who knew Japanese or who could learn it quickly. I wasn't eligible on either count, of course, but thus began a still astonishing series of events, which in the summer of 1943 actually found me, somewhat diffidently, being commissioned a second lieutenant in the United States Marine Corps Reserve.

NOTES

1. Julia Bredon, *Peking* (Shanghai, Kelly and Walsh, 1920). Peking was the foreigners' name for the city I grew up in. I use it in this book to give a touch of the foreigners' China. Beijing is much closer to the Chinese pronunciation. Beijing, meaning "northern capital," has been politically correct for Americans since the late 1960s when the State Department abandoned Peiping, "northern peace," then in use exclusively on Taiwan.

My parents' (center) wedding party. My mother said Dr. Chauncey Goodrich on the far right "looked the way God ought to look." She was being mildly sacrilegious rather than worshipful—I think. (Refers to p. 13.)

Wang Nai Nai and charge. (Refers to pp. 13–15.)

Beijing kindergartners——1919 variety. (Refers to p. 14.)

My mother's first class of kindergarten teachers in 1918. (Refers to p. 14.)

Mother (in left rickshaw) didn't like rickshaws in theory but rode in them every day. Enxiou (right) was the "compound rickshaw man" and regularly took me and two other compound children to the American School. (Refers to p. 23.)

Our Western-style house in Tongzhou. The Japanese used the porch and living room as a stable during World War II. (Refers to p. 31.)

"Skulls piled up by playful Japs" was the way we described our own thoughtless crude behavior to Life *Magazine in 1937. (Refers to p. 30.)*

Chapter 3

The Horse Marines

The Marine Corps has had a surprisingly strong influence on me, sometimes outweighing school and college, indeed any other institution, even, possibly, the Foreign Service. It goes beyond the pride that all Marines are expected to feel about the Corps and somehow continues despite intellectually accepting its faults. There are good reasons for these strong feelings; they are the Marines I knew.

Strangely for the child of a pacifist family, the Marine Corps was part of my life from the beginning. The barracks of the American Legation Guard in Beijing were at the corner of the Legation Quarter by the towering Qianmen (Front/Main Gate), next to what is now the southern end of Tiananmen Square and then against the mighty City Wall. During the Boxer Siege of the Quarter in 1900, there had been some heavy hand-to-hand fighting on the Wall itself, and the foreigners, thanks primarily to the Marines and the small Japanese detachment, held it, although just barely, thereby saving the Legations. After the Legations were relieved, the allies demanded control of the part of the Wall that ran along the Legation Quarter, and the Marines were charged with guarding it, which they did for forty years—a long connection with China that neither the United States nor China speaks about anymore. Among the sentries in the early 1920s was the young Mike Mansfield, later Senate majority leader from Montana, and longtime ambassador to Japan.

The wide top of the Wall (described in 1920 by Juliet Bredon as "wider than Fifth Avenue") had been made into a park with benches and little clumps of flowerpots. The Marines had also put up a 45-foot-high radio tower with its own little fence so that, I learned from an actual Marine, "the foreigners would never be cut off again" as they had been during the Boxer Siege. It didn't interest me at the time, but the rest of Beijing could be seen from the Wall, from the azure-tiled roof of the Temple of Heaven, just visible to the south over the roofs of Beijing's main railway station, and not far away to the north the yellow roofs of the Forbidden City; then further north, the Drum Tower and the massive gates of the northern edge of the City Wall. No Chinese except amahs with foreign children were allowed on that part of the Wall, so it was usually empty.

Because of the strictures on Chinese and Wang Nai Nai's feeling on the subject, I went there only with my parents or aunt, or other foreign children from the Legation Quarter. The point of a visit was always to talk to the sentry, who was usually taciturn and full of "sirs" and "ma'ams" in addressing adults, but was friendly, American style, with children. Probably sentries were not supposed to chat with civilians, because I remember my disappointment when with a slap, crash, and bang, one would suddenly shoulder arms and march off at the approach of another Marine. My father told me that the Marines were on the Wall all the time, and I imagined them there in the icy winds and dust of the Peking winters.

The famous Horse Marines were part of the Peking Legation Guard. Because they were unique in the world, their charge past the reviewing stand, sabres flashing, was an anticipated feature of the regular Saturday morning Dress Blues parades we watched sometimes before hockey or baseball games. The mounts were sturdy Mongolian ponies, small for cavalry horses but exceptional for endurance. This was a minor attribute because their military purpose, if any, was to enable the Marines to move around the city and warn Americans and other foreigners of danger, and perhaps in extreme circumstances to help them to the presumed safety of the Legation Quarter. As far as I can remember, the Horse Marines were never really needed.

In 1938 the Guard in Beijing was reduced and the Horse Marines disbanded. The ponies were sold to American families for ten U.S. dollars each, to prevent them from becoming cart horses or glue, or being eaten; several ended up at our school in Tongzhou. Stables were found for them in the village near the school, and we learned to ride from one of our teachers who had taken lessons at Smith College. The ponies had been used for polo before they became Marines and were very maneuverable, pursuing any ball rolling on the ground like a dog. Parades had made them used to lining up, which they would do whenever standing together, always in the same order: brown Avalon to the right of gray Tripoli, an inevitable name for a Marine Corps horse. In short, they were mature and settled in their ways; far more so than their high-school riders, who looked on them as liberating vehicles, the jalopies of transplanted Americans.

Lucian and I often borrowed two ponies belonging to our teachers, and well before breakfast we would put on their special Marine Corps saddles and ride off. Our operating theory was simple enough. Because the ponies would only gallop wholeheartedly back to their stables, we would prod them outbound for twenty minutes or so, cracking up the Chinese along the road by trying to post. When we or the ponies, or both, decided that the ride had lasted long enough, a touch of the reins and we were dashing home, racing each other, bent down like jockeys and swearing fiercely in Chinese and English to give the impression we had control over where we were going, madly loose among the carts and bicycles of Japanese-occupied China—teen-age foreigners, later both Marines.

BOULDER—JAPANESE LANGUAGE SCHOOL

To become a Marine I first had to join the Navy. This had been made clear to me during my screening for the Navy's Japanese language program. In May 1942, Roger Hackett and I had paid our own way by train to Ann Arbor, Michigan, to meet the redoubtable Commander Hindmarsh, a distinguished Harvard professor. Hindmarsh was the leading recruiter and motivating force behind the forced draft effort to provide the Navy with hundreds of Japanese language officers. Standards were necessarily high. In my five-minute interview, Hindmarsh had concentrated exclusively on my unproven, claimed capabilities to learn both written and spoken Japanese—and on serious intent. By that he did not mean ferocity against the Japanese Empire but on my willingness to pursue a year-long, high-pressure, scholarly endeavor—studying Japanese. Luckily, the doubts Hindmarsh must have had about me, a mere sophomore, were overcome by his assistant, Glenn Shaw, a former American Board missionary in Japan and good friend of my father's. Shaw showed me a first-grade Chinese primer, which I whistled through at second-grade speed proving, Shaw told Hindmarsh, that I had "a good start on Chinese characters" and thus could learn Japanese. This overstatement got me into the school. As to the Marines, all Hindmarsh would say was that "some graduates of the school will probably be taken by the Marines."

The Navy Japanese Language School at Boulder, Colorado, must have been the oddest naval organization anywhere. There was almost nothing Navy about it except for its commandant and his staff, with whom the students had little contact. True, we had traveled to Colorado using government transportation requests designating us exotically as naval agents of the Office of Naval Intelligence. A few weeks afterwards we were sworn into the Navy as yeoman second class—a rank for which I, for one, was unqualified by temperament, typing skills, or knowledge of naval regulations.

There were no controls on us except to turn up for classes and an awful two-hour exam every Saturday morning. We lived in college dormitories and fraternity houses, and we wore civilian clothes so that—sadly, I thought—there was nothing to distinguish us from the few young civilian males remaining on campus. Many, like me, were able to attend only because of the United States Navy's wasteful and ignorant prejudice against Japanese Americans for service against Japan.

The teaching methods at Boulder were similar to those used before the war in Japan itself to train American military and naval attachés: small classes of five or six with one instructor hammering conversational and written Japanese simultaneously into us for long, eight-hour days followed by private study; and proceeding with naval precision through the first five of the six famous (to students of Japanese) Naganuma Readers. Class procedures stressed drill, drill, drill, relentlessly introducing new ideographs—the *kanji*, which dominated our lives. In the beginning these were the childhood variety I was familar with from China but with entirely different pronunciations. There was a grammar new to me with the verb at the end. We were introduced to Japanese folk stories, for example, *Momotaro*, a nice boy who was found floating down the stream in a peach. He was adopted by an old couple and made them happy. He inevitably became known to us as the "son of a peach." There were simple-minded Japanese essays, for example, *keibajo*, "racetrack" in Japanese: life is a horse race and one should always run hard. We memorized the entire text of an Imperial Rescript, *kokubo*, "The National Defense," which had a fine, pompous ring to it in Japanese, starting with expressions of the universal hope for peace but after the first sentence *shikashi nagara*, "however," not everybody acts that way so Japan must be well armed and prepared for war. Grading was continuous and taken very seriously. I was worried all the time, but I somehow graduated.

Shirley came out to Boulder from Minneapolis for the ceremonies. She sat up for two nights on the train, having disregarded at my request the patriotic injunction IS THIS TRIP NECESSARY? which appeared in every train station in the country and dampened enthusiasm for travel by civilians without noticeably reducing it. She had agreed to become formally engaged despite some serious doubts, which I overcame by desperate long-distance calls, providing a positive answer to IS THIS CALL NECESSARY? On the moonlit tennis courts of the University of Colorado I gave her a ring with the smallest diamond to be found in Boulder. As she has done for the rest of our lives together, she made my friends hers. She said she admired my tailored new Marine officer's uniforms and happily attended the final ceremonies for our classes, which were in Japanese. Her presence made me less discouraged than I might have been when our valedictorian, who had covered exactly the same lessons I had, had taken the same exams, and had read no further than I in the Naganuma Readers, delivered a flawless speech in Japanese—and I understood barely half! We rode back to Minneapolis together, and for two weeks I strutted around Shirley's pleasant hometown of Faribault, south of the Twin Cities, already empty of healthy males my age. Still on a high, I left for Camp Elliott, near San Diego, to receive some actual military training.

GREEN'S FARM

About forty tightly knit "Boulder Marines," as we called ourselves, shared a training area with a Scout and Sniper School at Green's Farm. Although we bunked in a made-over barn, it was hard to see exactly what Mr. Green had farmed before he sold the property to the government, surrounded as it was by sharp ravines and sage-covered hills. Its isolation several miles from the main Camp Elliott did have advantages for the Marine Corps. It provided rugged terrain for the enlisted scouts and snipers to build on their already considerable skills in camouflage, quiet movement, night maneuvers, and marksmanship. On our trainers' side, it removed a group of awkward, unmilitary new officers from the distractions of the main base and, not incidentally, avoided questions, given our appearance, about our authenticity as officers. We resented the implication that we weren't already Marines, but there was some sense to the approach.

We learned proper deportment for officers, stressing military bearing and the honor of the Corps, organization, chains of command, discipline, and leadership. "Marines are like a string of spaghetti; they can't be pushed from behind, but can always be led from in front." We did close order drill, fired all the weapons of a Marine infantry battalion, learned to differentiate these from the lighter, faster sounds of their Japanese equivalents, practiced long marches, crawled under barbed wire well beneath machine-gun fire, and tried some infantry small unit tactics. We learned more than we needed to about Marine Corps trench warfare in World War I from our chief instructor, an oily voiced, heavily decorated major in the Reserves, given to graphic detail and dramatic emphasis. "And there it was, Gentlemen (the leg of the man near him at Belleau Woods), END OVER END, Yessir, right over our HEADS! GENTLEMEN, end over end, My! My!" I soaked it all up but realized that no one at Green's Farm knew what Japanese language officers actually did in combat. We would learn by doing in the fighting units we would join.

This would be three months later for the dozen of us who were assigned to the newly activated Fourth Marine Division than it would be for the rest of the group. While they went overseas and were soon involved in operations, we went to Camp Savage, just outside Minneapolis, where we were exposed to a cram course in Japanese military documents, courtesy of the United States Army and in the company of several hundred Nisei enlisted men. We learned a lot but could have learned more if it hadn't been for the lively Minnesotan hospitality.

As a small concession to our military status and on the assumption that Marine officers would naturally understand the procedures for the morning and evening formations, we took turns commanding companies of Nisei, all of whom were infinitely superior to us in Japanese. We were advised by the camp's adjutant, an unenergetic Caucasian major from Tennessee, that it was not necessary to render a scrupulously accurate accounting of our company's strength on each occasion but to shout out "'C' Company All Present or Accounted For Sir!" no matter what we actually had just heard from the first sergeant. The major's view, expressed rather wonderingly, was that "These people wouldn't go anywhere, even if they could."

We also learned to overlook the fact that most of our command was out of uniform, wearing a civilianized collection of towels, ear muffs, and bright-colored mittens as these thin-blooded transplants from Hawaii and Southern California desperately sought to cope with the big chills of Minnesota. Many of the absentees from roll call were scrounging wood for their stoves because they never could keep their battered uninsulated huts, inherited from the Minnesota National Guard, nearly warm enough.

FOURTH MARINE DIVISION

Our formal training in Japanese ended at Camp Savage. It had been the most practical that we had received because we dealt with actual Japanese battle documents and learned to tell their significance at a glance. But despite the aid more of this specially tailored study would have given us in combat, we were glad to receive orders in November 1943 transferring us to the gigantic Marine Corps base at Camp Pendleton, near Oceanside, California. There we joined the Fourth Marine Division, which was preparing hard to go overseas. I was assigned to the Regimental Intelligence Section of the Twenty-third Marines, one of the three infantry regiments in the division, and spent the rest of the war with that unit.

The Fourth Marine Division made four major beachheads in the Central Pacific. In historical terms it was the first division of any sort to go directly into combat from the mainland of the United States—a month-long journey of 4,871 miles from San Diego to the Kwajalein Atoll in the Marshall Islands. It was also the first step into territory that had been in Japanese hands before the war. All the other American operations had been to recover lands the Japanese had seized from others after Pearl Harbor.

Our second and third landings were on Saipan and Tinian in the Marianas; first on Saipan, the capital of all the Japanese Mandated Territories, only 1,485 miles from Tokyo, and then on Tinian about two miles south of Saipan. After its capture Tinian quickly became the world's biggest and busiest airfield, from which B-29s bombed Japan and the Enola Gay took off with the atomic bomb.

Our fourth major landing—on February 19, 1945—was on Iwo Jima, Japanese for "Sulfur Island." This was the final step the Fourth Division took in carrying the war to Japan. From there it was only 738 miles to Tokyo, an essential part of the relentless closing in. The United States needed a base for bombers crippled in raids on Japan, and we had to stop completely Iwo's use as an interceptor base and warning center against these bombers. Iwo was among the most heavily defended places in the world. Some 22,000 Japanese Army and Navy personnel, working together for a change, burrowed deeply into caves and tunnels and pre-plotted the fire of their guns to cover the whole island. They did not waste themselves in suicide attacks but had to be dug out. Their determined defense resulted in one of the most ferocious battles of the war.

All military achievements must be put into the perspective of their casualties. In January 1944, 17,086 Marines of the Fourth Division left San Diego. Nineteen months later the division had had 17,722 casualties of whom 3,298 were killed in action. Although replacements kept the division at battle strength between operations, some 75 percent of the original division became casualties.[1] Of that group the vast preponderance came from the nine battalions of the three infantry regiments—sometimes amounting to more than 100 percent of the strength that entered a battle, thus including masses of replacements. Beyond the fact that the Regimental Intelligence Section for the most part had less exposure than the men in the rifle companies, I had to have had considerable luck to have survived the war.

Whether because of our heavy casualties or just luck of the draw, the Fourth Marine Division returned to our camp on the slopes of Haleakala on Maui after each of our major operations. This required long sea voyages each way. We were unenthusiastic about the trip out but happy enough coming home to the same tents, to the same routines, while the division trained its replacements. We became known as the "Maui Marines." Many of us made friends with the predominantly Asian-American population on the island, taking advantage, as troops will anywhere, of a situation where most of the local males were occupied elsewhere in the war. This was especially so for the Japanese Americans, who had to reaffirm their patriotism by becoming the most decorated combat unit in the United States Army, far away from their homes in the cold and rain of Italy. For me it meant reaffirming my Asian connections with those Americans who, like myself, had felt somewhat foreign.

THE TWENTY-THIRD MARINES

The Two Section, as the Intelligence Section was called, was headed by Captain Richard Mirick who came, as was immediately apparent from his first words, from near Worcester, Massachusetts. Dick was en route to following his father as a prominent lawyer in Worcester when he was sidetracked by the war. His deputy was Captain William Hodge, also over six feet tall and a big-time athlete from Kansas. After the war Bill became a Protestant minister. Both of these officers demonstrated the skill and perception of the recruiters of wartime Marine officers. Both were unbreakably honest, absolutely reliable, and straightforward; both were conscientious and brave; both inspired loyalty and enduring respect. Both spent an inordinate amount of time trying to teach me the requirements for an officer in the Marine infantry. These are not sentimental judgments many decades after the fact but the way I described Dick and Bill to Shirley and my parents at the time.

David L. Anderson was the other Japanese language officer assigned to the Twenty-third Marines. He was a second generation American born in China. His grandfather had been a missionary there in the late nineteenth century, and his father had been in business in Qingdao and Shanghai before the Japanese intervened—three generations of the American presence in China. Dave had acquired his China coast foreigner's urbanity at the Shanghai American School and like me knew many "China Marines." He was a first-class golfer all his life (he died in the 1970s) and a track star in college in California. Dave was tall and dark, so it was easy to tell us apart and thus inevitable that we became known at first as "Tall Gook" and "Small Gook" in mid-war Marine Corps talk.

We were assisted by two enlisted men who had been trained a bit in Japanese. Dave worked more closely with a husky, calm corporal named Bingham and I with David Covell, a missionary's son who had spent some time in Japan. Covell was even younger than I but from the beginning I respected his judgment and his non-vindictive, gentle approach to the Japanese prisoners we captured—courtesy learned in his missionary family. Toward the end of summer in 1945 I had to tell him we had received information that his parents had been killed by the Japanese in the Philippines, something he had been fearing ever since all communication with them ceased after Pearl Harbor. I can no longer recall his reaction, but I know it must have been brave. Both of us were transferred shortly after and have lost touch, but Covell was with me for all the combat incidents I describe.

Everyone seemed colorful in the beginning, but the pale blue-eyed Colonel Louis Jones was the most. I heard, but never actually checked, that he had been in the Marine Corps as a sixteen-year-old bugler in

France during World War I—with many decorations from that war—followed by service in Shanghai, on battleships, in Nicaragua, Haiti, and other places famous in Marine Corps lore. Except on parade he was never without a cigar—even, I once discovered, in the shower, where he caught me trying to use his specially provided hot water. Surprisingly, Jones once told me that I could be made into a good officer, even a Regular Marine, if I tried. Jones never again referred to the Regular Marine Corps until we met in Beijing after the Japanese surrender, and he was my boss once more.

I have chosen a few from my many vivid memories of the war that convey both something of the atmosphere of combat and of my special kind of relationship with the Japanese enemy.

A FRIEND IS KILLED

The Regimental Intelligence Section of the Twenty-third Marines, five officers and about fifteen enlisted men, had three killed and several wounded on Saipan. These were not heavy casualties in comparison with the assault companies, but they seemed bad to me because by the time we landed, I knew everyone in the section very well.

Second Lieutenant Rolfe Hepburn, USMC, was a tent mate on Maui and my best friend in the regiment. He was a Regular Marine from Minnesota, four or five years older than I, and had been promoted from the ranks because he was a complete Marine—big and very tough, skilled at everything a Marine should know, from shining shoes (literally spit and polish) to firing machine guns, to interpreting regulations and how to get around them. He was an advocate for his men and their stern judge at the same time, and they were always first in his concerns. He taught me almost all I was ever to learn about Marine Corps responsibility and leadership, and these only by example. We shared a few crazy, drunken "liberties" on Maui and in Honolulu, slept out on the steel decks of the ships we were on together, and talked about ourselves and the future, but nothing at all about religion or politics—he having expressed early on disinterest in both. He died, like so many, in an almost incidental way.

Hep was killed the second night on Saipan. He had been wounded within a few hours after we landed with the assault battalions when a Japanese shell had knocked him into a tree. The aid station doctor tried to evacuate him to the hospital ship but he had refused, so they bandaged him heavily across the forehead, and he went on operating the Intelligence Section's observation post up on the front lines.

In the late afternoon of the second day, the Regimental Command Post, to our relief, was moved about a half mile from the beach, where we were still being shelled, to a battered banana grove on a low hill. I had been busy all day talking Japanese civilians out of hiding places bypassed by our assault companies and moving them to the assembly areas. Among the straggly, thirsty, frightened Japanese was my very first military prisoner, whom I discovered by luck as he was trying to pass himself off as a farmer. Dave Covell and I returned from delivering him to Fourth Division Intelligence on the beach barely in time to dig my foxhole within the new command post perimeter.

Typically, Hep had already made his foxhole—about thirty feet away from where I was to dig mine—and I wanted to say something to him, but he and the Marines nearest to him were busy with setting out fields of fire, or watch arrangements for the night. Besides, there had been small arms firing along our lines—some Japanese, mostly ours—and it was foolish to move and forbidden to shout. I never had another chance. Just in the final moments of the quick tropical dusk, during a few seconds of quiet, there was a single shot and a gasped, "Somebody help me," followed by "Corpsman!" from near Hep's hole. "Who was it?" I asked. "Hepburn," was whispered back to me. Then hours later when I checked to see that the men on watch were awake, one said, "Doc worked on him but he died."

The next morning there were several bodies covered with camouflaged ponchos lying on stretchers outside the aid station near my hole. "That one is Hepburn, do you want to see him?" "I don't think so," I said, and went away.

When the campaign was over I wrote to his widowed mother. She sent me a Christmas card in 1944, which I read in our old tent as we were preparing to go to Iwo Jima. "I'll never get over wanting him to come back. I can't believe that he is really gone." The correspondence didn't last. I remember him every Sunday at the right time in the Mass with Shirley, and when by myself, for some hidden reason I have an urge to be very sad, I just have to believe that I am the only person anywhere who thinks about him at all, fifty-five years later.

"SATCHEL CROSS" AND THE "CAVE OF HORRORS"

The Twenty-third Marines had no clear idea about using Japanese interpreters in combat, and it took us several days of trying to do everything at once on Saipan before we worked out a routine. Dave Anderson and I began alternating tasks because there were several distinct elements to the job. One was to find documents and useful items for intelligence. Of greatest tactical importance were battle orders or hand-sketched operational maps—often tucked into bloody shirts, or torn and smudged in small pouches lying under bodies, in bunkers, command posts, and other positions we had overrun. We sometimes were able to read these on the spot and pass the information on to the assault troops only a couple of hundred yards ahead of us, warning them of hidden Japanese positions. Most were rushed back to the Regimental Command Post where they were sorted for immediate use; for example, Dave took a Japanese map overlay showing the exact location of an ammunition dump, radioed this back to the Fourteenth Marines, our artillery regiment, and had the thrill of seeing a respectable explosion a few minutes later. Once we found some partially burned and heavily weighted red code books that we liked to think might have been helpful in breaking the Japanese codes. They probably weren't but we were praised for our alertness. We glanced through the many diaries to see the date of the latest entry before putting them in sacks to go back to the ships offshore, where they were looked at again.

The other more engrossing assignment was to try to capture military or civilian prisoners who might know something useful, questioning them on the spot, and then getting them back to the Regimental Command Post to determine their real value and how quickly they should go to the skilled interrogators at Division. Because Dave and I were equally weak in the language, we simply divided up by days. One day one of us would stay in the command post sorting documents and taking care of the Japanese civilians and the rare military prisoners. The other would go out with the battalions, roving between the reserve battalion and those on the line. We usually led a twelve- or fifteen-man team of a squad of engineers for blowing up caves and bunkers, a few scouts and snipers to find our targets or to discover the best way to surround a cave, a radioman so we could be summoned quickly, and a medical corpsman because some of the Japanese, civilians particularly, often needed immediate help. We would go along behind the assault companies checking out caves, clumps of trees, and other areas that had been bypassed in the initial attack. We surrounded these and tried to encourage any Japanese still alive to surrender.

We were seldom successful with the soldiers, and most often ended up blasting cave entrances shut, even though we knew there were living Japanese still inside. I achieved enough proficiency with a satchel charge used occasionally for that purpose (that is, I didn't kill myself or any other American) to get called "Satchel" Cross by Colonel Jones and others in the Regimental CP. I was never quite sure whether I should be proud or slightly ashamed. A satchel charge is just what it sounds like, very high explosives packed into a satchel-like bag with a protruding fuse, which could be slung, tossed, or lowered into a cave or bunker port.

After the first few days on Saipan we had a problem with the mixture of soldiers and civilians as the Japanese forces began to scatter into small groups. Many civilians did come out when they thought it was safe, but often they were held back by soldiers who had gotten mixed in with them and would force them to commit suicide when we got nearby, or shoot them if they responded to our entreaties. It was an awful dilemma for me because we couldn't leave an inhabited cave behind our lines, and yet I knew that there were possibly noncombatants in every cave we dealt with. If I had been able to speak Japanese better, I might have saved more lives.

Once, I disregarded my instructions to close every cave we could. We had gone to check an underground air-raid shelter, a cement room dug deep into the ground with a little doorway and hole for air on the top. I had started my shouting a few feet away from this shelter and heard some immediate chatter in high-pitched women's voices from inside, and then suddenly there were several clicks, the sound a Japanese grenade made before it exploded. The explosions themselves were followed by screaming from the women and children. I kept calling, but there was no answer, just shrieks and yells, and even these died down. I was afraid to go into the shelter myself, so couldn't order anyone else to do it, nor could I face blowing it up. After waiting around for awhile we returned to our headquarters. The thought that there might be children still alive in the shelter bothered me all night, so the next morning after promising my bosses to "neutralize" the shelter for sure this time, I went back with the same group of Marines.

There were no answers to my calls although we could hear children sobbing inside. So we finally just pulled a loose concrete slab and looked down in. What we saw became known as the "Cave of Horrors" in the American newspapers because, except for three Japanese soldiers who had blown themselves up with the grenades we had heard the day before, the rest of maybe twenty people had killed themselves by stabbing each other; the adults had apparently tried to kill the children. Three or four of these were still alive among the heaps of bodies, but they had had their throats slashed. I believe we managed to save all of them because the well-trained and kindly medical corpsmen held them in such a way that their heads wouldn't wobble and sever anything vital as they were passed up out of the shelter. We had an awful time moving them through some heavy underbrush to an aid station, where doctors temporarily patched their throats. Then gently, gently they were put into jeep ambulances and taken back to the base hospital area. Marines smiled and patted them as they went by. They are in their late fifties now; I wonder what they remember and what they think of the madness of their parents.

AN AMERICAN AGENT?

One time we found a batch of twenty-five or thirty civilians just standing in a clearing in the jungle, where the Japanese had planted some banana trees. They were mostly women and children plus a few old men, but prominent in the middle was a younger man, obviously a soldier wearing an almost white civilian shirt. I started to give the usual instructions to the group in Japanese, telling them that we would give them water because despite the almost daily rain, they were always thirsty, and warning them they would have to walk some distance before we could send them to an assembly area. Always alert to differences in behavior that set individuals apart and could signal danger, I noticed that the man was moving toward me, not saying anything but quietly separating himself from the other Japanese. He was unarmed but I unslung my carbine anyway and ordered him to raise his hands. He came right up beside me and when he was sure the other Japanese couldn't hear, he said in quite passable English, "I must ask to be taken to your headquarters immediately," adding, "I have an American friend, Lieutenant Commander So-and-So whom I knew in Tokyo." Dave Anderson jeeped him top speed back to Division and we never saw him again.

A few weeks later I happened to run into a half-Japanese American naval officer who spoke superb Japanese (his Caucasian father apparently made him acceptable to the Navy). I asked him whether my find had really been one of our agents in Japan. He, of course, denied it and claimed without elaboration that the man was a fake. Maybe not. I wonder where he ended up after the war.

THE JAPANESE

August 21, 1944 (on board ship after the Saipan/Tinian battles)

Dear Mom and Dad,

Everyone has a tremendous interest in Japan and China and now that people have seen some live Japanese civilians, they wonder what makes them tick. Something I wonder myself. Their seeming instinct for suicide, for instance. I believe that through fear and frustration, they actually become crazy. On the last days of the Tinian campaign, I talked with a loudspeaker to groups of Japanese civilians who had no hope of escape except to surrender or kill themselves. Although there were many individuals that came in to live on, others threw themselves over the cliff, pushing the sick first, or allowed themselves to be tied up in a circle by their soldiers, who then blew them up—all this in our sight. Soldiers shot each other, joined hands to jump into the sea, and so on. Those that came in, on the other hand, were almost nonchalant. The kids were the calmest of all and ate a tremendous amount of the candy which we had in our rations. They were very polite. Later on, when they were in the relaxed atmosphere of the prison camp, they would line the wire and shout, "Baitou," which was meant to mean "bait," or

Marine Corps slang for candy. The Marines would throw them some and they would say "Sanka you," or "OK." Seeing that there isn't any farming to do the kids can play all day with no school as yet.

September 2, 1944

Dear Mom, *(my father was in Free China and my mother was alone)*

Naturally, with all the patrols I went on, various things happened that were scary or exciting or disagreeable. I spent the last few days on Saipan floating around on an amphibious tank and trying to get the Jap civilians and soldiers to give up. They were caught on the cliffs and had to go up to our lines, sit there or jump into the water and drown. Some of the soldiers would wave languid hands or thumb their noses at us. They hadn't any weapons but they wouldn't surrender. We would bring the tanks up to within 50 feet of the rocks and talk to them, almost man to man. After four days of this, most of the civilians had left and I had charge of several of these tanks with orders to fire if the remaining soldiers didn't surrender. We fired but the waves were choppy so we missed quite a few of them.

HOME

December 3, 1944 (from Rest Camp Maui)

Dear Mom,

Tonight I am regimental duty officer. The whole camp is technically under my care. . . . Taps are (is) floating out over the camp. It is a peaceful sound with a sad connotation. It is the end of another day of war. All over the world men are dying and in pain and lonely. I hope that this will all end someday. Each bugler takes up when the other one stops; slowly the whole immense camp is put to bed.

Christmas Day, 1944

To Shirley,

We've really been having Christmas these last few days with good movies, carol singing, and even a lighted tree. The other night we had "Going My Way." Last night was really quite wonderful. I was invited to a friend's tent where we had hot buttered rum and sang carols and other songs. Then at 11:30 we went to Midnight Mass. It was outdoors but the theater stage was made into a beautiful altar. There was a good choir of Marines. It was moonlight and although that isn't exactly Christmas-like—a tropical moon—it was beautiful. I said a prayer for you.

The memory of the comradeship of us old-timers in the regiment is still fresh and poignant to me. We knew that we would be going aboard ship in a few days for another operation, but high up there on the slopes of Haleakala it seemed wrong for us to talk of it. Two of the five officers in the tent were killed and one was badly wounded a few weeks later on Iwo Jima.

IWO JIMA

The battle as I remembered it right afterwards (aboard ship back to Maui from Iwo Jima).

March 18, 1945

Dear Mom and Dad,

You have often asked me to write of my experiences or to give you some sketches of incidents which have happened. I've tried a little but it has been hard.

The main feeling I have now is of great loneliness. It is probably the same with all of the more fortunate veteran troops. It doesn't seem possible that so many of my friends and acquaintances should be gone. It doesn't seem possible that I won't have a drink or laugh with any one of a dozen good friends; yet, withal, the converse is true. And those who are left who were once merely acquaintances are now becoming good friends. It was that way after Saipan, too. It is a tradition, probably as old as war itself.

Iwo Jima first appeared to me as I walked out on deck to go to my debarkation station. On the left as we looked at it was Surabachi, a dirty brown mountain. At that moment, large puffs of brown smoke bounced off its sides as the fleet shelled it. To the direct front was the beach on which we were to land with the airfield above it. To the right was the northern part of the island where we were to have such a hard time later on. At the moment though, my sole attention was to the immediate front.

When we climbed down the nets into the landing craft, we were still too far out to see much of what was going on at the beach. It was an hour and a half before H-Hour at 0900, (time when the first waves hit the beach), and the bombardment was really getting underway. Unless one has heard one, it is impossible to describe the terrific noise of a naval bombardment. Noise is coming from every angle. We could see the orange flash of the guns on the ships, then the yellow brown smoke and after a wait, hear the noise. The big 16-inch guns sound like a heavy door being slammed, only much, much louder. The 5-inch guns were the loudest with a crack that made you tighten involuntarily.

Our boat had to go to what is called the Line of Departure because of our command functions. That is a line where the amphibian tractors and landing boats form into waves. We sat on the LD for a long time and had a view of the whole landing at first hand. A jeep was in my boat and I had taken off my pack to be more comfortable. I sat on the engine hood which was a good seat. We sat for a long time. This time we were to land quite late, compared with the first waves I went in with on Saipan, so I had more leisure to watch and less to worry about, for awhile at least.

As we rolled back and forth, we brought things to each other's attention. "Damn it, they seem to be fixing AA (anti-aircraft) over there." "They're really laying them on the right lieutenant." Or someone would say, "Is that the X over there, Mr. Cross?" For unavoidably, this was merely a show, never to be new to us, and yet not old. It was too important not to be watched every minute.

As H-Hour came nearer, the assault waves began moving around us. We were still far out in the water, and the men were sitting on the sides of the amphibian tractors. Occasionally a friend would go by, and in the Marine Corps way, he would give either a casual nod or boisterous greeting. Finally, the assault waves began to go in. As the tractors started roaring towards the beach, the men in them slowly slid down into the middle until all you could see were a few camouflaged helmets and rifles sticking up along the sides of the tractor, a geyser of water leaping behind each one. In the split second timing of such an operation, one wave after another followed into the beach.

We sat at the LD for two interminable hours. I smoke maybe six or seven cigarettes a day but found myself reaching for a damp cigarette about every half hour. We could see the shells hitting the beach and around the darker objects which were tanks half-way up the sloping beach to the airfield. We could tell it was a terrific beach and the men began comparing it to Saipan. The shells kept increasing in quantity and intensity. Occasionally someone would say, "Look at that." I'd look at the beach and see a dozen geysers at once shoot up in front of a line of boats going to the beach. Then all of a sudden, a boat growled up alongside and a naval officer shouted, "Proceed to Beach Yellow 2." And with a roar, we were off. In the next few minutes there was confusion in the boat. Everyone was scrambling for his gear and putting it on. Once these landing boats start for the beach, they go at top speed. I was hardly ready when I heard the unmistakable whistling sound of a shell overhead and a loud crash as it hit the beach about 100 yards to our left. Then a frightening thing happened. The beach was so messed up with broken vehicles, amphibious tractors, etc., that there was no room for us to go in, so we suddenly turned to the left and ran parallel to the beach looking for a place. We did this for only five minutes but it seemed longer than that. All the time shells kept going overhead, making a sound like that of a flock of flying pigeons except that the shell splashed into the water in front of us.

We finally found a landing place and went the remaining fifty yards into the beach. Everyone was crouched down and bracing himself for the moment when we'd run aground. With a jar the boat hit the sand and the ramp in the bow began to lower. All of a sudden it stuck, and I remember shouting, "Kick the damned thing down. Kick it down!" And seeing a Marine hurl himself against it sending it crashing to the sand. And then I was running hard. I went about fifteen yards and then stopped to see if the others were coming all right. I told all those I could see to go on up off the beach and after deciding to leave the jeep in the landing craft for it to go around and find a place where a jeep could actually drive up off the beach, I started up myself moving to the right up the sandy slope where the rest of the Twenty-third were, pausing only to rest here and there in a shell hole as did the men. It was all uphill, you see, and the sand was shifting and soft; I got tired quickly. No shell lit around me or my group on the way up and I reached the place where we were to dig in for the night.

(The following several paragraphs were not in this letter but seem to fit in here. They are from vivid memory.)

A few minutes after we had arrived at the Regimental Command Post, actually just some shell holes, a Marine jumped into the hole we were in and reported that a Japanese was lying out in the open about seventy-five yards from us toward the beach. He didn't seem capable of doing any harm but no one wanted to check. To me it was sign of battle experience—that he hadn't been shot out of hand. Taking only my carbine and a map of the Yellow Beach area on which I had marked some identifying features in Japanese, two Marines carrying a stretcher (one was Dave Covell) and I went over to my first prisoner on Iwo. Just as we got to him, shells began to crash all around us so I had to slide him back into the shelter of his shallow sandbag hole and prop him against two of his definitely dead comrades.

Blood was oozing out of his nose and ears and he had the vacant unfrightened look of the critically wounded. I shouted a question to him between shell bursts but he weakly raised a hand to his head, indicating that he was deaf. Interrogation was clearly out but I sensed that he might be saved for use later, forcing a knee-shaking decision to carry him to an aid station. We carefully put the silent but still conscious Japanese on the stretcher and with a little help from me struggled through the deep sand to the nearest aid station—really three shell holes crammed with wounded and nearly dead Marines. The doctor, who had been wounded himself, glanced hastily at our prisoner. "Can't do anything for him here—all the way to the beach—maybe they'll send him out to the ships—can't spare our stretcher bearers—he's up to you." Reluctantly, we went down the sandy slopes to the junkyard of the beach, where we put our stretcher in the line of those being coolly loaded onto the landing craft by Navy Corpsmen. Then we made our way back up the long slant throwing ourselves flat every few yards because the shelling had picked up again.

Resume March 18, 1945, letter.

Two of the men and I dug a foxhole (which was very easy because of the soft sand) near another hole where six or eight dead Marines were piled closely together. Just after the hole was dug, the shells began coming into our area and we stayed flat for the rest of the night. It was cold and all we had was a poncho to cover us. We were in our summer dungarees so besides the fear, we were also shaking from the cold.

During this night of D-Day, the shells kept screaming down. Some of them lit close enough to throw sand all over us and set our ears ringing. The shells going overhead made a whistling sound like a flock of birds or escaping steam, depending on whether they were high or flat trajectory. In a short while, we could tell whether they were going to be close or not and shivered or lay still accordingly. When one would land pretty close, the next one would be closer and then for a minute or two, they'd come down, a little nearer, a little farther, very close, a little way away, further away, nearer, a little nearer, close, very close and then WHAM and sand would come all over us and we would press into the ground as deeply as we could. Then the shells would fall further off and finally, switch to some other area and we would relax that awful shaking. After half an hour or so, we'd get worked over again.

The next morning they brought tanks up by our foxhole, which was torture because as they went by, the Japs would turn loose on them. After every barrage, there'd be the call, "Corpsman!" and the stretchers, walking wounded, and guys broken up by the shelling would wind slowly or crawl towards the aid station. The second night, the Japs hit a truckload of our ammunition about 25 yards away, and the shells in the truck would bounce out and explode about ten feet from our hole. The next morning it turned out that none of the shells had gone any further, but we didn't know that. I kept thinking how bad it was to be killed by one of our own shells.

CAVES ON IWO JIMA

After the Marines moved past the airfield areas, the Japanese resistance came from caves connected by tunnels, skillfully arranged so that they could support each other. Each had several entrances. Often the assault troops were pushed back after closing up some holes only to have the Japanese reappear from concealed openings behind or beside them. Casualties mounted as the Marines fought back and forth over the same rocks and ridges, firing in different directions, unable to avoid leaving unprotected gaps in the lines. Dave Anderson and I abandoned the one day in one day out routine we had developed on Saipan. Each of us had a team, this time augmented by a couple of war dogs (mine were Dobermans) and their handlers. We were just behind the assault companies much of the time, warily approaching holes that had been pointed out to us and trying to induce some surrenders. We used hand-held loudspeakers, which, when the battery was fresh, could dramatically project my poorly pronounced Japanese but I felt sure made me spectacularly conspicuous.

The technique was somewhat like fishing. I would put the bait out with offers of water and medical care, saying the battle was almost over, something no Japanese would believe given all the racket but which we hoped might have the effect of convincing isolated soldiers that they needn't fear their own side if they gave up. After awhile, if we were lucky, I was answered from inside the cave and then, following my instructions, an apprehensive Japanese would emerge blinking in the sunlight, hands held high. This was always a tense moment because the potential prisoner was vulnerable to being cut down by his erstwhile comrades who didn't want him to surrender, or Marines could get hurt if he were a decoy trying to draw us out into the open. I always felt that I was operating in slow motion when I went forward to search him.

As soon as he and I were sheltered from enemy fire, I delivered on my promise of water and a cigarette and, more often than not, medical aid. My interrogation initially concentrated on the cave/bunker complex itself. Where were the other entrances? Were there any others in the cave? Could he get them to come out? Some prisoners would even go back to the cave mouth themselves and call. I was especially alert when a man hesitated, because it showed that he didn't know if there were others or that he distrusted those still there. Once, I motivated a prisoner to try by indicating that we were going to blow the cave shut, but he got no response even though he called out the names of those supposedly still alive in the cave. He looked hopelessly resigned when the engineer squad and a tank bulldozer sealed up the opening.

THE END OF THE WAR

When the remnants of the Fourth Marine Division returned to Maui in mid-April 1945, we were greeted by the entire island. Schools were let out and children brought from all over to line the roads and cheer us back to our camp; even the big Native Hawaiian longshoremen with whom we had feuded when we jointly loaded the outbound ships four months before seemed glad to see us. Older mothers of all Hawaii's races, longing for their own faraway sons, stood in little groups on the corners crying and waving. Cases of canned pineapples were shoved into our trucks by grinning Filipinos from the canning factories. The island's mayors designated us the "Maui Marines." It was almost as if the war was over.

That was not really so. Dave Anderson and I went back into the same tent for the third time with another replacement tentmate; already our names were on regimental duty lists. During the next few days as replacements poured in, we began the tiresome process of learning new names and adjusting to new commanders. The Twenty-third Marines hardly missed a beat before we started our hard field training, the veterans wearily but thoroughly rebuilding their units. In the mornings the distinctive Marine sergeant's cadence rang out along the company streets; men appeared in clean dungarees; salutes were expected; even officers' tents were inspected. Dave and I spent whole days with the rifle companies translating (or pretending to) the writing on the blood-stained Japanese flags that the Marines had picked off the dead enemy, approving souvenirs ranging from swords and bayonets to postcards and Japanese cigarettes for shipment home. We used these contacts to lecture on the value of prisoners, speaking now from much experience. Life was stressless, yet we lived easily only in the present, not reliving the recent past, not speculating on the future.

The present became even more pleasant when the Fourth Division's language officers were assigned to temporary duty at Pearl Harbor. We went back to work in the Joint Intelligence Center Pacific Ocean Area (JICPOA), manned almost entirely by Boulder graduates who labored methodically in eight-hour shifts on captured documents. We searched unsuccessfully in the topics we were assigned to cover for clues to the Fourth Division's part in the invasion of Japan, already slated for the next fall. We knew enough about the Japanese people to anticipate that casualties would be high and that our language skills would be tested beyond anything that went before.

We were among the thousands who, conscious that their luck was bound to run out, felt saved by the Japanese surrender.

Johnny Rich, a Boulder classmate, and I, along with everyone else in Honolulu, celebrated V-J Day, August 14, 1945, to what could properly be called excess. Knowing that true popularity among the screaming mobs of citizens and servicemen depended on our finding wheels, we simply went to Camp Catlin, the huge Marine replacement depot and checked out a reconnaissance carrier, quite easy on that day—"What do you want it for?" "To ride around town in, pick up friends." "OK, official duty. Sign here"—and off we went, inching our way, gathering up friends and strangers. Somewhere, in one of our lifetimes of coincidences, we ran into Lucian Pye, also a Marine, whose until-then-secret mission would be taking him to China in a few weeks. Losing our caps, our faces and collars covered with lipstick, our shirts wet from spilled beer, until late on that mad day, the whole truckload, maybe twelve in all, arrived downtown at the Central Union Church for its service of Thanksgiving.

We were greeted with friendly reserve. The three of us Marine officers spectacularly out of uniform, the hatless sailor—an early recruit from the gate at Camp Catlin—less his black Navy kerchief, and the beautiful, now solemn, Asian-American girls who had joined us along the way, were somehow not out of place among the older, *haole* congregation. We wisely

joined in the post-service coffee, and I aroused some interest by introducing myself as Rowland Cross's son—my parents having been supported by the Central Union Church while they were in China. The minister, who I dimly realized too late was a longtime family friend, wrote to
my parents the next day, expressing the joy of the church that I had survived the war, with nary a word about my appearance.

Back at Pearl Harbor and sober, I struggled with my disappointment
that I had no profound thoughts about the war. Rather than gratitude that
the atomic bombs had made my future more assured, I lay in the double-
decker top bunk in my comfortable room at the Bachelor Officers' Quarters (BOQ) staring out through the window screens at the crowds of
sailors coming and going from the Fleet Landing, trying to rationalize my
mild depression that the war had ended the way it had. "There will
always be those Japanese who will never believe that we crushed them
beyond all power to recover before either of these things happened," I
wrote pensively to Shirley.

I have visited Japan often in the years since the war but have never
gone to Hiroshima or Nagasaki. I do not share in the guilt that some
Americans seem to feel over the first use of this unique and horrible
weapon. To me it was only the inevitable ending for a brutal period in
world history. I have thought about it long and deeply, especially after
studies appeared by youngish modern historians of American intelligence estimates available to the White House in 1945 but largely ignored
until the 1960s. These claimed variously that the bombs were not necessary to save American lives because diplomatic overtures were succeeding and Japan was in the process of surrendering; that our sustained conventional bombing and naval blockade would end the war without an
invasion; that General Eisenhower from the other side of the world had
told Secretary of War Stimson after the war that "Japan was already
defeated and dropping the bomb was completely unnecessary"; and that
American casualties in an invasion would not have been nearly as high
as the estimates given out shortly after the war. Implied in all of this was
that President Truman had reasons other than saving lives when he gave
the fateful order.

The whole dispute reflects the difficulties historians face in working
from documents to reconstruct the atmosphere in the summer of 1945,
although it might also reflect a general bias against American military
behavior growing from opposition to the Vietnam War. At the time, whatever the intelligence experts were later quoted as saying, there could be
no accurate estimate of American casualties in an invasion of the Japanese home islands. If the entire population fought for their own homes
throughout Japan as fanatically as they did for the territories they had
seized from others, American casualties could have been enormous and

those of the Japanese beyond comprehension. There was no way of knowing whether the Japanese military in Japan itself would have allowed the emperor to surrender; or whether the millions of Japanese soldiers scattered abroad would have obeyed; or whether a surrender negotiated as the result of conventional bombing and blockade would have produced the kind of occupation that transformed Japan. I never believed, even while the war was going on, that a political result could be brought about by bombing alone—a youthful understanding of the psychological effects of bombing that has colored my thinking ever since. But because of their unprecedented horror, Hiroshima and Nagasaki provided an honorable excuse for the emperor to quit. The surrender immediately after the bombs were dropped saved the American and Japanese lives that would have been lost in relentlessly battering or in invading an already defeated nation.

My high-school years were spent under the Japanese Occupation of North China and I served in a Marine infantry unit, so I find it impossible to accept the adverse judgments of these scholars on how our leaders ended that war. Historians critical of President Truman should recognize that there did not have to be any of the millions of Chinese, Filipinos, Indonesians, Vietnamese, Burmese, Dutch, Australians, British, Americans OR Japanese killed by war if Japan had not cruelly invaded its neighbors. Truman ended completely what the Japanese had begun—and I had seen that beginning with my own eyes.

THE MARINE CORPS IN CHINA

The Marine Corps seemed to operate its personnel system by mimeograph machine, with multiple copies of everything, sent everywhere. One always expected to be lost in the pile. So I was surprised when, shortly after the Japanese surrender, Dave Anderson and I—back once more in Maui—were assigned to the Marine forces preparing to go to North China, our previous residence there having been mysteriously discovered. We hurriedly said good-bye to our comrades in the Fourth Division, who were returning to the mainland. There followed a three-week series of "hurry up and wait" movements toward the Chinese cities where we were born: via Pearl Harbor, with quiet days on the already peacetime beaches of Kailua on the other side of Oahu. Next we were crammed onto a seatless Navy cargo plane for an exhausting, teeth-rattling ride to Okinawa where we succeeded in convincing a timid Navy transportation officer that we were much too tired to board the transports just leaving for China. We pleaded that despite the inconvenience, we would prefer to fly to Shanghai the next day. There we found that a

Japanese Colonel Saito of the defeated Japanese Army would pay our bills at restaurants, bars, and the world-famous Cathay Hotel. This amenity slowed our progress north for several more days, enabling the Marines to land and set up billets without our help. Finally in Tientsin, I found that my commander would be none other than Brigadier General Louis R. Jones, formerly of the Twenty-third Marines, and that I would be going up to Peking with the advance party for his headquarters.

THE COOK STORY

The very next day, dizzy from my quickening heart and unaccountably fighting tears, I stood on the lowest step of the car as the train slowly slid into the Beijing Station, taking the track closest to the big City Wall exactly as it had when we came into the city from our school in Tongzhou for our hockey games. A crowd of well-dressed Chinese officials and Lucian Pye, who had arrived a few days earlier, greeted us on the station platform. The colonel yelled, "Hey Cross! Say something to them!" So I supplemented the more practiced Lucian with a few words in Chinese about the United Nations, freedom, peace, and so on, which seemed to go down fairly well. But right afterwards one of the Chinese came up and said to Lucian, "We thank you very much for your speech, but a problem has arisen—the forces which are being brought back from West China have not yet arrived in any numbers, the Japanese who control the city have said that they are going to go back to their barracks, and the guards that we have in the city are only the former puppet soldiers of the Japanese. Meanwhile the Eighth Route Army (that is, the communists) are only about ten miles away in the western hills. So, what we would like you to do is show that American forces have arrived, and that the city will be guarded; and we would like to have you drive around to demonstrate this."

Lucian translated the Chinese plea for the colonel, who was not anxious to play the game. He said, "Hell, I just want to go around the corner here to the old Marine barracks, and I don't want to take our people all over town." But somehow the Chinese prevailed on him, and we piled the troops into some Japanese trucks that they had brought along. There seemed to be thousands of Chinese assembled to watch us come in. I climbed on the cab of a truck, and we slowly rolled through the shrieking crowds. After going through the Qianmen gate and a very short ways, I heard above the din and off to the side, "An Ning! An Ning!" my Chinese name. I looked down, and there was Da Shi-fu, the cook who had been in our family since my father arrived in 1917. I reached down and pulled him up beside me and he sat up there on the top of the truck as if he had done this every day of his life. When I had recovered sufficiently, I asked him, "How did you get here? How did you know that I was here?" And he said, "When you were a little boy you would come into the kitchen and you would say that when you grew up you were going to be a Marine, so when I heard that the American Marines were coming, I went down to wait for you."

This story has a sad ending. I prevailed on the headquarters mess officer to give him a job in the officers' mess; but he quickly became inadequate, too slow to provide the three huge meals demanded by ten or fifteen officers every day. He suddenly quit not only the Marines, but Beijing itself, and returned to his Shandong village. My Aunt Laura, who stayed on in China during the communist takeover, heard through the servants' grapevine that he had bought some land there and had become enough of a landlord to have been executed in the land reform. Maybe this wasn't true; there were rumors everywhere in Beijing before the communists came in; Da Shi-fu couldn't have bought much land or had time to make enemies. Anyway this saddened, decent, hard-working, honorable man, so much a part of our lives, left us without a trace.

Ostensibly, the Marines were in North China to take the surrender of the Japanese and repatriate them to Japan. Behind this simple concept was the deeply political motive of replacing the Japanese with Nationalist soldiers brought from West China by American ships and planes and establishing the latter in positions where they could prevent the communist Eighth Route Army from seizing North China and Manchuria. General Jones's little headquarters had the formidable task of coordinating the movements in the Peking area of both Chinese and Japanese units, as well as keeping the road and rail lines open to Tianjin in the face of some harassment by the communists, who were continually on the move themselves. I learned one of the facts of postwar international politics fairly early in this process.

One of my main duties was to attend the daily morning meeting of staff officers from our headquarters, the Japanese area command, and the arriving Chinese garrison. There, accompanied by Lucian for the Chinese part, we would discuss the movement orders for their forces the Japanese staffs had drafted overnight. Then we tried to describe accurately in Japanese and English the almost automatic objections to these moves followed by toning down in Chinese and Japanese the exasperation of the other Marine officers. Although the Chinese were quite credible in their choice of the monkey wrenches they threw into the Japanese plans (for example, availability of trains whose Chinese-controlled schedules invariably had rolling stock elsewhere), what was going on was clear enough to all sides. The Chinese were bent on keeping Japanese troops around Beijing for as long as possible, thereby assuring a continuing American presence.

The smartly turned-out Japanese lieutenant colonel would listen to my labored translation of the Chinese objection, solemnly begin to gather up his papers, and announce that his staff would have another proposal for the next day. Then adding in measured, plain Japanese that I could handle, "We understood that tomorrow there would be two American LSTs at Tientsin ready to load," leaving unanswered where those Japanese troops would be coming from. This usually set the American side off against the Chinese, and the meeting would go on for awhile, the remaining Japanese condescendingly aloof. One day a Marine colonel, desperately searching for some way out, asked Lucian, "Are you sure they understand what I'm saying?" He was about to translate that when suddenly out of the silence the Japanese officer, in perfect Canadian English, announced with a superior smile, "We Americans and Japanese have a hard time with the Chinese don't we?" None of the Americans changed expression, but I was jarred by the enemy's prophecy so soon after the war.

There are two postscripts to my Marine Corps story. They speak to a much different me and a much different Japan. Together they spell out the end of the war for me—an Asian full circle.

SAIPAN POSTSCRIPT

In 1981 I returned alone to Saipan on a hastily arranged, private visit just as Shirley and I were tying down the details for our departure from Taipei as head of the American Institute in Taiwan. The idea was that rather than a nostalgic or sentimental journey, my leaving Taipei for a few days would give both of us relief from the heavy good-bye Chinese feasts.

Saipan looked and felt very different. The battle sites in the island's interior were covered by *tangan tangan*, a vine-like tree often twenty feet high or, as in the place where Hep was killed, by small modern houses. The teen-aged sons of a Foreign Service officer serving with the American high commissioner of the Trust Territories drove me to the cliffs on the north end, where so many Japanese, soldiers and civilian men, women, and children, had thrown themselves into the sea. Here and there I felt the small tug of remembered sadness, but it had been too long ago and the stone monuments to the dead, the texts in English and Japanese, seemed almost as remote from my own experience as the stern statues at Gettysburg had been on our family's visits there.

My room at the motel-like hotel overlooked a beach where the Second Marine Division had landed. Half a rusted Japanese tank was the only visible souvenir of the fighting, unnoticed by the Japanese bathers. I watched these from the balcony of my room on the top floor. "Very quiet, you know, up here," explained the worldly teen-age Saipanese bellhop; "Japanese, you know, new married." They crunched over the volcanic cinder path to the light brown beach in their identical sandals, cameras slung over the beach bags of their tour groups and the bright towels provided by the hotel. Racing children, covered against the tropical sun by white T-shirts and colored baseball caps, led the parade. The young parents, father first, came next, overloaded with thermos jugs, rubber rings, and rafts. Grandparents, spotless in white long-sleeved shirts and gray dresses, followed slowly behind to sit briefly under the hotel's umbrellas and then to retreat to their own age groups on the shaded verandah. Mixed in were the honeymooners, not demonstrative, but not standing too far apart either. All of them, including the children, had gone by bus to the northern cliffs, but once they had performed their obligation to the souls of the thousands of Japanese dead of Saipan, they had settled happily into their holiday.

In the afternoons I walked along the beach or swam by myself in the soft, clear water—the only American, my white hair possibly indicating to anyone who thought about it that I might have been in the fighting. The Japanese, however, regarded me incuriously, and I, not at all lonely or out-of-place, felt an unaccountable—even disturbing—surge of affection for them.

I tried to put these conflicting emotions into words at a dinner given for me on the last evening of my visit. My host was the high commissioner for the Trust Territories, a man named High, easily remembered not only because of his title, but because he stood at least 6' 8". Throughout the steak dinner in the windowless small private dining room in the hotel and above the alternating purr and rattle of the hard-working air conditioner, High had discussed the battle for Saipan about which he was well informed. "And what do you think of it now?" he asked at the end.

I took him to mean the whole war, and in my slow reply I went back to my hatred of the Japanese for their atrocities in China, my contempt for the Japanese military leaders and the insanity of their code, the conflict between my urge to avenge Hep and others, and my job in the Twenty-third Marines to capture Japanese alive—and how all of this had happened when I was so young. I thought no one at the table would blame me if I were to have resented the way the Japanese seemed to be self-confidently taking Saipan back. Oddly enough though, I had reacted quite differently. For me, the sight of the young, well-off Japanese families playing unthreateningly on the beach, free of their past, had somehow turned the crushing defeat of Japan into something like a victory for them too. In that sense, I had concluded that modern Japan was an American gift to the Japanese people. I would agree that this was not a new thought for Americans and maybe one not readily accepted by the Japanese. Yet, even after many trips to Japan, I had not seen its truth more clearly than on this island, long after the battle.

IWO JIMA POSTSCRIPT

In June 1995 I returned to Iwo Jima, over fifty years after our landings there. Incredibly, I was a guest of the Japan Sumo Association, whose invitation read, "On the island of Iwo Jima, fifty years ago in March the United States and Japan suffered a great loss of precious human lives. Our wish is to pay respects to their souls and to promise them that the strong ties of goodwill and peace founded by the U.S. and Japan over the post-war years shall be everlasting and further strengthened." The crowning ceremony was to be a *Dohyo-iri* or "entering the ring," where sumo wrestlers step into the ring and go through a short ancient cere-mony—not a real bout—symbolizing they are driving out evil. Chosen for this were the two current *yokohana* (grand champions), a 450-pound, 6' 5" Samoan American from Honolulu, named Akebono for sumo pur-poses, and Takanohana of Japanese descent. They would "symbolize rep-resentation of the two nations who fought the war as enemies but have now become so close."

My presence at this quintessentially Japanese event was engineered by John Rich, a fellow Marine Japanese language officer from Boulder and the Fourth Marine Division. John had returned to journalism after the war, becoming a top NBC correspondent headquartered in Japan for many years. He had already been invited when he was asked by the thoughtful Sumo Association whether he "wouldn't be lonely among all the Japanese." He thereupon nominated me for this all-expenses paid journey. "How'd you like a free trip to Iwo Jima?" John asked from the Bahamas en route from Florida to Maine on his boat. The first Japanese I heard from was a cautious official of the Japan Defense Agency (JDA) inquiring politely—since we would be flying in a JDA C-130—whether there would be "any problem with the American military authorities" if I traveled to Iwo Jima. I replied that I didn't think so, because they hadn't objected the first time! His reaction to this sally was a disappoint-ing, "Ah, I see."

Seen from above, Iwo Jima had changed in the past fifty years from miserable gray- and black-scarred brown to green and gleaming white. It is a Japanese airbase again, manned by trim Japanese Navy and Air Defense Forces and shared occasionally with the United States Navy for training. The modern airfield and white air-conditioned barracks have sanitized the rocks, caves, outcroppings, and gullies in areas of the heaviest going in the battle for the Marines. Nevertheless, the simple, well-tended, almost austere, Japanese monuments to the dead and to peace and a few rusted leftover Japanese weapons, bashed-in block-houses, preserved caves, and the like are adequate reminders. John and I stood beside the memorial to the Marines on top of 560-foot Suribachi and looked down the long beach where two Marine divisions had landed. We wondered how we could have survived. From up there we could see the entire seven-and-a-half square miles of Iwo, still finding it incomprehensible that almost 7,000 Americans and some 22,000 Japanese could have been killed in that small space in just a few weeks—but we had seen it happen.

For many years the Japanese had debated how far her leaders should go in apologizing for the war. Reluctant-sounding statements of "regrets" in response to foreign pressures never have been accepted as adequate by the Asian nations who had suffered millions of Japanese atrocities during the war. Many Americans—more ambivalent—feel that, in their own interest, the Japanese should probably profess more guilt but that Japan was now our ally, had become democratic, and, in any case, the Japanese had been led into the war by a mad military leadership whose war criminals had long since been punished. A sizeable segment of those who think at all about the war—and perhaps put Japanese crimes mainly in terms of Pearl Harbor—seemed to believe that the massive slaughter caused by our unrestricted bombing of Japan in 1945 and especially the atomic bombs on Hiroshima and Nagasaki, being militarily unnecessary, somehow balanced things out. Others think that looking back detracts from our justified pride in our compassionate occupation and the resulting modern Japan.

Because the Sumo Association of Japan is, by its nature, a nationalistic, traditionalist organization, the ceremonies on Iwo probably expressed how the more conservative older generation of Japanese would now like to regard the war, centering memories on mighty battles between Americans and Japanese, both peoples led into the tragedy by policies of their governments.

Iwo Jima was an ideal—perhaps the only—place to give expression to such concepts. There never had been a civilian population to mistreat; it was not a jumping-off place for campaigns of conquest and had only been occupied at all for the defense of Japan; it had been skillfully defended, its brave soldiers annihilated only after inflicting enormous casualties on the American military enemy. There had been no atrocities to blot out the honorable fighting, an unsullied battle in a straightforward war.

There were two poems read at the ceremonies expressing these thoughts: one by a Shinto priest at the shrine in the northern end of the island and the other by a Sumo wrestler at the Dohyo-iri ceremony itself.

They both said the same things. I've reproduced an English translation of one:

> Spirits of those who lost their lives to the War
> Rest in peace on the isle of Iwo Jima
>
> The United States of America with her bountiful land
> And Japan known for her fresh and bountiful rice,
> Fought the War here on this land,
> Surrounded by the borderless sea.
>
> The people of both nations risked their lives
> All battling with the sole purpose
> To protect their mother nation
> For thirty-five days and nights gun-fire filled the air,
> Turning the quiet isle suddenly into hell.
> A tragedy claiming 30,000 lives.
>
> Marked in history as a land once badly scarred in battle,
> Fifty years now past
> Both nations have overcome hostile feelings
> They now shake hands on an everlasting friendship
> Praying that precious souls lost at war
> Have found their eternal peace.
> The Sumo held here today is in commemoration
> Of the promise between the two peoples.
>
> Yokozuna Takanohana born here in the land of Japan,
> And Yokozuna Akebono born in America,
> Today step up to the Dohyo
> To vow peace to each other and to all.

The actual "entering the ring" at the main "Peace Shrine" by the two grand champions followed the playing of the two national anthems and several declamatory speeches. The American one was delivered by George Ariyoshi, former governor of Hawaii, in good, if unflowery, American accented Japanese, the rest in the sonorous Japanese style. As our names were called, members of the audience placed white carnations on the altar to the front, led off by a joint march forward by both enormous top-knotted champions in special purple loincloths. These vastly overweight pouty young men rolled back a bit later, wearing braided blue and gold half-skirts held up by thick woven belts of purest white. They ceremonially bowed, squatted, clapped their hands, raised each leg high in the air, coming down with a stamp, and then paraded off, watched in reverential silence—although busily photographed—by all.

John and I were the only Americans in the party who had fought on Iwo. We were treated most respectfully in outgoing friendly ways by the sons and male relatives of the Japanese who had died in the battle, but I felt little in common with them or the several dozen Japanese television commentators and newspapermen. We shared the unique experience of the battle only with the few Japanese who had been captured on Iwo, and we became friends of sorts. Now, growing old, that seems important.

We learned, too, that the humane treatment of Japanese prisoners had paid dividends not only in the intelligence they gave us without coercion, but in their friendly and trusting approach to the United States as well.

One individual had had his nose blown off in the process of being captured and had been paralyzed by a rifle shot to the back. (He pulled up his shirt and showed us the small hole at the base of his spine—perhaps to prove that he had been unable to resist or kill himself.) American surgeons at a military hospital in Honolulu built a new nose for him, rather large for a Japanese and with visible veins but obviously still an interesting subject to him and the other Japanese. "I'm a little bit American," he said, pointing to his face. He was also given treatment and therapy for his back. For the three years it took for him to advance from wheelchair to canes to stumbling walking, he had a job on the hospital grounds. He returned to Japan in 1948 and still marvels that the United States government paid him lump sum wages for his work, enough to start a business. One of the other ex-prisoners admitted without prompting on our part that "Japan would not do that!"

We rode back to the military airfield near Tokyo in the same olive drab C-130 military cargo plane that had taken us to Iwo Jima. Some of our Japanese fellow veterans faced us across the narrow cluttered aisle. For the first few minutes they busily showed each other the tapes of their visit on the little screens of their camcorders and then, like soldiers would anywhere, anytime, they napped the rest of the two-hour, forty-minute rattling flight. Compelled to look inward anyway by the earplugs distributed to all the passengers, I began my private search for meaning to the previous twenty-four hours. I knew that I would have to speak gratefully to our attentive Japanese hosts about my experiences, but I worried that they would expect more than formal thanks, looking for some reaction to the spirit expressed in the sumo lyrics that I have quoted.

It would be hard to do. Personally, I had never believed—even in the dark early months of the war—that we Americans were simply defending our "mother nation." Instead I had been dedicated to defeating Imperial Japan and stopping her from enslaving the rest of Asia. Indeed, I resent the implication that the United States and Japan had anything in common in our war aims as expressed in the poem.

However, over the years I had relearned the lessons of my upbringing and had no residual ill feelings toward Japan—and never did have them toward the Japanese people. Thus, I had not looked at the visit to an old battlefield as a chance for reconciliation; nor would the Japanese I met on Iwo Jima this time wish to be forgiven for anything. I had not been moved by the ceremonies themselves even though the Dohyo-iri had been for the souls of Americans as well. I had tried to bring forth the faces of dead Marines—usually easy to do at memorial services at home—but the atmosphere was too Japanese for even that habitual gesture. But watching the snoozing old fellows, camcorders resting in their arms like weapons—some in red T-shirts printed gracefully down the middle with the gold *kanji* for Iwo Jima; others dressed in proper, neat business suits, all dignified and composed even sound asleep—I was struck that we in that part of the plane were the only men on it who knew what Iwo Jima had really been like or appreciated the enormity of our luck. What the hell, I thought, they know and we know, America won the war. In their hearts they know how it started. Formal words of apology couldn't change anything. What mattered was the quiet respect we had for each other—we who had shared the battle, setting us apart from the others on the plane.

Back in Tokyo for a night I said that the experience had left me feeling *kanzen* (meaning "complete" or "whole"—possibly also the sense of being satisfied), a word provided me by John's son Whitney, a Tokyo businessman, who like all the Rich children is bilingual in Japanese. *Kanzen* was a wise choice because the Japanese I used it with were pleased.

NOTES

1. From the Foreword by Robert Sherrod to *The Fourth Marine Division in World War II* (Washington, D.C.: Infantry Journal Press, 1946).

At Green's Farm. How could the Japanese have hoped to prevail? (Refers to p. 44.)

My friend Hep, Lt. Rolfe Hepburn, USMC (right) a few hours before he was killed on Saipan, June 1944. Gunnery Sergeant Sands (left) and Staff Sergeant Bancheek (center) survived the war. (Refers to pp. 48–49.)

With radio operator (left) on Saipan, July 1944. (Refers to p. 50.)

I (third from left) talked the mayor of Tinian town (center with microphone) into encouraging Japanese soldiers and civilians to choose life rather than to throw themselves off the cliffs (to our right). He was successful with several hundred women and children but only a few older men. (Refers to p. 52.)

Yokazuna Akenobu performs the Dohyo-iri on Iwo Jima in June 1995. (Refers to p. 68.)

Before one of the American monuments on Iwo Jima, June 1995. (Left to right) Sumo assistant, John Rich, Akebono, former governor of Hawaii George Ariyoshi, and me. (Refers to p. 67–68.)

Chapter 4

After the Marines

My brief service in China with the First Marine Division was the last duty of my military career. It almost wasn't, because General Jones had been in the process of appointing me his aide de camp: "It will help you with a regular commission." Fortunately, I had already received my return orders before the general and I had discussed the matter. Just before Thanksgiving I sneaked off without saying good-bye, arriving at my parents' New York apartment the evening of December 23, 1945, to be greeted by the boisterous elevator operator, my happily crying mother, and my grinning father.

My formal transition to inactive status was accomplished at the Navy's Great Lakes Training Station outside Chicago on January 6, 1946. It was an unsentimental occasion, made more so because somewhere along the line I had lost my pay account, which all officers were required to take with them wherever they traveled. According to the paymaster—a Regular Marine—this had never happened before in the then 170 years experience of the USMC, and much as he regretted it, "Sir!" I would have to reenter civilian life unpaid for my nearly two years overseas. This did not appear to either Shirley or me as a serious obstacle compared to the war itself, and we were married on January 12, 1946, by a kindly Father Foley, Shirley's pastor in Faribault, Minnesota.

Two weeks later I picked up my studies at Carleton under the benign auspices of the GI Bill. We moved into the first of our four residences in Northfield, and Shirley got a job in the bank that had been robbed in the 1870s by the infamous Jesse James gang—a group of thugs secretly admired in town as the source of its only excitement in eighty years. Our financial situation improved further when we received an unexplained U.S. Treasury check for $85 in late February, another one for $175 in March, and a final check for $1,050 in April. Both the Marine Corps and I understood that a normal accounting to close the books on Lieutenant Cross would not be possible.

Everything at Carleton looked the same—the buildings, the serene snow on the campus, the familiar professors, imposing but glad to see us. Carleton produced its usual sorry hockey team, with me on it; our first daughter, Ann, was born in the Northfield hospital; all was as it should be.

I graduated from Carleton in June 1947. The continuity of a family connection with Carleton and China, disrupted by the war, returned when my father gave the baccalaureate at my commencement. His relief work in Free China from 1943 to 1945 was added to his previous twenty-five years service to China in the citation for his honorary degree. Our short-term future was ensured by Lucian and Mary Pye, who between them had wangled a handsome scholarship to Yale Graduate School for me. That help plus the GI Bill meant that we could make it financially, especially when we were able to find a cold-water flat in a New Haven tenement renting at $21 a month. I switched back to Chinese from Japanese.

Life in New Haven was pleasant. The ambiance, hearty with Yale's prestige, was beguiling, but by the spring of 1949 we realized that we had to make some fateful decisions. The reason lay in the couple of points by which I had flunked the French section of the Foreign Service exam that I had taken the previous fall. French was regarded then as an essential language of diplomacy while Japanese and Chinese were not. I should have passed the easy test in it, but I thought the sample I had seen was so simple that I reviewed other subjects—mostly American diplomatic history—instead. I passed the rest of the hard exam acceptably, but my casual approach to French meant that four years later I had to go through the whole two-and-a-half days' ordeal once again in Hong Kong—this time successfully.

The discouraging word from the Foreign Service meant that I should look elsewhere in the foreign affairs system. During the spring break in 1949, I took the train to Washington and made the rounds, using an elaborately compiled Yale "Old Boy" collection of introductions: first, to the infant but already high-powered CIA, then to the State Department's own Intelligence and Research Bureau. The bureau was still largely staffed by the Office of Strategic Services analysts who had chosen not to go over to the CIA and were in the Civil Service rather than the Foreign Service—an important distinction to me because they would not ordinarily be assigned abroad. Almost as an afterthought, I went over to the Pentagon, where I was interviewed by the Office of Naval Intelligence, which suggested a scheme whereby I would return to the Marine Corps. Finally I checked the United States Information Service, then formally a part of the State Department.

I received offers from all of these agencies but chose USIS because I liked the enthusiastic people I met. They seemed genuinely convinced that psychological and cultural elements were essential to effective diplomacy.

I survived the intensive security check despite one aunt in Beijing. She was still making a determined effort to understand her beloved students who were welcoming the communist rulers of China. She had to be included on the form I filled out for the FBI under "Relatives Living Abroad," but I did not admit to another aunt on the West Coast who had been a Communist Party member in the '30s, nor mention that my parents advocated getting along with Mao Zedong as a policy for the United States. All our neighbors in the red brick building were supportive, although one may have misinterpreted the FBI's interest in us. Shy, wispy Mrs. Landon, who lived right above us and for whom once a month I hauled a large can of kerosene up four floors from the basement to her tiny, immaculate apartment, knocked lightly on our door one evening. "I thought you ought to know, the FBI is lookin' for you," she whispered, and skittered away.

As became customary when the Foreign Service moved us around the world, I unfairly left the complications of packing to Shirley and on June 15, 1949, reported to our new—and only—employers for the next thirty-two years.

Chapter 5

One Path to the Foreign Service

Sometime in high school at Tongzhou, I became attached to the idea of joining the Foreign Service. Perhaps it was because of an extraordinarily effective history teacher, Frank S. Argelander, a Methodist missionary detailed to our school. With months-old *Time* magazines he was able to reinterpret the Japanese-censored Chinese and English local newspapers so that we could understand quite well the alarming developments in Europe during the late 1930s. Argelander somehow created in me an abiding, at times nearly fanatical, interest in current events.

Perhaps it was hearing my father, who was not uncritical of the American government, speak approvingly of the consular and military officers who had learned Chinese and understood Chinese ways. These included O. Edmund Clubb, the consul general in Beijing, who became a recognized scholar of Chinese and whose promising career was later shortened by McCarthyism; and Colonel Joseph Stilwell, the military attaché stationed in Beijing, whom my father first met in famine relief in Shanxi Province in 1921. Stilwell later became the American commander in Free China during World War II. He spoke both a rough soldier's argot and reasonable Mandarin. Major Samuel V. Constant, Stilwell's assistant, who was also an excellent Chinese language officer, lived next to us in Beidaihe. I spent several active, mischievous summers together with his sons, Tommy and Victor. And then there was Captain David Barrett, another of Stilwell's assistants, convivial, liked by all Chinese who knew him. His later career was curtailed because during the war he was chosen to head the so-called Dixie Mission to the Chinese Communist headquarters in Yanan, back in the hills of Shaanxi Province. Barrett's thankless job was to assess the Communists' contribution to the war against Japan and whether the United States could assist them. The Dixie Mission reported favorably on the communist guerrillas as an effective force against the Japanese, recommending that they be helped, thereby earning unfriendly attention to its members from the Chinese Nationalist government in Chongqing and Chiang Kai-shek's political supporters in America.

Perhaps it was because my mother spoke occasionally about a distant relative, Charles Tenney, who had left missionary work for a position in the American Legation in Peking. He had risen several times to be chargé d'affaires during the early years of this century because of his competence in Chinese. He had some glamour in my eyes.

Most probably, though, it was a "C" in chemistry and the consequent discussion with my young teacher about my languid approach to science—in fact study in general—that indicated that others were discounting my tall talk of becoming a doctor.

Medicine's lucky loss among my ambitions was not automatically replaced by a fervent single-minded preparation for a diplomatic career. The Japanese invasion of China in 1937 and the excitements and dangers during my last three years of high school were too distracting. I did sense that my pleasure in literature, history, and government classes—and the resulting good grades in those subjects—vaguely hinted at some sort of life work that would not be impeded by the kind of precision required of those choosing the scientific path. I wisely kept this odd illusion to myself and fortunately shed it completely before I actually joined the Foreign Service.

In fact, I consciously studied for the Foreign Service at Carleton after I returned from the war. There I was unusually fortunate in having David Bryn-Jones, a small eloquent Welshman, as my faculty advisor and professor of international relations. "B-J" often wore stiff, detachable white collars and parted his hair in the middle. He sported spats and bland bow ties, yet he looked far from debonair in his rumpled ash-strewn suits. He was an ordained Baptist minister and, although I was never at ease with him, I understood his moral approaches to the world's problems and detected quiet warmth behind his curious appearance.

B-J was technically the best academic lecturer I have ever known. Too short to speak from behind the lectern he moved back and forth in front of his small classes, his thoughts marching in disciplined order through each class session, tracking clearly week after week, until all was summed up in three masterful lectures at the semester's end. His appeals to genuine internationalism and the cause of democracy in the world were more polished and organized than what I had heard at home and school. Consequently, they were more appealing, as if they were somehow new. His vivid descriptions of the 1917 Bolshevik Revolution in Russia and the rise of fascist dictatorships in Spain, Germany, and Italy created permanent yardsticks in my mind for ideological behavior by which I was to judge international politics. Later, of course, Yale and the Foreign Service itself tempered my idealism as I became conscious of the hard realities of national power, more discriminating and pragmatic in my conceptions of American national interests. This sharpened the clash of idealism and reality and would persist throughout my Foreign Service career.

There were heavy reading assignments in all my courses plus a special Carleton stress on term papers, essays, and long written exams. This was valuable to me later at Yale as I hastened through the usual one or two weekly book reports for each course and the several comprehensive seminar term papers required at the graduate school level. Reading and writing skills are essential to the work of the Foreign Service, and the two-and-a-half-day Foreign Service written exam demanded fast writing for essay questions and accurate, quick reading comprehension. In short, Carleton and Yale prepared me reasonably well for the Foreign Service.

The whole exam process, which included (and still does) a calculated winnowing-out oral assessment of the relatively few candidates who had first passed the written exam, was frankly aimed at securing an elite Foreign Service. Probably hidden away there was some social snobbery and Ivy League bias but not nearly as much as was portrayed by the Service's numerous critics, who have charged administration after administration with running a Foreign Service unrepresentative of the American people. Over the years, the State Department has widened the base of the officer corps by including a greater variety of pre-Service expertise in those it commissions, encouraging specialization and recruiting more women and minorities. These efforts were necessary because the United States routinely took on more responsibilities, and thereby more interests, as part of the Cold War.

I didn't learn very much about what people did in the Foreign Service from my month of training for my tasks in the Information Service while in Washington. The week allotted to the workings of the State Department (of which USIS was a part) was filled with exposure to the forms for collecting one's pay, submission of travel vouchers, applying for leave, and some general warnings about the punishments for violations of the security regulations. We were given some interesting advice on in-Service protocol by the head of the Foreign Service Institute, whom I remember chiefly for a suspiciously grinning approach to important subjects such as calling cards, calling on American senior officers and their wives (claiming that as USIS officers we would not be calling on foreign diplomats). If I had not been somewhat matured by the Marines and marriage, I might have taken seriously the even then outdated bits of pomp and circumstance: "A vice consul is entitled to a five-gun salute, and I assure you, he hears every one of them," he confided. We USIS officers were supposed to be the explainers of American foreign policy to the world, but our briefings by junior Foreign Service officers were perfunctory, usually a tentative "They'll let you know when you get there."

Chapter 6

Taipei I—1949–1950

Altogether it took us nearly a month to get from Washington to Taipei, our first post—an utterly unearned vacation before a day on the job. Not afflicted by conscience, we enjoyed the SS *President Wilson*: the pool, the bar, the endless food, and the playroom where two-and-a-half-year-old Ann could charge about under the guidance of a heavily tipped baby-sitter. We sat with others from the Foreign Service at meals and received biographically tinged advice about colleagues at our new post. It struck me then—and still does—how much Foreign Service people know and talk about each other. Shirley thinks that perhaps this is just as well, because as we move around the world, our colleagues and their families in some ways gradually come to replace our own extended families.

We changed ships in Hong Kong, leaving there for Taiwan on a miserably hot August afternoon on board the *Wing Sang*, a small coastal passenger ship-cum-freighter run by Jardine Matheson, the original and then still the greatest British trading house in Hong Kong, indeed, in all China. I took special pleasure in pointing out to Shirley the wrought iron grill separating the passenger and ship's officers quarters from the third-class dormitory sleeping areas, our protection against pirates. The piratical technique of the day was for the pirates to board a ship as deck passengers and then at a given moment seize the first-class area and the bridge, taking what loot they could forcibly extract before rendezvousing with a junk somewhere in the dark. An attempt of this kind had even occurred on the *Wing Sang* during the past year that had been foiled by the alert crew. The pirates were returned to Hong Kong where, according to the first officer, the British authorities were not especially soft hearted about this kind of thing—hinting for our benefit but without proof at a hanging.

Keelung, the port for Taipei, has one of the highest rainfalls anywhere. It was drizzling lukewarmly when we tied up beside a small vessel unloading cement. We and our numerous big bags took our turns in the chain of coolies as they trotted, staggering slightly, over a narrow gangway to the crowded pier, each carrying a crushing bag of cement. Out in the harbor were ships full of Mainland Chinese crowding the decks, many of whom had to stay on board for weeks until the slow-moving security authorities cleared them to come ashore. The United States had bombed Keelung heavily, especially in the last few months of World War II, and in the heat and the rain Taiwan appeared dispiritingly battered and gray.

Taipei, a half-hour away by the consulate's tired car, was a Japanese provincial city, with many heavy red brick government buildings connected by muddy streets and alleys. Taiwan University, where Shirley began teaching American literature shortly after we arrived, was partially destroyed. Her classroom was covered by a huge slanting tarpaulin strung from the only standing wall in the building.

Several of the consulate families had found comfortable Japanese-style houses in the city, but these were hard to locate and to furnish in desperately crowded Taipei. We settled on sharing a sort of annex to a mansion owned by a wealthy Taiwanese with Scott George, a tolerant officer in the consulate general. Scott's tour was almost up and his family had already left so he was happy to have Shirley take over the running of the household. In return he showed us the social ropes of Taipei's small foreign community. We looked out of a small screened porch at a partially developed Japanese garden. Ann had a dog for a playmate, the first of six such around the world, all named "Archie." Social life on the porch and in the garden was marred by the presence of a large outside toilet a few feet away belonging to one of the newspapers that had moved over from the mainland. The paper began printing about ten in the evening, and we were not easily lulled to sleep by the SWISH-CRACK-KWAM of the antiquated presses. Early morning sleep was not encouraged by the landlord's four turkeys that roamed and gobbled just outside the barred windows of our ground-floor bedroom.

The end of the Nationalists on the China Mainland was approaching fast by the summer of 1949. Chiang Kai-shek had not yet arrived in Taiwan, but no one expected his dissolving forces to resist the communists on the mainland much longer. U.S. policy was up in the air, hovering between the Democratic attempts to find some sort of working relationship with the Chinese Communists or conceding to unwavering Republican support for Chiang. As it has been ever since, the American political conflict was played out on the island—among the people it most affected. Republican Senator William Knowland of California came several times in 1949 to attack the Truman administration, before large handpicked audiences, for "selling out China." In Washington, meanwhile, the

State Department argued that the collapse on the mainland was due to negotiated mass surrenders and desertion to the communists by erstwhile Kuomintang (KMT) leaders.[1]

A fall through treachery was much less likely after the Battle of Kinmen (Jinmen in *pinyin*) in October 1949. There, a stubborn, outnumbered Nationalist garrison decisively defeated the communist forces when they attempted to seize this island just off the Fujian coast. Militarily, Jinmen has no significance for the defense of Taiwan, which often caused Americans to discount its value during the many years it has remained in Nationalist hands.

On Taiwan at the time, we could sense the surge of confidence created by even this small victory. My work in USIS had already made me conscious of psychological trends, and I began to realize that confidence in the future was the supreme political requirement for Taiwan, and that depended primarily on appearances. I was to argue this thirty years later when the American attitude toward Taiwan was still crucial.

I started to work the very afternoon of the day we arrived in Taiwan according to Foreign Service custom. (Shirley had actually beaten me to it. Just as we were sitting down to lunch with my boss in USIS, Robert S. Sheeks, and his family, a messenger arrived from the consul general's wife requesting Shirley to accompany her to call on the British consul's wife, who lived in an old Dutch fort in Tamsui, a half-hour's drive away. Shirley was instructed to wear gloves and bring her calling cards, neither of which she had. She went without complaint, leaving little Ann with the Sheeks's rather skeptical amah, returning in the late afternoon to report that the British consul's wife was a charming and informal Australian.)

But for the first few weeks I felt we were floundering. It's easy to admit now, five decades after the fact, but I didn't really know what USIS was supposed to be doing. I had learned at the beginning of my training in Washington that "information" meant presenting a truthful, balanced picture of the United States to the rest of the world. In particular, this was supposed to include accurately conveying U.S. policy, although our policy toward Taiwan was still undecided. Anyway, everything the State Department said was being contradicted in Taiwan by the American political opponents of the administration. Talking about the United States in our output even seemed out of place. I felt that few Chinese on the island really cared how great/progressive/democratic/strong the United States was. What they really wanted to hear were assurances that we would protect them from the Chinese Communists, doubting that they could do so on their own.

However, the Chinese Mainlanders on Taiwan seemed to have understood the way the American system worked better than we did ourselves.

In late November 1949 after the consulate general had duly reported on the effects in Taiwan of the Jinmen victory, cautiously intimating that Nationalist morale had lifted (although those on the staff who had been through the retreats on the mainland warned against taking official Chinese optimism at face value), I was asked to travel to the eastern side of the island to call on the local military and civilian officials in that seldom visited area. In the process, I was to contact the American missionaries scattered in those remote parts and suggest to them that because the island was by no means secure, they should consider leaving their isolated posts while the going was good, perhaps moving to Taipei or Kaohsiung on the western side, where it would be easier for them to participate in any U.S. government arranged evacuation. Neither of the two families I was able to meet were interested in the slightest, which, as a missionary son, I had foretold.

USIS did not have a jeep to spare so I had to hitch a ride from Taipei to Hualien, the small seaport halfway down the eastern side of the island, with O. J. Todd, an "old China hand" engineer, who was to check on a dam being strengthened in the Taroko Gorge area (now part of the modern, well-constructed East-West Highway system). Julian Todd had been a good friend of my father's since the early '20s when Todd began his life-work of redirecting the flow of the Yellow River so that it would be less "China's Sorrow." "Todd Almighty," as he became known in missionary circles, was hard driving, irascible, dedicated, and extremely competent. Much of what he had accomplished was destroyed by the Chinese forces in 1937, when they deliberately flooded a large area of north central China in vain attempts to slow the Japanese advance. Todd was reportedly bitter over this setback and the frightful loss of peasant life that occurred, but he returned to his work of helping China right after V-J Day and retreated to Taiwan with the Nationalists. Chinese admired him despite his rough ways as did I who was glad to see him again.[2]

The trip did not start smoothly. Todd had become enraged at the already apprehensive interpreter who had loaded his large suitcase into the backseat. Todd had lifted the young Chinese bodily and placed him firmly, if precariously, on top of the suitcase. "I want you to stay there," he growled.

I spent most of the morning while we rocketed along the stony, washed-out road reassuring the silent unresponsive interpreter in Chinese that Todd really wasn't upset with him. This colossal misstatement of fact was having some soothing effect when we came to a notoriously dangerous stretch of road cut from the sheer half-mile-high cliffs, so narrow that only one-way traffic was possible, reversing itself on a two-hour schedule. Todd began instructing the driver through me, usually in the form of questions: "Ask him why is he going so fast?—or poking along?—

or too near the edge?" (a recurring thought to me because there was no railing). Finally, the interpreter turned to me, now the middleman, "Tell him not to be so nervous; all the BAD drivers have been killed." I thought this local joke was funny but Todd didn't.

Todd dropped me off at Hualien's government guesthouse, a long-established Japanese inn. Besides a large communal bath, it had added pleasant Chinese touches of a continual cheerful racket and excellent fish dishes from its kitchen. For three days I walked the unpaved but neatly kept streets and alleys of this Taiwanese town, never far from the fresh smell of the sea and its fish, hearing no recognizable English, speaking more Japanese than Chinese, pleased to be on my own.

Everywhere I went I received the most friendly Chinese treatment: expansive lunches and dinners, effusive toasts and long briefings by the mayors, school principals, medical doctors, and the commanders of the East Taiwan Military Region and an army communications training school. In each case I was told of the shortages in equipment and supplies, the inadequate buildings, the broken-down cars and trucks, and then asked outright for American assistance. "We thank you for coming to investigate our situation. You are our friend. Please influence the American authorities to send us what we need quickly so that we can start—enlarge—fix—our service to the people." The military added the thought that their particular functions were more deserving of immediate aid than similar units elsewhere on Taiwan.

I tried to appear properly judicious, occasionally nodding thoughtfully and taking notes. I knew I shouldn't be effusively sympathetic, thereby inviting follow-up calls and letters when I got home to Taipei. Also, just before I had left Taipei, the Truman administration had announced another of its periodic "reassessments" of our military aid programs to Taiwan, which, in any case, had almost ceased, and was not committing itself to large economic programs beyond those already underway.

On the other hand, I was sure of the needs of these particular people and felt the United States should help. What I did was to fall back on the truth. My "face" boosted by my Beijing accent and perhaps bolstered a bit by some still serviceable Japanese (for the Taiwanese who were present), I explained that I was an insignificant member of the organization; that as far as I could tell the questions of assistance to Taiwan were still being discussed in Washington, and while I understood their difficulties, there was little I could do.

My excuses were greeted with flat disbelief. Why would the Americans bother to send even such a lowly person if they had nothing in mind for all these worthy programs? The prevailing view was expressed by the commander of the communications training school who said simply, "The United States cannot but help us [also a Chinese construction]; so when the aid begins in large volume, please try to find ways of sending some to our school." Sure enough, when I got back to Taipei ten days later, a new policy of substantial military and economic assistance had been announced. A few weeks after that I heard that communications training equipment had been included.

In the late fall of 1949 the State Department became worried that despite the Nationalist victory at Jinmen, Taiwan was the next step in what seemed to be an inevitable complete defeat of the KMT and the unification of all China under communist control. As part of the worrying procedure, the department sent a Foreign Service inspector named Kenneth Krenz to talk to all of us at the consulate general about the possibilities—my first experience with anyone from this feared group, one that I was to join many years later. This old-timer, who had earlier served in Taipei, called in the married staff one by one and gave each of us the flat choice of evacuating our "dependents"—preferably all the way back to the United States—or being transferred as a family to a presumably less precarious post in the area.

Some of us argued in different ways that the department was being unnecessarily cautious because the Nationalist forces on Taiwan were notably different from the losers on the mainland, being "the distillation of defeat"—a clever description that we thought had emerged from much talk within the consulate general. What we meant was that those military who had reached Taiwan had chosen to stick with the KMT even when they had had plenty of chances to defect. Defeat after defeat had "distilled out" these hard-core Nationalist supporters, and we could, therefore, count on the island being seriously defended.

Krenz quickly spotted a flaw in this argument in that most of the troops coming to Taiwan had had no choice and had left their families on the mainland; their only realistic hope of getting home would be a communist victory in Taiwan. I suppose that some of us went further than others in defending our views, but feeling a Marine Corps–like discomfiture in my first Foreign Service confrontation with higher rank, I merely said that I thought Taiwan would not fall. Krenz followed with the standard senior to junior argument in any organization and asked me how long I had been in the Service. He was vocally unimpressed by my qualifications for judgment when I told him, "about seven months," adding uselessly that I had been born in China. The result was that those of us who had mildly resisted evacuating our families were all transferred. The Crosses were ordered to Jakarta, at that time still in the hands of the

Dutch and called Batavia. Others were sent to places like Rangoon and Saigon, also wildly more unsafe than Taipei. The few who chose the evacuation route passed many placid months before they were able to see their families again.

I took the transfer to Jakarta personally. While there was nothing we could have said to have achieved in our six months in Taipei, I felt we had started well in our first post. We had many contacts, good relations with the Americans and Chinese in the USIS office, the consulate general, the increasingly effective American aid organizations, which were setting high standards of Sino-American cooperation in several fields, and the American correspondents—some like Albert Ravenholt of the *Chicago Daily News* would become our lifelong friends. Most of all I thought we were quickly acquiring a sense of how to operate in the tense, confused, and yet surprisingly hopeful, atmosphere.

Also, the transfer, as they always would, presented huge problems for the family. Shirley, expecting our second child, had made careful arrangements with the only adequate hospital in Taipei and was under the care of an excellent Canadian doctor. She had gained devoted students in her course on the American novel at Taiwan National University by sharing their bombed-out classrooms, giving them individual attention, and producing their reading material. She typed fourteen copies on her portable—carbon paper, small type—of Stephen Crane's *Red Badge of Courage* to supplement the university's editions of *Pilgrim's Progress* and *The Compleat Angler*. She joined David Osborn, also then of USIS and a brilliant Japanese linguist en route to becoming an accomplished Mandarin, Cantonese, and Burmese speaker, in an English-language radio program he developed. She played the role of a Mrs. Chase to Dave's Mr. Li, who spoke excellent English with a slight Arkansas accent. The two met on trains to Kaohsiung or in well-known restaurants in Taipei, greeting each other formally and then proceeding to get reacquainted and, in the exciting part, laying plans for the next meeting. Texts were sent out to a subscriber list that grew to over 20,000 after only two episodes. Mrs. Chase received much fan mail, some of it proposing alternatives to Mr. Li. It was Shirley's first of many experiences of having to leave major endeavors important to my job and personally satisfying to her, just as they were becoming successful.

Hardest of all, our Chinese friends, Mainlanders and Taiwanese alike, acted as if we were abandoning them. Our too robust assurances of their continuing safety sounded hypocritical even to ourselves. Having so vigorously made ourselves known, the symbolism of our departure in the face of no obvious threat took on added political significance—a mistake in American diplomatic style we would remember throughout our service.

Besides, our disappointment at this purely administrative decision was shared by Ambassador H. Merle Cochran in Jakarta. His messages to the department, with copies to Taipei, were polite enough but flatly asked that we not come, listing accurately that there was no suitable housing for his already overinflated staff, that the hospitals were inadequate, and that the security situation was bad. Embarrassed, we watched as Washington firmly overruled one of its senior ambassadors and in the same message ordered us to inform the American embassy in Jakarta of our arrival time.

NOTES

1. The State Department issued a monumental study in August 1949 called the *White Paper: United States Relations with China.* Secretary of State Dean Acheson, in transmitting that formidable document, asserted in phrases that put him under permanent attack by the China lobby, "Nothing the United States did or could have done within the limits of its capabilities could have changed that result; nothing that was left undone by this country has contributed to it. It was the product of internal Chinese forces. . . ." Transmittal letter p. xvi.

2. Jonathan Spence included Todd, an engineer, among the missionaries, educators, doctors, and revolutionaries in his fascinating study of those who tried to change China. Jonathan Spence, *To Change China: Western Advisers in China 1620–1960* (New York: Little, Brown, 1969), 205–216 in the Penguin edition.

Chapter 7

Jakarta—1950–1951

Nobody asked whether we knew anything about Indonesia before dispatching us there and we made no claims to expertise. However, in one of those lucky coincidences that would regularly come to our aid during our career, I had whiled away a few hours at Yale interrupting the studies of Francis X. Galbraith, whose little cubbyhole carrel in the library was near mine. The State Department had sent Frank to Yale for a year to learn Indonesian, and he was rapidly acquiring the skills and knowledge that in a few years would turn him into the U.S. government's leading expert on that country. Indonesia was much in the news in 1948, and Frank tolerantly explained the details of the desultory fighting between the Dutch and the Indonesian guerrillas and the complicated negotiations—the United States playing a key role—leading the Netherlands to relinquishing its 300-year-old colony. He became a political officer in the American Embassy, Jakarta, transformed from Consulate General, Batavia, a few weeks before we arrived in January 1950. Frank and his wife, Martha, were our guides to operating in this milieu—our first experience of the flowing excitement of a newly independent country.[1]

Like most Americans we were psychologically inclined to be anti-colonial anyway, and our experience on the Dutch ship that took us from Hong Kong to Java via Singapore made us strong Indonesian partisans. The officers on the SS *Tjitjalengka* were all Dutch, the crew all Indonesians. Most of the officers had been born in the Netherlands East Indies, and a couple were hard-faced Eurasians who, under the Dutch system, were officially classified as Dutch for jobs, treatment, and privileges. They and the several Dutch passengers complained in common about what was happening to them in harsh, high nasal, or growling voices and in perfectly correct English. We began by weakly sympathizing with their prospective loss of a certainly attractive way of life, although that had only existed "Before the war," as they prefaced everything they said. As the evenings in the bar wore on, however, the tone changed to bitterly, "Why did the United States do this to us?" (that is, help engineer the peaceful transfer of sovereignty). New to the game and becoming uneasy, I pointed out that we had been responsible for the liberation of the Netherlands from the Nazis and that could be regarded as an important service. This was irrelevant in their eyes because, they argued, their own government was also letting them down, "You support the British and French; why not us, we're anti-communist too, and Indonesia is more valuable to the West than their colonies."

Our arrival in Tandjongpriok, the bustling, disorganized, dangerous port for Jakarta, did not inspire much affection for Indonesians either. The Dutch had formally given up control of the country and were in the process of repatriating their forces, including those Indonesian-born members of the Netherlands East Indies Army who wished to leave the warmth of their homelands for cold, gray Holland. Others would disband and join their erstwhile enemies in the Indonesian National Army. Some did neither, however, and began to form little groups that coalesced with extremist Muslim guerrillas to oppose the new Indonesian government. One of these gangs was led by "Turco" Westerling, a renegade Eurasian Dutch Army officer who had gathered together a force of about 200 men and was rampaging murderously throughout Western Java. He had reached the outskirts of Jakarta just as our ship arrived and the nervous Indonesian authorities had closed the road between Tandjongpriok and Jakarta.

This meant that no one from the embassy was on the pier to meet us. The Dutch captain put us ashore immediately because we had not paid for our lunch in advance. Shirley stood on the pier with Ann and the luggage while I searched in vain for a telephone. For several hours we watched the piratical Indonesian longshoremen unload our ship and others, dropping crates (no containers yet in 1950) from deck heights onto the concrete pier, where they broke open. Two trucks pulled up and the longshoremen loaded their pickings onto one and what was left over for the shipper onto the other. I learned my first words of Indonesian when one of the huge crates crashed a few feet away from me as I was strolling worriedly from office to office. A dockhand, not unfriendly, but very quietly said, *"Mau mati nanti, ya bung?"* meaning I learned later "You want to die soon, buddy?" Eventually, we were met by John Nalley of USIS-Jakarta, who came with a station wagon flying the American flag (to distinguish us from the Dutch), numerous passes, and a few *rupiahs* for bribes to drive us uneventfully into town.

We adjusted quickly to the tropics but it was hard. It wasn't the heat, it wasn't the high humidity, it was the sameness that got the family down a bit. We had no air-conditioning in the two houses we lived in during our tour, and we soon made pleasant concessions to the tropics: early afternoon naps under antique ceiling fans that stirred the lukewarm air in bedrooms; lots of baths—a simple procedure of dipping water from a big earthen jar in the bathroom and pouring it over one's head; methodical frequent changes of underwear; as little as possible walking in the sun; tennis in the early morning or late afternoon. Most foreigners tried to escape crowded Jakarta to the highlands on the weekends although the security situation and the abysmal traffic made for a hazardous journey.

Our family left town only twice. Once we stopped at the former Dutch capital at Bogor—the site of an admired garden founded by Sir Stamford Raffles during the brief British rule in the early nineteenth century—to call on the flamboyant chief of the embassy's intelligence effort. This friendly gentleman also had a large residence in Jakarta where he entertained more people than the ambassador did—to the latter's irritation. He had established the Bogor hideaway—actually right on the main highway—to ease the strains of Jakarta's social life but was hospitable as ever to embassy travelers.

We were greeted enthusiastically and hurried to the upstairs verandah overlooking a muddy *kali* or stream. Drink orders were taken before we sat down—*air jeruk,* an Indonesian lemonade, for Shirley and little Ann, gimlets (gin and Rose's Lime Juice—lukewarm because of an ice-cube problem) for our host and me and apparently two other guests. These soon appeared and were introduced as Don and Mabel, a pair of gregarious orangutans, who after shaking hands, sat down sedately beside Shirley. They were not entirely free of their jungle habits because they drained their gimlets in one long slurp, and threw their glasses over the railing. Don familiarly put a long arm around Shirley and looked her in the eye. Ann, who had regarded all this as standard adult behavior, asked politely to go to the bathroom. There, she and Shirley found a three-foot crocodile in the bathtub. We thanked our host profusely. Ann waved good-bye. Don and Mabel watched from the balcony as we drove off.

Shirley and I immediately began to study *Bahasa Indonesia,* the *lingua franca* of the 2,700-mile-long, 3,000-island Indonesian archipelago. After a few weeks we acquired enough facility to get around a bit. This was necessary for Shirley because we had no car for nearly a year and she had to direct the *becak* drivers around the strange city with her dictionary always tucked under her arm. (The driver of this Indonesian version of the Asian pedicab pedaled from the back—putting his passenger in a more dangerous position on the overcrowded streets of Jakarta than his front-riding counterpart did in Taipei.) She also directed the activities of the customary astounding number of servants: the *kebun* or gardener, who tended a few bushes near the cement driveway; the *jogga* or guard, whose protective capabilities were augmented by his alliance with other *joggas* in the neighborhood, each of whom briefly stayed awake in turn during the night; *koki,* the lovable, good-natured lady cook, shrewd in market ways; Asna, the nubile fourteen-year-old baby amah called a *babu;* and a laundress named Ahs.

All of these servants were under the ineffective control of Amat, whose other undemanding duties consisted of serving the meals, answering the phone, greeting guests, and organizing the occasional *selamatan,* a quasi-religious ceremony to celebrate new children, housewarmings, and the like. Everyone was related—meaning that none could be fired without lots of trouble, but also that all were responsible for each other. They were paid according to rank, with rations of rice in quantities measured out by the embassy Administrative Section, and had relatively roomy quarters behind the house. Inflation complicated the small cash wages. Twice in the first few months we were in Jakarta the fledgling Indonesian government literally cut the paper money in half, making the payer carry around a pair of scissors and twice the money needed. Shirley and Amat worked together on the tactics of ice and vegetable preservation while the electricity was entirely off for one day in four, and for days at a time at the end of the month if our area used more than its unpredictable monthly allotment. Strangely for people who had gone barefoot all their lives, almost everyone suffered stubbed toes, causing a run on our Band Aid supplies brought from America. A nightly 10 P.M. to 5 A.M. curfew confined evening social and representational functions within livable limits for many months after we arrived.

Soon Shirley again began teaching, this time at a prestigious girls high school that catered to the daughters of leading politicians. Several of them, who had benefited from the combination of classroom lessons in English and tea party conversations at our house, became the graceful wives of Indonesian diplomats whom we later ran into in London and Washington.

Shirley and Martha Galbraith helped form the International Women's Association, a project to enlarge contacts between Indonesian women and those of other nationalities living in Jakarta, putting relationships beyond reception superficialities. It was a time when the women's half of the American presence was watched carefully by everyone in the countries emerging from colonialism and had direct impact on the role of women in those societies. When we visited Jakarta over thirty years later, Shirley was encouraged to learn that the association was still very active under Indonesian leadership.

Shirley was also doing other things.

On July 7, 1950, our second daughter, Kathy, was born in Jakarta's Tjikini Hospital. She was the first American born in Indonesia after independence.

The event was attended by some excitement. The Dutch doctor, disgruntled at being interrupted from his bridge game, turned up in dinner jacket and black tie just moments before Kathy did. Quickly Shirley and the baby were securely wrapped Dutch fashion in cotton blankets. The doctor returned to his club. Shirley urged me to hurry back across town to check on daughter Ann, who was in the unreliable hands of our alcoholic housemate, the servants having decamped to celebrate the end of Ramadan, the biggest of their many holidays.

Just as I swung past the wide hospital gates, machine guns began firing from the Indonesian Army barracks next door and shot out the streetlights. I turned off the headlights and jumped out of the car. In the sudden darkness I was relieved to see the red tracers from the guns fanning out over the hospital, obviously not aimed at anyone. I went on, spurred by rapid fire elsewhere in Jakarta, soon the only car on the streets and thus the subject of special attention by flashlight-waving troops who were hastily establishing checkpoints. The diplomatic license plates on the borrowed car got me through three heavily armed groups, and I reached home to find Ann and our emergency baby-sitter safely asleep. The Indonesian soldiers had merely been demonstrating for a larger holiday bonus.

Meanwhile, Shirley had just been wheeled to another pavilion and our newborn whisked away to a faraway nursery when the gunfire erupted and the lights went out. She argued anxiously with herself about trying to find a nursery she had never seen and decided that safety lay in staying put. When, in about half an hour, the firing seemed to have stopped, one of the unflustered Indonesian nurses brought a safe and sleeping Kathy to her. At dawn, however, Shirley was sad to see that one of the deer that had grazed in the courtyard of the pavilion had been shot. The nurses said that three people in the hospital area had been killed by stray bullets.

Shirley and I found USIS work in Indonesia absorbing from the beginning. There was a sense of being involved, of contributing to the process, as the Indonesians switched from the struggle for independence to the frustrations and confusions of actually running their own affairs. In 1950, USIS had the widest sweep of Indonesian contacts of any section in the embassy, many of them acquired before *Merdeka* (independence) by Willard Hanna, the tall redheaded acerbic public affairs officer. In 1942, Willard had been my classmate at the Navy Japanese Language School at Boulder, Colorado, where he floated near the top academically. Only eight years later in 1950, he graciously recalled that briefly, before ability grouping had taken hold at Boulder, he and I were in the same six-man section. Before the war he had taught English in a Chinese middle school in Fujian Province, resulting in two novels, which he called "thrillers" but wouldn't let anyone read. Short on athletic skills and cocktail party finesse, Willard typed and talked rapidly, dryly, and penetratingly about Indonesia all the time—in English and Indonesian. The Dutch had regarded him suspiciously when they were in charge because he ignored them in favor of expanding his relationships with those Indonesians he could see would be taking over after Merdeka.

One long-range beneficial result of Hanna's looking forward was an outstanding Indonesian national staff in USIS. They seemed to know every medical doctor, potential university leader, dramatist, novelist, newspaper editor, top army officer, and certainly all the politicians from Sukarno on down. Hanna was cagey about sharing his contacts with the rest of the embassy, except with Frank Galbraith of the political section, but he was liberal with introductions for his own staff. Shirley and I were swiftly taken in as friends by a rapidly expanding group of Indonesians, most notably in our case those around Sutan Sjahrir, a socialist, former prisoner of the Dutch colonial regime, and with Sukarno one of the heroes of the Indonesian Revolution. Sjahrir's reasonable socialism made him ineffective in the pell-mell Indonesian politics after Merdeka, but he was a thoughtful guide to Indonesian aspirations for foreigners.

I was the most junior officer in USIS so my first tasks were designed to get me around the country. I started by accompanying the USIS mobile movie teams as they went from one *pasar malam* (night fair) to another, first in the Jakarta suburbs, and then, as the security situation improved, to outlying villages. We carried our own generator. The soundtrack was dubbed in Indonesian or the operator turned it off and commented when he chose through a loudspeaker about the not-too-engrossing documentaries on the TVA, or river traffic on the Mississippi. Those on World War II battles were very popular because the audiences had not actually seen the Japanese defeated and were watching to see how the fighting came out. The American Constitution was of lesser interest.

A perk of this job was to try out new films at home for suitability and appeal—or even understanding. One evening we showed the household a good documentary on New York with several panoramic shots of the Manhattan skyscrapers. *Koki* had not been enthralled. "We have bigger mountains here," she sniffed.

I never felt that showing documentary movies indiscriminately to mass audiences was a good use of USIS resources—sort of scattering our shots without hitting anything—and I argued only that they created interest in America, an end in itself. I was pleased when USIS in Washington began sending out specially selected films dealing with science, technology,

health, and other educational subjects for use with specialized groups—
an ever more sophisticated process that continued for the rest of our time
in the Foreign Service.

THE OVERSEAS CHINESE

Most of my travel outside Jakarta came after I was assigned to work with
the Overseas Chinese, those descendants of immigrants to the Netherlands East Indies from South and Southeastern China. It was my first real
contact with a different kind of Chinese from those I had known before.
They would become a major element in our professional lives in other
Southeast Asian countries from then on.

In 1950, the Overseas Chinese in Indonesia ranged from those whose
sense of ethnic identity had been diluted by living for many generations
among the Indonesians, mostly as small shopkeepers, through newer
arrivals recruited by the Dutch in the late nineteenth and early twentieth
centuries to work in mines and large plantations, to the latest batches,
who usually came individually, fleeing China's troubles and the Japanese
invasions in China during the 1920s and 1930s. Through the years, the
upwardly mobile of all these groups had become clerks, accountants, and
even "native managers" in foreign companies and international banks,
cosmopolitan journalists, businessmen, exceedingly wealthy but unobtrusive owners of large trading companies, and medical doctors, to name
just a few of the types we met. They came from different places in China,
spoke different Chinese dialects at home, if any Chinese at all, but
learned Mandarin in their higher schools. Families were tightly connected in clan, commercial guilds, benevolent associations, Buddhist
temples, sports teams, and other activities—mostly based on provinces of
origin in China. All these groups, despite being competitors to some
degree, banded together in times of trouble for the Overseas Chinese as a
whole. There were around three million of them scattered throughout
Indonesia in 1950, essential to the Indonesian economy, bringing to bear
on it innate Chinese trading skills and sharp intelligence.

Extracting introductions from one to another, I called on the Chinese
leaders in the distinctive Chinatowns of the big cities: Jakarta, Semarang,
and Surabaya on Java and Medan in Sumatra, not spending much time in
the countryside, which the security situation made impractical. The
Overseas Chinese had deep, undefined worries. They spoke of pogrom-
like violence in the countryside against Chinese shopkeepers, which also
flashed up in the cities, sudden arbitrary actions by local authorities in
closing Chinese schools, petty corruption beyond anything they had seen
under the Dutch—matters really outside their control.[2]

I did not learn the extent of the confusion of the Overseas Chinese over their own future in Indonesia until after repeated talks over tea with the same people. Their past successes as a group had come from adjusting to Dutch rule, making themselves an indispensable element in the colonial economy, obeying the Dutch laws, and minding their own business. Their protection by the Dutch had disappeared with the Japanese invasion in 1942, when they were brutally treated as enemies, and their later ambivalence toward Indonesian independence had made them suspect to the new rulers. Now, developments in China itself had become a further complicating factor in their lives. It was apparent to me, after I was able to overcome the practiced caution of the Chinese I met, that the more modern-minded Chinese were attracted by the sense of power and prestige the New China was able to project and were quietly responding to appeals to "return to serve the Motherland"—a place they had never seen.

This was a phenomenon of youth. Older Chinese, counting on experience, were occupied with the tactics of adjusting to new Indonesian officials, holding on to what they had and even playing down their ethnic Chinese backgrounds. Younger ones, as we would experience later in Malaya, had become discouraged as to their future in an independent Indonesia; they did not wish to assimilate into what they had been raised to look down on as a lesser culture and which might have meant embracing Islam. More and more, Overseas Chinese youth began to seek ways to identify with the PRC.

The conflict within the Chinese community was sharpened by the PRC embassy, which systematically went after the old KMT-dominated Overseas Chinese institutions. The Chinese Communists concentrated their fire on the Chinese schools and the Chinese language newspapers—the two main areas of USIS activity—effectively using the theme of China's new place in the world in their propaganda and privately cajoling or threatening their way into control by playing on their embassy's official status in Indonesia. The KMT fought back with the only means it had, which were to urge the older wealthy Chinese to withdraw funds from schools that had changed direction and not to sell their newspapers to the communists. USIS could not really help in this form of ideological struggle, although I was able to obtain some anti-communist publications from USIS in Hong Kong as an indication of American backing. These evidently had limited success in changing minds at the school administration level because we continued to receive formal jargon-loaded cancellations of USIS materials from the Chinese schools.

Also, officially engaging in Chinese political warfare through USIS was out for the American Embassy for policy reasons. In the early 1950s, President Sukarno was putting himself in with U Nu of Burma, Nehru of

India, Tito of Yugoslavia, and, most significantly for the Overseas Chinese in Jakarta, Zhou Enlai of the PRC, as one of the leaders of a loose grouping of nations claiming to walk a line between the two "blocs" led by the Soviet Union and the United States. Sukarno had not yet advanced very far along this path, which led to his hosting the Non-Aligned Conference in Bandung in 1956, and certainly was not eager to have well-organized Chinese Communists active in his country. It was clear he would not like a confrontation in Indonesia between the U.S. and the PRC over the Overseas Chinese either.

Willard Hanna, responding to Ambassador Cochran's cautions, suggested that I channel my efforts into developing closer contacts with fewer individuals, learning more about the Chinese community and reporting on developments in it, building up lists of presumed anti-communists, and generally putting my activist inclinations on hold. I agreed and did so. I had received some invaluable lessons on the limitations of American public diplomacy in situations common to Southeast Asian countries and a sense of the phenomenal appeal of an exciting, strong China to young, ambitious Overseas Chinese. I found that both lessons were helpful in all our subsequent Southeast Asian posts.

Ambassador Cochran discussed my reports on the Overseas Chinese with Shirley and me at tea in the residence on our last day in Jakarta. We had not expected this old-fashioned Foreign Service touch and were doubly appreciative when he volunteered that, on the basis of our work with the Overseas Chinese, he had recommended that we next be assigned to Hong Kong.

NOTES

1. This period is well covered in the first five chapters of Paul Gardner's *Shared Hopes—Separate Fears: 50 Years of U.S.-Indonesian Relations* (Boulder, Colo.: Westview, 1997).

2. Daniel Chirot and Anthony Reid, *Essential Outsiders* (Seattle: University of Washington Press, 1997). Chirot, a wide-ranging sociologist at the University of Washington, and Anthony Reid, a Southeast Asian historian at the Australian National University, have edited this important study of ethnic and national identities of the Overseas Chinese in Southeast Asia and Jewish communities in Central Europe. They look, inter alia, at the potential for violence and peaceful adjustment between the Overseas Chinese and Indonesians.

Chapter 8

Hong Kong I—1952–1954

Hong Kong had the unmistakable sense of a British colony when we arrived in 1952, although a precarious one. Crisply uniformed Chinese policemen, shining black leather belts and holsters and hobnailed boots, strolled through the streets in pairs, alert eyes and impassive faces, symbols of control. Young British military officers in uniform left swagger sticks and caps on the table as they sat for tea in the Peninsula Hotel, coolly contemptuous of the civilian world. "God Save the Queen" (actually "King" in 1952) blared out at the end of every movie showing, non-British foreigners standing rigidly at attention with the British while the Chinese in the audience, as a convenient gesture of anti-colonial principle, vigorously pushed past them to the exits. One of the British-mandated indications of a separate identity for Hong Kong was that signs and public notices were in English. The Chinese spoken by British officials—if at all—was Cantonese and not the Mandarin being required in the rest of China. On Queen's Road, the Hong Kong and Shanghai Bank Building competed with the adjacent Bank of China Building for the honor of being the most prestigious in Hong Kong. At strategic points in the hills one could find the slit trenches and firing points where the Canadian and Hong Kong volunteer forces had been prepared to make their last stands against the Japanese during the desperate days of December 1941 before their leaders surrendered.

The American presence was already the predominant non-British foreign element in Hong Kong. A U.S. Navy destroyer escort had obtained a permanent mooring, somewhat behind the line of Royal Naval vessels but nevertheless a prominent place. Its crew competed in the Senior Softball League as did a team from the American Club (on which I played a questionable second base) against teams of Eurasians, old Westernized Hong Kong Chinese families, and even Britishers bored with cricket. Mighty vessels like the battleship *New Jersey* came down from Korea for

R&R when the war slowed, and then stopped up there. As always when there are Americans, there was action everywhere. Shirley and I were seized by the excitement of the big-time and thrived on the purposeful, innovative work of USIS, involving as it did close contacts with Chinese of all kinds.

There is a common shorthand explanation that the Korean War and Hong Kong's being British were indirectly responsible for the astounding economic growth and ultimate prosperity of the colony.

Prior to the Second World War, Hong Kong had been a far second to Shanghai's British-dominated International Settlement in the British trading system in China. There a skein of trading centers in the treaty ports were linked by the coastal steamers and riverboats of the great trading houses of Jardine Matheson and Butterfield and Swire, often garrisoned by British troops, and regularly reinforced and visited by the Royal Navy. It was a profitable system for trading IN China, as against trading WITH China. Hong Kong's value to the British in those days was that Hong Kong was entirely theirs, whereas the treaty ports were shared with other countries.

After the war it all changed. Great Britain joined the rest of her Western allies in giving up extraterritoriality; the treaty ports officially disappeared, although the distinctive nineteenth-century-style colonial buildings even now give an old-fashioned flavor to parts of immense, modernizing Chinese cities; and the Chinese civil war and the advent of the communists ended the old ways in China proper. Hong Kong was all that was left for the West.

When we passed through Hong Kong en route to Taipei in 1949, there was some talk, mostly from British "Old China Hands," about an early resumption of full-scale trade with China.[1] The proponents' short-lived optimism came from a naive acceptance of the communists' initial appeals to "patriotic elements" among Chinese capitalists and even some British managers to stay on and help in China's reconstruction. These were coupled with the standard foreigners' belief that "The Chinese (sometimes, unhappily, 'the Chinaman') has to do business; that's what he knows best; China just has to get over the present nonsense, which it will after awhile." They were sure that because of its geographical advantages and its 99 percent Chinese population, Hong Kong would be the leader in the revival of the China trade. These dreams became reality in ways unimaginable in 1949—but only beginning thirty years later.

By 1952, however, Hong Kong was already finding a future outside China. As a military participant in the Korean War and observing the United Nations' embargo on trade with the PRC, Great Britain was required to limit the historic entrepôt function of Hong Kong. The process of trading its own products with other countries—especially with the

United States, which required that everything we bought from Hong Kong had to be produced there—made Hong Kong what it is today, one of the great manufacturing/trading/financial centers in the world. The British provided the framework: the fair enforcement of contracts, non-political law and order, and a hands-off-the-economy approach (except for sophisticated intervention in the currency); the Americans and others—but not yet the Japanese—provided investment and became the markets; and, above all, refugees from China brought energy and unceasing effort, brains, entrepreneurial genius, and flowing masses of hard-working, quick-learning, and nonunionized labor.

The Chinese came in by the hundreds of thousands, quintupling the population of V-J Day in 1945 to over two million by 1952. New housing had been built but it was not enough. Multitudes lived in huge squatter settlements of tin-roofed shacks crawling precariously up unused hillsides. Families gathered in unruly lines for water at standpipes, searching incessantly for jobs, and subjected to the often bloody competition for control over them by the communists and the Kuomintang—all prey to the Triads, ancient criminal gangs founded in South China centuries before.

For several years, the Hong Kong authorities balanced the health and other services they provided for this class of refugees between enough to keep them alive and not so much that they would be encouraged to remain. The policy had come from Hong Kong's experience in the prewar past, that most refugees would return to their homes as soon as the current upheaval had died down. What changed the British approach was a spectacular fire in a large squatter town that in two hours made some 50,000 people homeless.

Shep Kip Mei was not the only fire in Hong Kong that year, just the worst. All the fires had two things in common: they were not preventable because of the wood construction. They were uncontainable because the settlements were usually perched on steep slopes in undeveloped areas with little water and poor access for firefighters—everywhere the same awful recurring danger to people by fire. Despite this, the new breed of refugees defied tradition and did not go back to China; rather, they rebuilt in the same shantytowns or crowded into others. The problem would not go away and could only get worse.

Shep Kip Mei jolted out the Hong Kong government decision to intervene; and shortly, gray, unattractive but livable, eight-story blocks of Hong Kong government-built flats began to appear everywhere. These were followed by nicer and taller buildings in the New Territories. Within a decade, miles of high-rise flats were built for the not-really-poor in Kowloon, extending to the New Territories and filling the rugged edges of Hong Kong Island. Once it was clear that the British rulers were serious about providing for their Chinese population, private builders followed right along. Old homes in the mid-levels on the island were torn down and replaced by tall glistening apartments for the ever-increasing numbers of Chinese pretty-rich and foreign businessmen, topped by penthouses for the very rich—mostly all Chinese, boasting of paying some of the highest rents in the world.

Along with these came hundreds of office buildings (some of them strikingly designed) and innovative, multileveled, vertically integrated, modern factories crowding out the earlier jumble of sweatshop tenements. Huge container ports, using landfill from leveled-off hills, pushed into the harbor. New roads blasted through solid rock were immediately overloaded. Dams for a massive water supply system made Hong Kong less dependent on water from China. Tunnels under the harbor and a smooth, comfortable subway system and much, much more—including several million more people—came within twenty-five years. The British, by moving decisively and efficiently in an emergency, showed in ways the people could understand that they were committed to staying in Hong Kong—confidence again the central factor in an Asian future.

Realism dictated that this could only be a moral commitment. The British could briefly at best resist the PRC communists if the latter chose to seize the colony by force. Certainly American military power could not save Hong Kong; that would be applied to evacuating Americans if called upon at all. Hong Kong's separate existence, therefore, depended on Chinese—the leaders of the PRC and the Hong Kong Chinese. The PRC's official position on Hong Kong (and the Taiwan-based Republic of China's too) was the same as that of my parents' Chinese students thirty years before: the treaties giving Hong Kong to the British were "unfair" and the colony should be "returned" to China. This Chinese principle obviated the time limits set by the ninety-nine-year lease on the New Territories surrounding the colony due to expire in 1997, because the communists could demand the turnover whenever the British "mistreated" the people—a pretext that could be invented at will. The PRC never pushed their principle to the point of serious armed confrontation during the intervening forty-five years, but in the 1950s, it regularly tested the determination of Hong Kong's rulers.

We saw one of the most serious of these efforts to shake British control in 1952. The communists had sent a delegation from Guangzhou to "comfort" workers from one of the unions they controlled, who were being "oppressed" by the "running dog imperialist police" (for resisting one of Hong Kong's strict labor regulations). The British, trying to avoid an armed confrontation at the border, allowed the group to come across by the regular train. They were met by a crowd of their organized supporters at the Mongkok Station in Kowloon, and violence began immediately with attacks on the police.

Foreigners in the area were caught by surprise. Five-year-old Ann and I drove the just-delivered family Morris Minor, top down, right into the communist-engineered riot. After turning off Prince Edward Road in Kowloon toward the harbor, I saw smoke from burning vehicles mixed with puffs of white tear gas and further down a huge crowd milling around in the middle of Nathan Road (already becoming one of the world's famous shopping streets). When I tried to turn off to the side, we immediately ran into another gang who began to hit the car with their placards, shouting in English "Kill you." I instructed Ann, who responded perfectly, "Don't look at them; don't smile; don't cry" and drove through the mob slowly. We then doubled back to Nathan Road and watched safely from behind the police lines.

The front row of riot police stood calmly under their British flat steel helmets, holding clubs but not armed. In the second row a few armed men stood on chairs. They were clearly under the orders of a hefty Chinese sergeant recruited from the northern province of Shandong. Symbolically, only one British officer was on the scene, sitting out of sight of the crowd in the front seat of an imposing police van. Every few minutes four policemen charged forward, clubbing their way into the slogan-screaming mob, grabbing the loudest, dragging, beating, and kicking him for all to see, and then throwing him into the van with Cantonese curses. After each flurry of activity the whole police contingent would move forward a few paces, the sergeant would officially order the crowd to disperse with the bullhorn, and when they didn't, more rioters were violently arrested. Ann and I left when the police ostentatiously donned their gas masks as a warning that they would next fire tear gas. This process of breaking up the demonstration was repeated in the other affected areas of Kowloon and the riot sputtered out by dark.

I felt, along with others in the consulate, that two major long-lasting political symbolisms determining Hong Kong's situation for decades grew from the Mongkok riots. The Chinese in the Hong Kong Police proved to be reliable, disciplined, and very efficient. The Chinese Communists were not able to expand the incident nor stir up general support. Hong Kong would not fall to the communists from within, as had happened in China proper.

The Chinese who slipped, bribed, and schemed their way into Hong Kong were not a homogeneous group. Most were Cantonese-speaking laborers from nearby, but many were from further north and east and provided the shrewd entrepreneurs driving Hong Kong's growth. Along with them came intellectuals from all over China: university teachers and students who had become disillusioned with the New China or had been made to feel unwanted, disaffected journalists who had tried to get along but found the revolutionary regime even more restrictive than the old

Kuomintang had been, and graduates of the influential American-founded universities like Yanjing in Beijing, Lingnan in Guangzhou, St. John's in Shanghai, and the nationally known women's college, Jinling, in Nanjing. Sitting amidst the racket in their crowded flats or in much more comfort in ours, they described desperate escapes using forged papers, enduring months of "struggle sessions" with erstwhile colleagues before they could get away, and tricky contacts with the "Yellow Ox Gang,"[2] who smuggled them into Hong Kong from as far away as Shanghai. Thus USIS had several kinds of "audiences," "customers," "clients," or in jargonese, "targets" for its programs.

USIS produced two magazines for the general public: *World Today,* a monthly collection of features, articles, short stories, and book reviews sent out from Washington in English, recrafted by USIS Americans into more appealing formats, and finally transformed by our adept Chinese translators and editors into popular reading; and *Four Seas,* a *Life* magazine-like pictorial, which proved to be so popular that it eventually went off on its own, taking along its Shanghai staff. Both of these magazines were also designed to appeal to the Overseas Chinese in Southeast Asia and to Chinese on Taiwan.

The wide readership—*World Today* grew to a paid circulation of 125,000 in a few years—and governmental attitudes called for thoughtful, close editing. For example, Taiwan liked strong, direct anti-communism combined with a pro-Kuomintang slant; this would be all right for Thailand, whose leaders were friendly to the Kuomintang. Anti-communism was in favor with the British in Malaya, but they were against strengthening ties between "their" Chinese and any political grouping in China itself. Indonesian authorities were even more cautious about publications in Chinese aimed at its Overseas Chinese that could create enthusiasm for a separate Chinese identity. The search for new and appealing angles was continuous and expert, calling for sophisticated interplay between the Chinese and American staffs in USIS.

Once, we arranged through a contact of a Chinese staff member for Henry R. Luce, the publisher of *Time* and *Life,* to purchase a series of photos of the brutal land reform then winding up in South China. These created international attention when they were printed in *Life,* and USIS reproduced them for our own publications.

The photos were clearly taken with official sanction. They showed in cold black and white the entire land reform process at a South China village, starting with the "explanation meetings" conducted by party land reform cadres from outside the village to taut assemblies where villagers were divided into landlords, rich peasants, middle peasants, and poor peasants/landless peasants based on really small differences in their land holdings. The contorted faces of the members of this last group could be seen as they accused the others of specific crimes and mistreatment. Then there were close-ups of the executions of the six landlords of the village, who knelt in a row beside a narrow stream and were shot in the back of the head by a People's Liberation Army soldier, all watched unemotionally by their former neighbors. Finally, the prosaic photos of the meetings to divide up the landlords' and rich peasants' lands, houses, and tools—the logical end for the reform. I knew about the ruthlessness of the land reform campaign, which the communists didn't try to conceal and sometimes even emphasized for ideological reasons in their propaganda, but I was unprepared for the chilling, overwhelming sense of finality and horror the pictures conveyed.

Although I was proud of our little coup, I thought there was a defect in atrocity propaganda in areas such as Hong Kong that were threatened by the communists. Instead of creating a renewed spirit of resistance to them, it would only add to the fear. If, as was obvious, the United States was unable to do anything about what was going on in China, the Chinese "target" in Hong Kong would likely think of how hopeless the situation was—facing such cruel power. Building confidence in the future was a better way to success in Asian political propaganda.

BOOKS AND PEOPLE

The USIS–Hong Kong book translation program was the most immediately effective in encouraging confidence in a personal future for many Chinese individuals and groups. It was started by Richard M. McCarthy, a former University of Iowa track star, whose literary interests had been inspired by Iowa's strong English department. Dick had noticed that few good books were available in Chinese in Hong Kong and realized how the process of producing translations of major Western works would fit USIS aims.

In the first place, they provided thoughtful works on anti-communist, pro-democracy themes to a wide receptive readership in Hong Kong and among Overseas Chinese, for example, *Darkness at Noon* by Arthur Koestler—a sad, bitter novel by an ex-communist. Choosing translators capable of handling nuances from English to Chinese put USIS in touch with Western-educated Chinese refugees in a quickly expanding circle of contacts. Enlisting editors, publishers, printers, and distributors began to generate possibilities for new independent publishing ventures that soon became self-supporting. The atmosphere in the ever-widening refugee intellectual circles changed slowly from dreary to hopeful to active—a vital factor in Hong Kong's vibrant future.

CHINA WATCHING

The consulate general's large-scale China Watching (so-called, I suppose, because we were looking at China from the outside like ornithologists on the edge of a woods) began during our first tour in Hong Kong, although, of course, reporting on China had always been a major function of Chinese language officers in the Foreign Service. The United States had to change some of its methods of analysis when travel, personal observation, on-the-spot interviews, and the other ways of learning about developments directly were denied to Americans in China itself.

The chief resources became what the Chinese Communists were saying about themselves in their totally controlled press and radio, which required obtaining newspapers and journals of many kinds from inside China—often at serious risk to the vendors because of the strict bans on exporting provincial papers from one area of China to another. American officers culled and analyzed these materials. Portions were then translated by the Chinese staff and published almost daily in the consulate's *Survey of the China Mainland Press* (SCMP). The consulate general and the institutions it nurtured[3] quite soon became primary sources on China developments for the United States government, journalists, and scholars and indeed for a good portion of the rest of the world as well, until China really opened up in the early 1980s. It was an effort pursued one way or another by most of the consulate general's political and economic staffs, including USIS.[4]

The consulate general's China Watchers also systematically interviewed Americans who had been "expelled" from China. I talked for hours with a distressed John Hayes, a Presbyterian missionary from Beijing, a Rhodes scholar and family friend, who "confessed" to spying after months of sleep deprivation and interrogation. His captors had transposed items of furniture in his house until he finally said that his ordinary radio was a sending set. Hayes understood what had happened a day after he arrived in Hong Kong and had had some sleep, but he could not shake the feeling that he had failed his Catholic priest housemate who had not broken.

The study of "brainwashing" came into prominence as a result of "confessions" by American POWs in Korea and was part of China Watching. We puzzled over why the communists bothered to extract a confession that the interrogators knew was false when all that they got in the end was a written document that the victim only had to sign anyway. Like so many aspects of communism, we could describe the techniques and psychological effects but not the whys.[5]

The easiest but saddest victims for me to understand were those foreigners who had been in China for altruistic reasons—Protestant missionaries who wouldn't confess under torture but succumbed to suggestions that they were in China to mislead or exploit the Chinese. We had to discourage another Presbyterian missionary from crossing back into China at Lowu—"I have something I didn't tell them,"he pleaded. He had spent his entire working life selflessly running a universally praised industrial arts school for poor Chinese boys in Beijing and couldn't imagine Chinese turning on him—somehow blaming himself for what had happened. My Aunt Laura B. Cross died broken-hearted in 1960 after searching her conscience for years for reasons why her students had turned against her and had gloated over her house arrest in Beijing.

There seemed to be two classes of foreigners who couldn't be broken— Catholic priests, who were often tortured but didn't doubt their purpose in China, and beachcombers, who didn't doubt theirs either. I talked briefly to one of the latter who had been imprisoned for months in Shanghai without explanation or trial and then released suddenly after a brief and painless interrogation. He was still mystified in Hong Kong: "They asked me did I admit to trying to make money off the Chinese people? I told them why the hell else would I be in China? I signed a paper in Chinese and they let me go."

My own small special part in China Watching was to produce a weekly survey called the *Chinese Communist Propaganda Review*. The theory behind this effort was that we could tell what the Chinese were planning to do domestically by their instructions to their cadres contained in several publications like *Xuexi* (Study) specifically designed for the purpose. We determined the location of the next major campaign in the land reform movement, for example, by instructions to the cadres in those areas—what they should say to the people at each stage and so forth— followed by our pointing out changes in nuance. This modest attempt to know what the Chinese were planning was often redundant to other material in the Survey of the China Mainland Press and was stopped anyway by budget cuts in 1953—an example of the Republican distaste for the State Department in the '50s, which outweighed their ideological desire to "know the enemy."

NOTES

1. "Old China Hands" covered a wide range of foreigners who had lived in China and was loosely applied—often by themselves—to those who had lived there the longest. When they were actually working in China, my parents, who qualified by any criterion, avoided the term because it lumped them with those whose only real experience with Chinese—they thought—was in the concessions and in exploiting the Chinese. After the war, separation from China and Chinese

made them much more understanding, and they eagerly joined groups of OCHs of all kinds in New York and California with whom they found much in common in their affection for the country. My generation has kept up the OCH tradition and unofficially reduced the qualifications for those who had lived in China before Pearl Harbor to only a year. We meet mostly in reunions of our high schools. We even have a black necktie of our own significantly embroidered with dragons for the Manchus and thin stripes for the Nationalists, warlords, and communists of our pasts, and are kept in touch by well-written newsletters like *The China Connection,* published by Oscar Armstrong, and *Tungchow Re-Collected,* published by Gladys Smith. Long removed from our family prejudices, we are really very close.

2. Corruption was inevitable at the Hong Kong/China border because both the British and the Chinese authorities limited movement. The "Yellow Ox Gang" was the generic term for a host of operators who brought people by boat past patrols on both sides to outlying Hong Kong islands, or through wire on the land borders, or sometimes directly past the immigration officers of both jurisdictions. Our resourceful cook brought his wife and five children several hundred miles from Hankou using the auspices of the "Yellow Ox" combine. Hu himself had paid the smugglers in installments to get the family as far as Guangzhou, but the final payoff soared to several hundred Hong Kong dollars, or Hu's salary for two months, and we had to help him out. I listened just outside the kitchen in our consulate-owned flat on Prince Edward Road in Kowloon while Hu (a northerner) bargained in fractured Cantonese with a nervous, quick-gestured, chain-smoking bag man of the Yellow Ox. The next day, Hu and I drove out to a planned rendezvous in the restricted area along the border, using my consulate identity to pass the checkpoints, but no one showed up. A week later, after another meeting in the kitchen where Hu mentioned my nonexistent police connections, I dropped Hu off at the Shatin railway station in the New Territories and watched a smiling subdued reunion from a distance. This kind of personal engagement in bribery and smuggling activities was discouraged by the consulate's administrative officers, who were responsive to the Hong Kong government's "we'd rather you not" get mixed up in what was becoming a common practice among foreigners. Hu had worked for higher-ranking Americans before us and appreciated my risk. He responded by refusing to leave us for better-paying jobs until our tour was up. Hu and his again augmented family departed from Hong Kong soon after we did, went to Bangkok, opened a restaurant and, we heard, became rich.

3. The Union Press was the organizational name for a group of young student refugees from China—mostly from Beida prior to 1948—who had become disillusioned with both the Kuomintang and the Chinese Communist Party and were vaguely trying to find a "Third Force" to support. They never fully abandoned the idea of a middle road in Chinese politics, but their longest-lasting achievement was the establishment of the Union Research Service, which, before the age of computers, built extensive files on almost every conceivable subject in the PRC. These were made available to journalists and academics and were useful from the outset to the consulate general's China Watchers. They later gradually turned their files over to the University Services Center in Kowloon, which became an international resource for scholars studying PRC developments.

4. The China Watchers I list below are those I remember being engaged one way or another in that fascinating activity when we first arrived in Hong Kong. It is important to mention them because they were the pioneers in a capital post–World War II Foreign Service achievement.

Ralph Clough—the quiet, scholarly Political Section chief oversaw the whole process, assigning priorities for subjects to be covered by the entire post, noting gaps in information, writing his own analyses, and contributing to the consulate's weekly summary report to the State Department called, prosaically, the WEEKA. After he retired from the Foreign Service, Ralph became a formal member of academia, conducting research at the Brookings Institution and teaching at the Johns Hopkins School of Advanced International Studies. He is recognized for his wise books on Taiwan and Korea.

Howard Boorman—the first editor of the SCMP, devoted and thorough, had begun his reporting work with Edmund Clubb at the consulate general in Beijing before the city fell to the communists and Clubb ran afoul of McCarthyism. (Clubb was famous among Foreign Service Chinese language officers for his insistence on high performance in the language.) Howie followed Clubb's practice of adding several new Chinese characters to his collection every day while shaving; he began and then expanded enormously the systematic organization of biographical information on PRC leaders/officials. He went on to teach at Vanderbilt University for many years, publishing biographical studies on the PRC.

Doak Barnett—only temporarily in USIS, earlier with the *Chicago Daily News* in China during the civil war and later the Universities Field Staff. One of the United States' leading scholar/writers on contemporary China, he saw the early need in China Watching for constant systematic discussion of China issues. He formed a prestigious discussion group in Hong Kong, transplanted it to Washington, and led it until his death in April 1999.

Robert Burton—a USIS officer working mostly on VOA news reporting, made especially good contacts with the young Chinese refugees in the Union Press group. Through them he met Zhang Guotao—a founding member of the CCP and a major rival of Mao Zedong at one time. Bob introduced others in USIS to Zhang. I recall long afternoons on the verandah of the old red brick Foreign Correspondents' Club hearing Zhang describe in detail the ups and downs of the CCP—his own roles, ideologies, and Mao Zedong. Bob later taught at the University of Kansas, where he produced a two-volume study/memoir/biography of Zhang— valuable to students of the CCP.

Arthur Hummel—the second head of USIS while we were in Hong Kong, beginning a brilliant career in the Foreign Service, later rising to the highest rank of Career Ambassador, and becoming the American ambassador in Beijing—the first of three China-born ambassadors, excellent spoken and written Chinese, helped by years with Chinese Nationalist guerrillas in Shandong after his escape from internment camp in World War II. He is hard-headed, perceptive, and skilled in dealing with Chinese of all kinds.

Douglas Forman—replaced Howard Boorman doing political reporting, superintending translations for the SCMP, and interviewing people leaving China. Doug received his language training in Beijing.

John Heidemann—thorough economic analyst, stayed with his specialty throughout his career, becoming one of the United States government's top experts on the Chinese economy.

Alexander Peaslee—another very busy reporter on the Chinese economy, Sandy later became a lawyer and with his wife, Kay, edited a newspaper in Charlottesville, Virginia.

John Holdridge—serving the first of two tours in Hong Kong as a China Watcher, John came to Hong Kong after extensive study at Cornell and Harvard. He continued in the China field for most of his career, taking part in the historic Kissinger trip to China in 1971, and serving as the deputy chief of the United States Liaison Office in Beijing and as assistant secretary of state for East Asian Affairs in the first Reagan administration.

Arthur Rosen—also a Cornell- and Harvard-trained Chinese language officer, his initial work in Hong Kong was to acquire publications. He became president of the National Committee on U.S.-China Relations during the period of its greatest growth and influence.

Then there were the others whose professions made them prime members of the Hong Kong China Watching community:

Father Lazlo Ladany, SJ produced a small newsletter for experts; had his own press clippings and files, was indefatigable, and always available for discussion. I was to see more of him in our second Hong Kong tour.

Tilman Durdin, longtime *New York Times* reporter on China, was scholarly, thorough, and cautious. He developed excellent contacts and superb Chinese assistants, one of whom, Vincent Lo, came to provide the institutional memory in the consulate for many years.

Robert Elegant—friend from Yale; excellent Chinese and with Durdin he was one of the longest lasting—forty years—journalist scholars on China and the rest of Asia, with *Newsweek*—later the *Los Angeles Times*. Among his several books on the PRC was *China's Red Masters* and much later a broader look at Asia, *Pacific Destiny,* and the highly successful novels *Dynasty* and *Manchu.*

Richard Harris of the *London Times* also had a China background; provided a British but not official viewpoint.

5. See Edward Hunter's *Brain Washing in Red China: The Calculated Destruction of Men's Minds* (New York: Vanguard Press, 1951) for a frightening picture of the process.

Chapter 9

Washington and McCarthyism

We were returned to Washington in 1954 where for a year I was a policy guidance type in the United States Information Agency. John Foster Dulles had succeeded the year before in "divesting" the State Department of direct responsibilities for "informational" activities, thereby adding to the supporting bureaucracy in the new USIA, duplicating some State Department functions, and further complicating the coordination by the United States government of its voice to the world.

I had a head down, powerless kind of job having to do with China, not requiring much expertise and only useful in learning how to draft brief clear themes of American anti-communist purpose on the China Mainland. The only accomplishment I can remember was to argue successfully to stop an American offering of wheat to China during one of its food shortages. The ploy was to publicize the fake offer and then make propaganda hay from the inevitable Chinese refusal. I felt that playing political games with food would not go down well in other hungry areas of the world and would be exposed as a heartless hypocrisy. (I still do.) The undemanding work was made painful because McCarthyism and a cowardly—as I saw it—USIA leadership forced out my predecessor and several other talented and conscientious colleagues.

I started on the job earlier than I had planned. I had come into USIA headquarters at 1776 (naturally) Pennsylvania Avenue to clear up a few last-minute details before heading off to Minnesota to begin our leave at Shirley's home. I was stopped on the ground floor near the elevators by a dapper man who, after giving me his name, assured me that he was from a prominent Virginia family. He said he was a personnel officer and wanted me to postpone my home leave for a few weeks. Tensely I objected, "Well, Bob, whom I'm replacing, isn't going to Indonesia (where he had been assigned) for two months so why do I have to give up my leave?" Personnel responded with a cool smile, "Bob (using his surname) is resigning as of the close of business today." Having nothing left to argue with, I agreed to stay on in Washington and took the elevator up to Bob's cubby-hole office. Just as I entered I heard him say politely, "Personnel on the ground floor? Yes, yes, I'll be right down." I had been told before they let him know that he had been fired. I went on down the hall and when I came back in an hour Bob had gone; I never saw him again.

Something like that happened to Isabelle a few weeks later. I had just gotten to know this helpful, attractive woman who had served in the Office of War Information, the propaganda agency for the United States during World War II, and had been pleased to be asked to join her and others of the Policy Guidance group in their daily mass exodus for lunch. But when we stopped to pick her up, her office was empty, only a note propped on her heavy black typewriter saying good-bye, that she liked working with us, would remember us all, and wished us good luck.

There wasn't much talk among us about either case, but I knew that Bob, while stationed in Taipei a few years earlier, had been sympathetic to the indigenous Taiwanese then being mistreated by the Kuomintang on Taiwan. This could have caused him to be labeled a "pro-communist" by the Nationalists, which would have been noted by the "loyalty" network in Washington. Isabelle had a past that included work in the Institute of Pacific Relations. This scholarly, but generally leftist, think tank funded primarily by the Rockefeller Foundation had come under fire from Senators McCarran and Jenner, who headed the Internal Security Sub-Committee in the Senate concerned with loyalty of government employees.

McCarthyism's shots only hit around me and then only on officers considerably senior to me for anti-Nationalist reporting or behavior during the war, when I was engaged elsewhere, or still in college. Thus I was too young and far too insignificant to have "lost China," which the Nationalists had given up themselves anyway, shortly after I joined the Foreign Service. Like everyone else in the Service, I was affected by the rumors that individuals were "in trouble," so that good assignments fell through for them or promotions were held back. Increasingly, a new breed of employee turned up in the State Department and USIA: the security careerist. Ignorant and fundamentally uninterested in foreign affairs, recruited through Republican Party connections, they seemed to set themselves against the Service as a whole. The everyday gossip of the Foreign Service took on dangerous edges of guilt by association in the heavy unfairness of Washington.

John Foster Dulles's grubby administration of the security area in the State Department, accompanied by his pompous self-righteousness, tarnished his memory. But what it did to the conduct of America's foreign relations and the making of foreign policy is harder to judge.

Certainly it negated the influence on China policy-making in the State Department of a well-trained, competent, conscientious, and patriotic group of specialists on China: John Service, John Davies (both China missionaries' sons like me), John Carter Vincent, and Edmund Clubb to name those whose cases were the most publicized and who were forced out of the Foreign Service. Several others such as James Penfield and Philip Sprouse had interesting and useful careers, but their knowledge of China was not fully utilized.

However, that generation of Chinese language officers had experienced a different China and a different United States than they would have faced in the 1950s, even had they been given a fair chance. The China they had known and reported on suffered the Japanese Occupation, was engaged in resisting the Japanese, or, in the late 1940s, was wracked by its revolutionary war. They based their political assessments on watching the incompetence and flagrant corruption of the Nationalist Chinese military bureaucracy in crowded Chongqing, which they measured against more controlled looks at the Chinese Communists in the isolated, peasant areas of Northwest China. They came out that the communists, because of their ability to organize and motivate rural Chinese, could have helped to defeat the Japanese and thus deserved a share of the supplies the United States was giving to China. They added to this an implied corollary that the Nationalists couldn't mount a similar appeal to the Chinese masses and, therefore, Mao Zedong would win the country no matter what the United States did or didn't do. It would thus be to American advantage to find some means of accommodation with him.[1]

As I saw it in 1954, proposals to do that were already out-of-date as practical policy; the chances for accommodation had passed if, in fact, they had really existed. The communists in their drive to power had mistreated our diplomats in China who could have been a link to a better relationship. Mao Zedong had signed a treaty of alliance with Stalin in 1950 and later that year threw his armies into Korea, reinforcing the image of "monolithic communism." The United States had ensured that Taiwan could not be captured by arms in 1950, when President Truman, in one of his first moves to meet the invasion of South Korea, had interposed the Seventh Fleet between Taiwan and the mainland. Later the Eisenhower administration formally incorporated Taiwan into the ring of containment alliances around the "communist bloc," substantially aiding Chiang Kai-shek's Republic of China. American policy toward China was nailed down and remained so until President Nixon spectacularly revised it fifteen years later. Then another line of well-trained China experts from the Foreign Service aided in the quiet preliminaries and well-managed follow-through.

When President John F. Kennedy's New Frontier reached Washington in 1961, some of its academic cadres such as James Thomson, down from

Harvard, regarded the Far Eastern Bureau (FE) as the most hide-bound area in the State Department, unable to move quickly on anything, much less come up with dynamic solutions for the problems of the area. It seemed frozen on China policy.

The newcomers ascribed the malaise to McCarthyism. The alleged lack of experienced advice from State Department China experts was later seized upon by critics of the United States' intervention in Vietnam as one of the fatal weaknesses in the decision-making process. This was not true; it begs the question of what Jack Service, John Davies, or Edmond Clubb would actually have advised about China's intentions during the excited atmosphere of the early 1960s. The PRC was then reeling from anti-rightist campaigns, recovering from one of the greatest famines in Chinese history resulting from the wild policies of the Great Leap Forward, and Mao Zedong was planting the first seeds of the Cultural Revolution. It is not important anyway. The American national leadership, thanks to President Kennedy's encouragement of new thinking, was overloaded with informed advice from all directions from which they picked and chose, in the end going the way they inclined, driven by the habits of the Cold War. I shall be discussing Vietnam at length later in this book, but I say right now that blaming McCarthyism for the mistakes of the Vietnam War is a cop-out.[2]

There is an ethical point to be made here. Inevitably, as the new and vigorous replaced the stale and tired, a mild reverse form of McCarthyism came in, complete with its own forms of snobbery. This was again directed against those officers who had centered their careers on Asia but this time had been duty-bound to support the Dulles policies. In some of the criticism there was a distressing implication that they did so out of fear. David Halberstam in *The Best and the Brightest*,[3] his enthralling, long, imaginatively slanted, anecdotal characterizations of the personal motives and interpolated private thoughts of a multitude of American government objectors and supporters of the Vietnam War, says that because Service and others had been destroyed by McCarthyism, their successors in the Bureau of Far Eastern Affairs "had been men willing to serve in Asia under the terms dictated by Dulles, terms of the most rigid anti-communism where viewpoint and rhetoric had very little to do with facts." A few sentences later he concludes, "At FE, loyalty came before intelligence."[4]

Like much else in this influential book, these aspersions were thoughtless and unfair. Anti-communism was the bipartisan national policy; Eisenhower was the overwhelmingly elected president and Dulles the legally appointed Secretary of State. Refusal by career officers to carry out national policy would not only be self-defeating—because then they would be unable to influence the nuances of tactics, or serve as brakes on foolishness, or quietly voice dissent, all of which they did during the Dulles era—but would have been counter-democratic and unconstitutional. A career service must exert its best efforts to support the policies of the elected administration—even while possibly working within house to change them. Otherwise it would operate on its own and thereby subvert democracy itself.

Our assignment to Kuala Lumpur resulted from the bureaucratic changes in USIA, which now had a new independent career path for its officers, some of whom needed Washington assignments. Shirley and I were asked our interest in the political officer's post in KL and responded enthusiastically to the invitation to "regular" Foreign Service work. But I never lost my affection for USIS nor my feeling that its work has been essential to modern American diplomacy.

NOTES

1. Harvey Klehr and Ronald Radash, *The Amerasia Spy Case—Prelude to McCarthyism* (Chapel Hill: University of North Carolina Press, 1996), interprets Service's actions less benignly than did his 1950s supporters in the Foreign Service. The authors, working with FBI reports and other material that only became available much later, say that while allegedly passing classified documents to *Amerasia*, a small publication with a known leftist bias, in a determined effort to affect U.S. China policy in favor of the Chinese Communists, Service may have been duped into teaming up with possible Soviet agents. I thought the book unconvincingly polemical. It also contains some careless errors, for example, it has Congressman Walter Judd of Minnesota on a "fact-finding junket" to Japanese-occupied Beijing in 1944! What it shows, however, is that the government's supposedly sloppy security procedures, the alleged leaks of classified reports to undermine the hapless American ambassador to China, Patrick Hurley, combined with the appearance of a cover-up by the State Department, looked to the American public like a pro-communist conspiracy at high levels in the Democratic administration. The conspiracy theories were then shamelessly embroidered and expanded upon by McCarthy. In that narrow sense Service, by his actions rather than his analyses and recommendations, may have contributed to the vicious excesses of McCarthyism.

2. Robert S. McNamara in his examination of conscience makes this claim specifically. *In Retrospect: The Tragedy and Lessons of Vietnam* (New York: Random House, 1995) 32–34. Pre-eminent among those whose expertise was rejected by the high policymakers was Paul M. Kattenburg, a middle-level Foreign Service officer in the early '60s. Kattenburg, who had had extensive experience with Vietnam, argued that the American approach to Indo-China was bound to fail because it misjudged the nature of Vietnamese nationalism and the capacity of the United States to deal with it successfully—burdened as our leaders were, with the habits of straight, un-nuanced anti-communism. Kattenburg's thoughtful study, *The*

Vietnam Trauma in American Foreign Policy, 1945–75 (New Brunswick, N.J.: Transaction, 1982), is the best presentation of this view I know. A similar slant is provided by Leslie H. Gelb and Richard K. Betts in *The Irony of Vietnam: The System Worked* (Washington, D.C.: Brookings, 1979). This classic study shows that the decision-makers followed established paths in reaching the wrong policies. Their reactions, neither foolish nor uninformed, were again conditioned by the Cold War.

3. David Halberstam, *The Best and the Brightest* (New York: Random House, 1969).

4. Halberstam, 189.

Chapter 10

Kuala Lumpur—1955–1957

British style tends toward the undramatic, and the tide of the communist insurgency that had risen in 1948 had ebbed by early 1955 when our plane landed at Kuala Lumpur. Nevertheless, the sandbag barricades, the Malay police in field uniforms slouching purposefully around the airfield, the cold-eyed Chinese and British immigration officers in their sharply creased khaki shorts and shirts methodically interrogating our recently airsick Overseas Chinese fellow passengers, all showed that the Emergency was still on. Indeed, in Singapore that morning I had read the *Straits Times* account of the ambush and murder of a British planter and his Malay body-guards at a rubber plantation near Kuala Lumpur. He was an acquaintance my age from Beidaihe, the beach resort of my childhood and youth in North China, who had left China in the fall of 1939 to join the British Indian Army. The *Straits Times* story nailed down the realities for me.

KL was possibly Shirley's favorite Foreign Service assignment of all eleven. She taught English at a Chinese Women's Normal School after being specially vetted by the Police Special Branch, which regarded all Chinese schools as recruiting bases for communists, and the colonial education authorities, who worried about dilution of the language as it might be taught by an American. Her students came for tea and wondered guardedly about their future in a Malay-dominated independent country. A moment of recompense for her hard, astute work came when the American 103-piece National Symphony played in KL on its first international tour after the death of Toscanini. She had succeeded in arranging tickets for two hundred students from her school at this USIA-sponsored concert and watched the girls' ordinarily closed, bespectacled faces turn to joy as they were lifted out of their dull, controlled, and worried lives by the soaring music of this premier orchestra of the world.

KL was my first political job. It was mostly reporting in Kuala Lumpur rather than negotiating with foreigners because there were no political or international problems between the United States and the Federation of

115

Malaya before independence. Political reporting depends on building contacts, as does everything else in diplomacy. My predecessor, Oscar Armstrong, also a missionary's son from China and already an accomplished reporting officer, turned his carefully compiled, comprehensive contact list over to me, as is customary and professional. In a long series of briefings, Oscar described why each contact was important, what each knew about, what each would tell, what each wouldn't or couldn't, and assessed his reliability and how best to approach him. Then, during the crowded week we overlapped, he introduced me to many of those on his list in calls at their offices, at long lunches, cocktails, or other social events—all fundamental to our becoming part of the community in a hurry, a Foreign Service virtue.

I was fortunate that my first boss, Eric Kocher, also did political work. He had reported on labor matters in Europe previously and, with his strong anti-stuffiness bias, was skilled in making contacts among both Malays and Chinese. Although he left me pretty much alone to choose subjects for reporting, he was an excellent guide whenever I needed help.

Eric was succeeded as the consul general by Thomas K. Wright—a businessman before World War II, in the United States Navy in the war. Ken was full of nautical expressions such as "clean ship" for the consulate general running smoothly, "clear the decks" for preparing for action—usually a VIP visitor—and particularly noteworthy, in describing a bureaucratic impossibility, "You can't piss up a rope." He was less directly interested in political reporting but would scrupulously pass on everything he heard.

There couldn't have been a better time to be doing political reporting in Kuala Lumpur—and being the only political officer for most of our tour. I arrived in time to watch the preparations for the first countrywide elections and left just after describing in detail the final drafting of the constitution under which Malaysia has lived since. I heard at first hand of the confidential, intricate balancing of interests, selection of candidates, and drafting of slogans between the Malayan Chinese Association (MCA) bankrollers of the Alliance Party and the militant Malays in the United Malay National Organization (UMNO), the predominant voters in the Alliance. These arrangements allowed the Overseas Chinese to retain most of the economic domination they had won under the British in return for not opposing the political hegemony of the Malays and thus assured Alliance victories at the polls.

Tunku (Malay Prince) Abdul Rahman, the Alliance leader, was the key to political progress. I have always been grateful that Eric introduced me to him right after we arrived. Easy-going, friendly with everyone, tolerant, and honorable in relations between the races, the Tunku was the only absolutely "right man—at the right place—at the right time" I have ever met.

The British, who unobtrusively backed the Tunku, were always somewhat uncertain about him. He seemed unabashed by his reputation as not very bright and too genially malleable; his anti-communism appeared too mild and, because of Alliance politics, did not have the anti-Chinese overtones usual from a Malay leader. Some speculated that he would be outwitted and cowed by Chin Peng, the Overseas Chinese leader of the Malayan Communist Party, at their historic 1957 all-conclusive meeting in a jungle clearing on the Thai border. The consulate, which had not shared these doubts, proudly reported that Rahman stood firm in denying the MCP any place in an independent Malaya unless it disarmed, came out of the jungle, and submitted to the democratic process—thus assuring that the MCP would continue the "struggle" but ever more ineffectively. The British were privately relieved.

THE EMERGENCY

I was first plunged into the stuff of counterinsurgency during our tour in Kuala Lumpur. My thinking from then on was affected by this experience. I watched the British adroitly combine military and political measures designed to advance the self-government process and political independence in a multicultural society while at the same time eliminating threats to these—and succeed. The differences between Malaya in the mid-'50s and Vietnam a decade later when I got there were enormous and crucial. But having seen a genuine Chinese-inspired communist insurgency defeated and a new, independent country safely created, I never lost the feeling that it could be done again—and I understood that it had to be done right or it would fail.

Fortunately, I had come to Malaya with a substantial head start in knowledge about the insurgency. In another of those helpful coincidences in my life, while we were packing up in Washington, Lucian Pye was putting together the final report on his in-depth study of the influences that produced the Malayan Communists (almost all ethnic Chinese) with resulting insights into their vulnerabilities. He had been in Malaya for several months in 1953 to conduct some systematic interrogations of communist terrorists who had surrendered to the British to determine why they joined the communists, why they left their families, their backgrounds, and so on. On the last weekend before we left for Kuala Lumpur he spent several hours outlining his conclusions for me while I took notes. After Lucian had given the British a summary of the results of his work, *Guerrilla Communism in Malaya* was published in 1956.[1] It was immediately recognized by political scientists as a significant pioneering effort, combining information from extensive interviews of participants

in an Asian communist movement with wide-ranging analysis. Following along behind the scholars were a group of military planners, State
Department and CIA officers, all kinds of consultants to the U.S. government who, thinking in terms of anti-communist politics, realized they
needed much better understanding of the psychological motivations
behind these Asian revolutionaries.

The appeal of "People's Liberation Communism," as Pye described it,
was "intimately related to a general process now going on in most under-
developed areas of the world. Large numbers of people are losing their
sense of identity with their traditional ways of life and are seeking rest-
lessly to realize a modern way."[2]

The thought was not new to me; the impact of the West on Asia and the
struggle between ideologies had always been part of my life, as it was of
my parents'. Pye sharpened my understanding of how the revolutionary
communist structure provided young Asians a form of "personal security" where they would have an acknowledged and admired role, a
means of advancement, adventure, all in a changing world that otherwise
might pass them by. This is somewhat different from the urge to do good,
produce a better, fairer society, and so on, that we who were concerned
with the subject thought drove the young communists and where we
devoutly believed the Western democracies were most competitive.
Lucian clarified my thinking further when he established the connection
between ideology and power: "Communist literature was essentially a
literature of power, not in the sense of either glorifying power or calling
for the maximizing of power at every opportunity but in the far more
fundamental sense of first ascribing political significance to all aspects of
life and then identifying politics as power."[3]

Thus the Overseas Chinese–dominated Malayan Communist Party
and its guerrillas, emotionally tied to the powerful, successful Communist Party in China, had as its plain objective seizing control over the Chinese community—and then using what they regarded as that ethnically
superior group to supplant the British and rule in their stead. This was a
monumental miscalculation. It alienated the Malays, the majority population, and negated the MCP's anti-colonial propaganda; it frightened the
Overseas Chinese living among the Malays and hoping for long-range
political accommodation with them; and it simplified the task for the
British, who had to fight only a violent fraction of a minority.

THE BRITISH COUNTERINSURGENCY WAY

One of the first official calls I made in Kuala Lumpur was on Lieutenant-
General Sir Geoffrey Bourne, the Director of Operations who com-

manded all the armed forces in the Federation and was responsible for the coordination of the myriad activities of the Emergency. Bourne was a bluff, one-armed, friendly gentleman. He had an intricate way of serving in tennis and played successfully in the matches that were very much part of the scene in Kuala Lumpur. At our first meeting he said he liked Americans and was used to them from his experiences during World War II. I'm sure he liked us and understood us too, because the first drink he offered me was an ice-cold, quite dry martini, served in his deeply air-conditioned study.

Counterinsurgency, as the British practiced it, was an immensely complicated process calling for a firm yet subtle touch as policies were set at the top by the British and then skillfully sold to each military and administrative level, emerging after innumerable meetings as joint British-Malayan plans. Although the Emergency was really a war, the British were scrupulous about not calling it one officially. To them, the armed members of the Malayan Communist Party were always "CTs," communist terrorists, individuals who were breaking the law, not members of a great world movement, as the CTs tried to label themselves. Military operations were described in government handouts as "in aid of the Civil Power." Everything was aimed at reinforcing the concept of a functioning government fully in charge, making the point that because Malaya's independence was inevitable and would be defined by British power, it would be advisable for everyone to fall in line—particularly, of course, the ethnic Chinese living in the Federation.

The overall British strategy was directly responsive to that of the communists. It was methodically to separate the guerrilla fish from the sea of their almost entirely Chinese supporters—to paraphrase one of Mao Zedong's colorful sayings on guerrilla strategy. A natural corollary to that was to provide sure and continuing protection to those who, willingly or not, were on the government side. Chinese squatters tending small vegetable plots or groves of rubber trees on the fringes of the jungle, and other Chinese thought to be vulnerable, were concentrated—often not too gently—in the so-called New Villages. Initially, these were poorly equipped camps, tin-roofed structures thrown up in a hurry, surrounded by barbed wire, and fortified so that the population could be both controlled and protected. They eventually became permanent, self-governing small towns with their own schools and, natural for Overseas Chinese, centers of small businesses.

Life in the New Villages must have been grim in the beginning because the primary emphasis was on control. Often the protection was inadequate, especially as the guerrillas knew that they had to be able to contact their supporters or be destroyed. The struggle was relentless on both sides. The British instituted iron restrictions over the movement of food outside the cities; even in 1957, when the emergency was almost over, there were areas where the possession of food of any kind outside the designated zones was forbidden. People who worked away from the towns and New Villages were thoroughly searched when they left, and arrangements were made to feed them in groups at the rubber estates and tin mines—though they often had to go without. The tougher the British were on such things, the more ruthless the CTs were in forcing help for themselves and intimidating those they suspected might fail them. Again, for the British, protection of the affected population was essential to success—a lesson I was to learn over and over in Vietnam.

The most dangerous time for the guerrillas was when they came out of the jungle from their base camps to ambush, or more often just to seek food (nothing much grows in the perpetual twilight of the deep Malayan jungle). The CTs were helpless unless they had reliable intelligence on the movement of their targets or enough "outside" supporters who could cache supplies where they could be quickly picked up and transported back into the jungle. The British, naturally, also depended upon intelligence to exploit the advantage they had in dominating the populated areas.

This exciting and often remarkably dangerous work, particularly for the ethnic Chinese officers, was in the hands of the Police Special Branch who infiltrated "outside" cells of the CTs, arranged the defection and "turning" of cell members, and planted false instructions leading to the ambushing of armed CT units, to mention only a few of the Special Branch operations I knew about. The Special Branch were aided in their tasks by the harsh Emergency Regulations, which permitted holding suspects for long periods without formal trial. The threat of the death penalty was often used to extract information, and was a powerful deterrent.

General Bourne's instructions to his staff to be forthcoming with the consulate general made it possible for us to know many of the Special Branch officers and their families. We grew to admire them. They were not only courageous and patient, but shrewd in analyzing their adversaries' personal motivations, exploring such aspects as home life, schooling, and prospects for the future, cutting beyond ideology, which, as they might have learned from Pye's studies, was not always the major reason the CTs joined the party. I thought of the comprehensive dossiers the Special Branch was able to compile on individual CTs when we were trying to organize the same kind of information for the Phoenix Program ten years later in Vietnam.

The Special Branch occasionally allowed us to see them in action. A new Foreign Service officer, Howard B. Schaffer, and I once made a trip to Johore, the princely state in the Federation just north of Singapore, as part of Howie's introduction to political work. Kuala Lumpur was his first Foreign Service post, and he was being rotated through all the sections of the consulate general; his presence doubled the Political Section. Howie's later career concentrated on the subcontinent, and he became one of the Foreign Service's leading experts on India and later was ambassador to Bangladesh.

Howie and I traveled all over Malaya. This time we planned to pay a formal call on the Sultan of Johore, a famous playboy who passed much of his time in London but who had some influence over the more moderate Malays (that is, less anti-Chinese) throughout the Federation. We hoped to talk politics with His Highness, particularly about the hot issue of the future status of the nine Malay Princes in an independent, multiracial, democratic Malaya. How two strange visiting Americans were going to introduce this delicate subject to royalty forty years older than we, was a problem. We had no tiger-hunting stories of our own to break the ice nor London nightclub experience, possibly a better opener. In the event it didn't matter. We somehow missed the sultan entirely and were received with unpretentious Malay courtesy by an aide, who professed mystification about our inquiries. We signed the guest book and went on our way to Singapore.

At the suggestion of the Special Branch headquarters in Kuala Lumpur, we were to spend the night in the small town of Kluang in central Johore, one of the worst remaining "black areas" in the Federation where CT activity was still high. We were to be the guests of Ian, the Special Branch chief for Johore, a hospitable Welshman who paid for his occasional trips to the United States by lecturing on the Emergency to what I'm sure were rapt audiences. Detroit was his favorite stop for some—possibly romantic—reason.

We arrived at the sandbagged police station in Kluang in the late afternoon. Our host hurried through the briefing—mostly sightings of CT bands—then, reveling in indiscretion, suggested, partly as a way to amuse us, but mostly, I think, because our Chevrolet was bigger than his British Morris Minor, that we should load up our car with supplies and drive out to rendezvous before dusk with a secret patrol operating nearby. He hoped to deliver the supplies quickly before it got too dark for the patrol to slip back into their jungle camp. Howie and I naturally agreed, knowing full well that our American and his British superiors back in Kuala Lumpur would disapprove.

We set off in a two-car convoy with the Morris Minor leading the way and drove on suspiciously empty roads, with only an occasional clearing in the jungle on both sides, until we came to a large rubber estate and its perfectly aligned rows of exactly the same-sized whitish trees. We turned off the highway onto the estate's own straight road leading a half-mile up to the fortified complex where the British manager and his guards lived and where the tapped rubber was processed. Halfway to the houses I was instructed to stop the car, get out and lift the "bonnet," pretending to have engine trouble. The Morris Minor went on to the estate complex to prevent anyone from coming down the road from there.

At that point we were only fifty feet from the edge of the jungle. I didn't know it until then but the deep jungle floor is oddly clear of shrubbery and grass because there is little direct sunlight through the high canopy of treetops. But at the edges, where the sun can get at it, there is a thick curtain of bushes and low trees, twenty to thirty feet high and maybe thirty feet wide, called *blukar* in Malay. Paths in and out of the jungle had to be cut through the *blukar* where it is thinnest, and we had stopped where I could see that there was a small opening.

We were cautioned against making any noise. Although Ian had the Welsh flair for drama, I could sense tension in him and the two Special Branch Chinese who also stayed in our car. Howie and I stood there for not more than a couple of minutes appearing—I hoped—to be competently inspecting the engine, when one of the Special Branch officers glanced at his watch and gave one sharp birdlike whistle. This was immediately answered from the *blukar*. Suddenly in seconds, as if from a mist, a bunch of armed Chinese in nondescript uniforms stood silently at the jungle's edge. I saw little red stars on several of their caps and ducked behind the car when the Special Branch officers began to grin. I realized that we were being shown one of the most secret of their operations—one in which ex-CTs and hardened young Chinese Special Branch agents who pretended to be CTs lived in the jungle acting like regular CT units.

The length of time these defectors stayed in the jungle depended on the deals they had made with the British. I gathered that some of them had never actually left there but had been recruited or captured somewhere inside and had been "turned" to serve the British. They would stay in until they had proved by some special act—such as killing, capturing, or arranging to ambush their former comrades—that they were fully hooked, always an open question with people like that. The Special Branch had the cultivated reputation of not being easily reassured.

These units were led by British police officers, usually ex–British Army NCOs who stayed with the group for maybe a month, which was about as long as a Britisher could live in the jungle under those conditions. The leader of this particular patrol was obviously tired. He had three or four more days to go, and all he was interested in was his mail, which he burned after reading it quickly so that there would be no evidence taken back into the jungle other than his face and his smell that he was not a Malayan Chinese. He said that he tried to stay out of sight when the group was actually in contact with real CTs and one of the Chinese Special Branch officers would pose as the leader. It was all enormously risky. My initial jump at seeing the little force come out of the jungle was not entirely due to my unadventurous spirit; some of these operations had gone sour and British officers and loyal ex-CTs had been killed. Just as quietly as they had come, the group was gone, taking with them their slightly augmented real CT supplies. Howie and I had learned a lot—about techniques and about character.

Counterinsurgency was not entirely British. It would have failed if it had been. Although they had commanding positions wherever it mattered, control was more often than not exerted indirectly, in the best traditions of British colonialism. It was a well-thought-out process: When the color of districts shifted from black to white on the charts at General Bourne's headquarters indicating that the CTs had been eliminated in them, British district officers were replaced by Malayans, who in turn became responsible to elected officials. The Emergency regulations were eased or eliminated and the people were given a sense of what life would be like after independence. Control was replaced by guidance, direction by persuasion. It took time and undeviating perseverance.

The British also recognized the moral and practical military value of being able to show that their efforts were supported throughout the Commonwealth. Australia and New Zealand sent sizable contingents from their regular forces, and the then remaining colonies such as Northern Rhodesia (now Zambia) and Fiji provided units.

The Fijians' dress uniform featured a kilt-like white skirt, called a *lava lava*, with jagged hem. They sometimes paraded in bare feet. They and the Maoris from New Zealand performed war dances at parties featuring deep bass chants and thunderous foot stamping. Both led in rugby football. All of these units had active combat roles, and the nonwhite colonial troops often came out ahead of the British regiments in the inevitable competition over soldiering skills.

Best of all were the Gurkhas, superbly disciplined, light infantry from Nepal. I had first heard about the Gurkhas in 1940, when several of my British friends, a year or so older than I, left North China suddenly to receive officers' training in the British Indian Army. During World War II the Gurkhas won more Victoria Crosses, the highest British decoration for bravery, than any other units in the entire British Army. Their superiority seemed to be accepted by other forces in Malaya, even the otherwise fanatically unit-proud Britishers. I once saw a cartoon in the Malayan Police Officer's weekly that showed a couple of police officers sitting morosely at a bar looking out past the barbed wire to the jungle. One said to the other, "I can tell you this; if they'd a had Gurkhas at Bunker Hill, I'd be Chief Police Officer—Texas by now." A decade later in London I heard some desultory talk about the United States "renting" some Gurkha

battalions for use in Vietnam. This got nowhere because no British government could run the political risk of taking a direct part in the Vietnam
War. I think, on the American side, our military had doubts about introducing forces that had not been trained by Americans in our own, but not
necessarily better, ways.

It was clear by early 1957 that Malaya would become independent
under a constitution that, while assuring the Malays of continuing political domination due to their majority status, would also allow the Chinese to retain their pre-eminent economic position. Statistics showed the
Emergency steadily winding down as district after district was declared
white, until only the small CT concentrations in Johore in the extreme
south and along the border with Thailand in the north were left in the
Federation. Whether these trends would survive the final transfer of
power to an elected Malayan government depended on the leadership of
the Alliance Party. And, in that respect, our reports pointed reassuringly
to Tunku Abdul Rahman, who would be the new prime minister.

Independence meant that the consulate general would become an
embassy. There would be an ambassador, more staff, and, inevitably,
more hierarchy. Some of the contacts Shirley and I had made among
Alliance officials would go to higher-ranking officers in the new embassy.
All these changes were natural, even desirable from a wider viewpoint,
but Kuala Lumpur looked like it might not be so much fun anymore. We
were actually relieved at receiving orders in early spring 1957 to Alexandria, Egypt. I was replaced by John Farrior, also a China missionary's son
and Chinese language officer—the third such Political Section chief in a
row—and a fellow Marine student at the Navy Japanese Language
School at Boulder, Colorado.

We sat in our assigned seats far back in the stands at the last great
British Commonwealth parade in the Federation of Malaya peering
around and between the heads of the high-ranking British and Malayan
officials. Across the *padang*, Kuala Lumpur's wide, central playing field,
the weak orange lights from the Selangor Club, known as "The Dog," sil-
houetted members gathered on the verandah. We had been asked to
arrive an hour before the parade was to begin, even before the thoughtful organizers put lighted coils of punk under each seat, whose smoke
sometimes slightly discouraged mosquitoes from our ankles. We and the
other non-Malayans smelled of citronella. At three-minute intervals we
had risen and stood silently when, timed to the second, crested Rolls

Royces pulled up to the curb behind us dropping off Tunku Abdul Rahman, now the official director of operations en route to becoming prime
minister; the Sultan of Selangor—the princely state surrounding Kuala
Lumpur—whose name and titles took up two lines of the program; and
finally Sir Donald MacGillivray, the high commissioner, who for a few
more months would outrank everyone else.

Exactly at seven, the floodlights flashed on and there they were,
stretched in a long line in front of the Dog: two battalions of the Malay
Regiment wearing their white dress uniforms, with the traditional elaborate short blue apron-like *sarong* shot with silver threads and a shining silver emblem on their black *songkoks*, the Malay Moslem cap; the Fijians in
their red and white *lava lavas*; Australians in slouch hats and immacu-
lately creased khaki; Africans from Northern Rhodesia, their height augmented by red *fezzes*, led by their almost-as-tall, mustachioed British officers holding heavy sabers unwaveringly upright; New Zealand
paratroopers in red berets; and, of course, the Ghurkas. The bands
massed before the reviewing stand, the high commissioner walked stiffly
to his dais, and out of the loudspeakers came a series of yelps (not from
him), seconded by the commanders on the field, as the troops were called
to attention. Then the long screech "ROahaaLL SALOOOT" and the
crash, crash, stamp as 3,000 soldiers of the Queen presented arms, a long
rattle of drums, the lights went out, a spotlight fixed on the flagpole and
when the Royal Standard was shaken loose in the breezeless night, the
bands thundered into "God Save the Queen."

We sat down. The bands marched and countermarched, pipes and
drums alternating with the others. There was a *feu de joie* as the front
ranks of the riflemen fired single blank shots in unbroken sequence all the
way down the line of troops—a long rolling machine gun sound. The
units passed in review, and then off the field, marching to their own
drummers and regimental tunes, one stiff arm swinging high as the
British do.

The last to go were the Ghurkas. As they disappeared under the great
banyan trees to the right of the *padang* at their own special quick march,
the lights dimmed; the bagpipes' heart-quickening mournful wail faded
too, leaving only the cadence of the drums. The guests began moving
toward the Dog for a drink and dinner.

The gaunt, pale-eyed wife of a senior British official smiled at us and
we went along the aisle with her. Like many of the British women who
had suffered in the Japanese camps during the war, she was chronically
ill and desperately tired of the tropics. We had sometimes pitied her and
yet admired her because she had been in Malaya too long but never complained. We stood silently together looking at the Malayan crowds on the

padang until she turned shyly to us, "It was grand, wasn't it?" She was describing the parade; I was thinking how proudly the long British rule was ending with its gift of independence. "Yes," I replied. "Yes, it really was grand."

NOTES

1. Lucian W. Pye, *Guerrilla Communism in Malaya* (Princeton, N.J.: Princeton University Press, 1956).
2. Pye, 7.
3. Pye, 21.

Chapter 11

Washington Again

After a quite different but absorbing tour in Alexandria, Egypt (1957–59), we began a happy, grinding four years in the State Department, where I toiled at the bottom of the policy and operational "line" as a desk officer in the Office of Southeast Asian Affairs, followed by a professionally valuable year at the National War College.

"Desk officer" is the generic title for the person who is supposed to be the focal point, source of information, coordinator of action, drafter of papers and instructions, initiator of policy proposals, point person in inter-agency battles, guardian of the bureaucratic turf, and much more—just about everything to do with United States relations with a specific country. Desk officers have much to say but little authority over what happens. During my day, in an effort to give them more wallop by title, they officially became officers-in-charge, an embellishment that enabled them occasionally to have desk officers under them, without changing their purpose. They lived in turmoil because Washington is crammed with serious, hard-working people having real or assumed interests in everything that goes on in every country and who fight for a piece of the action. Desk officers would get in early to be able to brief their many layers of supervisors who also came in early. They worked fast all day and stayed on in the evening until the last message was sent off to the field, and they were often awakened at night. Their hardest work was frequently O.B.E. ("overtaken by events")—or, having waited impatiently to be allowed to argue for a proposal, they were finally told, "You're pushing on an open door; you won an hour ago and the message has already gone out." Most desk officers liked it; I did. They are not decision-makers though, and their intricate, essential function in the foreign affairs process is often overlooked. Presumably now, new devices have eliminated some of the tedium of their tasks; but while computers can keep many things in mind at once, decision-makers can't— or shouldn't try—and some human has to know the state of play.

I was the officer-in-charge of Burma affairs during the last year and a half of the Eisenhower administration (1959–60). Burma (now Myanmar) could have made some progress toward modernization—we thought— and thus by our logic become less a possible victim of communism than was generally assumed. General Ne Win was yet to show all the paranoiac, xenophobic characteristics he did later, when he presided for decades over the decline of his country. He was even briefly popular in Washington for his professed anti-communism—a common misjudgment of the era. I knew nothing about Burma, had never been there; thus, blindfolded but with a strong sense of purpose, I plunged bravely into the politics of foreign assistance, aided by reading in manuscript another of Lucian Pye's books *Politics, Personality and Nation Building*,[1] about Burma's political culture and the search for an identity by a colonized Asian society in transition to modern independence. Wisely advised by Richard Usher, a conscientious, workaholic boss who had served in Burma, I found that the more individual Burmese one met, the more one liked them and their country. One also had to realize that the charmingly fey Burmese ways, while not actually clashing, were unable to meet the American urges for unambiguous responses, clear commitment to joint purposes, forward planning, and genuine enthusiasm. There was competence and seeming goodwill on both sides, but the two seldom came together. The experience left me with firm opinions against our using economic aid to show support for individuals.[2]

LAOS DESK

In the spring of 1961 I became the officer-in-charge of Laos affairs. I had never been to Laos either, but by that time I knew a lot about the Washington end of its affairs. Laos received direct attention from President Eisenhower. In his final day in office, Eisenhower briefed it as his hottest foreign affairs problem to President Kennedy because it looked like the North Vietnamese were en route to seizing the entire country. Eisenhower argued that Laos could be the first "domino" to "fall" in Southeast Asia if the United States stood passively by, endangering our ally Thailand and thus the entire U.S. position in the area. The "Domino Theory" was to become a compelling American foreign policy maxim for both political parties.

Presidential interest ignited bureaucratic passions, and Laos crowded out other subjects in the daily staff meetings of the Office of Southeast Asian Affairs. During most of 1959 and all of 1960, earnest, worried people dropped in; the *Today Show* called; congressional staffers wanted news— the atmosphere in our crowded offices became tense. Christian Chapman, my predecessor who had served in both Laos and Vietnam, deftly avoided being overwhelmed by the continuous pressure but occasionally needed some simple help. I would rush along the brightly lit, multihued corridors of the brand new, enlarged State Department bearing messages for clearance. While advocating Chapman's proposals and defending them against the obligatory resistance of our colleagues, I became aware of many of the developments agitating the American government—all colored by the Cold War. I still wonder how, through no fault of its own, this remote country of two million gentle, fun-loving (I have heard) people could seize the attention of the major powers in such unhappy ways.

THE GENEVA CONFERENCE ON LAOS 1961–1962

My first duties as OIC-Laos were as a delegate to the Fourteen-Nations[3] Conference on the Neutrality of Laos in Geneva, which began in May 1961 and ended with the signing of the Laos agreements in July the next year. The conference and its follow-up effects on U.S. policy in Indo-China became my professional way of life for two and a half years— engrossing, wearisome, and inconclusive.

The conference has long left the list of major diplomatic events of the Cold War because it did not prevent the widening of the war in Vietnam. But for a flicker of time it seemed to offer a distant chance for an internationally backed peaceful settlement in Indo-China. Unfortunately, it soon became apparent that the North Vietnamese were not going to abide by the parts of the agreements that would interfere with their aims in South Vietnam. I suppose that after the fact there are few who would admit to having been sanguine.

At the time though, the varied national interests of the fourteen participants faintly stirred hope. As described below in shorthand, they sound elementary, but the mixture of motives for attending looked like angles to work on—international ways out of a Vietnam War. Our dim optimism then is a splinter of history.

General Secretary Nikita Khrushchev of the Soviet Union had agreed with President Kennedy at the otherwise unyielding 1961 summit in Vienna that Laos should be a neutral state.

The People's Republic of China, not yet in the United Nations, would welcome becoming formally, but passively, re-involved in Southeast Asian affairs—as would France.

All of Laos' neighbors—Burma, China, North Vietnam, South Vietnam, Cambodia, and Thailand—would accept a government in Laos under centrist Souvanna Phouma, albeit for different reasons and different conditions—Thailand and South Vietnam under pressure from the United States.

Almost lost among the overlapping or conflicting national aims of the others was poor Laos, whose competitive leaders were inaccurately lumped ideologically into "right," "left," and "neutral" political groupings ("les trois tendances" as they were referred to in French). Although the American record of arranging things in Laos did not inspire confidence, even in the State Department, it seemed quite possible on entering the conference that the "right" could eventually be maneuvered into teaming up with the "neutral" Souvanna Phouma and limiting the power of the "left."

India, Canada, and Poland were the three members of the International Control Commission established to oversee the Indo-China settlement of 1954. A revitalized ICC would be essential to any scheme for "neutralizing" Laos. It was already organized under the "troika" (from the Russian three-horse sleigh) principle then being touted by the Soviet Union as a "peaceful co-existence" device for Cold War situations around the world. Its usefulness to the United States depended on its chairman, India, the "neutral" middle horse, guiding the "right" horse, Canada, and the "left" horse, Poland, down an honest middle path. Canada could be counted upon to be a robust supporter of a genuine ICC, but it was assumed from the beginning that Poland would slavishly obey the Soviet Union in everything. We knew that India would be handicapped by the anti-American, pro-Soviet prejudices of its fiery-eyed foreign minister, V. K. Krishna Menon, but might try to show itself capable of playing a "neutral" role and support some autonomy for the ICC. The prognosis was not good for an effective ICC, but it seemed possible that Canadian skill and enthusiasm would gather international support. This could, at least, allow the ICC to publicize North Vietnamese violations of the agreements.

The United States and Great Britain wished to mobilize international support to prevent Western Laos from falling into North Vietnamese hands without having to use U.S. ground forces. The best nonmilitary hope of impeding the NVN would be to reverse a solid Cold War policy of the Eisenhower administration and endorse a "neutralist" arrangement for Laos itself, backed by international agreements on how Laos was to behave and how the world was to behave toward it. If this worked, it conceivably could provide leads to some sort of negotiated long-term scheme for Vietnam.

How the United States was going to pursue such substantial objectives was a mystery to me when I boarded my first trans-Atlantic jet for Geneva in late April 1961. I knew I was not alone. A couple of weeks earlier I had been infiltrated into a small semi-secret working group set up under Kenneth Young, a former State Department officer and an expert on Southeast Asia. Having lost out on becoming ambassador to Saigon in the seething personnel situation of the young New Frontier, Young was soon to be appointed American ambassador to Bangkok. Young brought to Washington three officers who had served with him previously: Patricia Byrne from the consulate general in Izmir, Turkey; Lewis "Skip" Purnell from the Political Section in London; and Tom Corcoran, assistant political adviser to the commander-in-chief, Pacific at Pearl Harbor. I had been added at the request of the Office of Southeast Asian Affairs (SEA) mainly to keep an eye on what Young was up to. Nevertheless, I was received well, and we talked, wrote, and argued into the evenings over position papers. However, we had only a brief meeting with Averell Harriman, who was to be the chief negotiator, and we left Washington with only unagreed drafts of our proposals.

It took some time for the U.S. delegation to focus. With twelve other nations and the three "tendencies" of Laos involved, there was much initial American milling around, hurried unannounced high-level meetings without real preparation, and multiple competing press conferences. Secretary of State Dean Rusk brought along an enormous group to help him attend the opening, as did Assistant Secretary of Defense Paul Nitze, mindful of the far-ranging military implications for the negotiations. Even after the Washington crowd left with Secretary Rusk in a few days and Harriman could trade his small desk in the front reception room for the delegation chief's private office, problems of coordination between representatives of the different agencies remained—a lack of cohesion that was noticed by other delegations.

Fortunately, William H. Sullivan, my predecessor on the Burma desk, possibly the best younger officer in the Foreign Service then for bringing people and policies together, soon became the number two on the delegation. Decisive, quick on his feet, alert to the bureaucratic tangles in Washington, he was able to give Harriman consistent support and created a disciplined team from the delegation. Harriman made it easy for Sullivan by sharply cutting out all the higher-ranking officers. We began the systematic work of contacting all the other delegations.

Initially, I was the only member of the delegation who talked to the Chinese. As the conference developed its own routines and settled down to genuine negotiations, the Chinese became less formal. In a casual way I learned a bit about dealing with the Chinese Communists.

My opposite number in the PRC delegation was its secretary, Han Hsu, a crew-cut, smiling man about my own age, known to us as a protégé of Premier Zhou Enlai and a participant in the 1954 Geneva Conference, which Zhou had attended and which had arranged for the departure of the French from Indo-China. Han, who died in 1994, later became an active player in Sino-American relations, serving in Washington from 1973 to 1979 as the popular deputy chief of the Chinese Liaison Office and from 1985 to 1989 as the PRC's ambassador to the United States. When I first met him in Geneva I mentioned that I was impressed by his excellent, if somewhat rusty, English, which he said he had learned at the American-established institutions of Yanjing University and of Yuying, the elite boys high school in the American Board Compound in Beijing. These connections from our pasts slightly eased our relationship.

Our first brief meetings were to exchange the formal statements, press briefings, notices of meetings involving our two delegations, and other papers—the fodder of conference diplomacy. Later, as the conference dragged on ineffectually, we began to meet more casually as part of a conference routine that wisely provided long breaks for coffee and drinks through a device known as "The Language of the Day."

There were four official languages for the conference: French, Russian, Chinese, and English; and there were facilities for translating Lao or Vietnamese into one of these. Even though each speech was adroitly simultaneously translated into the other official languages during delivery by experienced translators from the United Nations, there was a formal retranslation into a rotating "Language of the Day" or, if the speech was in that language, into another official language. This crazily complicated, time-consuming process must have been deliberate—maybe to ensure the accuracy of the official published account, but most likely to provide opportunity for delegation leaders to meet informally and others to arrange appointments or consult among themselves on press guidance, or in the case of the American delegation, to begin preparing our daily reports to Washington. While the delegates were milling purposefully around the Delegates Lounge, someone from each large delegation had to stay behind to watch their papers and briefcases. During plenary sessions, which were held in the ornate council chamber of the old League of Nations, Han and I would occasionally chat in the spectators' area above the twelve empty seats allotted to the Burmese delegation that separated the massive presence of the Chinese from the much smaller, but still huge, American delegation. Because most of the listed two hundred PRC representatives were young trainees sent to Geneva to learn interpreting skills, many stayed in the room to listen to the formal retranslation, Han really didn't need to guard anything. I began to hope there was some substantive purpose in his hanging around.

I was briefly encouraged in this direction when one day after the conference had meandered for over two months, Han suddenly departed from our bland small talk and asked me flatly, "How is the State Department organized?" I busily drew wire diagrams of bureaus, offices, and chains of authority on the back of an official statement. I was sure Han already knew everything I told him but he picked up the paper, thanked me, and went his way. I waited for a few days before I made my modest first move. "Mr. Han, you asked me about the State Department; I wonder whether you could tell me how your Ministry of Foreign Affairs is organized." A slight smile and looking me in the eyes, "Just like the State Department," he offered. My opening closed.

HARRIMAN THE DIPLOMAT

Although W. Averell Harriman turns up in all accounts of the great American foreign policy events from the early 1940s to the mid-1970s, the only comprehensive biography of him that I have read is the appropriately titled *Spanning a Century* by Rudy Abramson.[4] Abramson had access to Harriman's papers and interviewed scores of people who had worked with this remarkable man. During the ten years it took to complete the project, Abramson also talked at length with Harriman himself—not that easy to do. In his nineties Harriman's eyesight was failing, and hearing was always a problem; and he was habitually reticent about his childhood and personal life. The book is a full account of a restless shifting of scenes as Harriman moved from a polo-playing near-playboy to big business success in railroads, shipping, airlines, Sun Valley, and international finance, to the Roosevelt New Deal, to strenuous roles in Great Britain and the Soviet Union during World War II, to secretary of commerce, head of the Marshall Plan in Europe, governor of New York, and presidential candidate. Finally, he served as a trouble-shooting diplomat in the Kennedy and Johnson administrations, the short period in his life when I joined several younger officers in the State Department in repaying his confidence in us—which we had earned by our own very hard work—with lifetime loyalty and affection.

I experienced Harriman for the first time in April 1961 at an overcrowded meeting in the State Department. He sat tall but hunched over at the head of the long conference table, looking uncomfortable as the hard of hearing do when people talk at once, blurting out their little speeches. The crowd was supposed to be discussing plans for the Laos conference. Harriman had asked for suggestions on negotiating strategy, which then came at him without order, often more aimed at establishing credentials for the speaker than conveying substance. Most of us had become inured to this kind of gathering by the tiresome, inconclusive meetings of the tail-end Eisenhower era; but I wondered why Harriman would bother, given his impressive reputation for highest-level personal dealings. Moreover, in this first sighting he seemed ineffectual—mumbling rhetorical questions in his upper-class New York accent. It took me time and many similar incidents to realize that I had been seeing Harriman's total immersion in the task at hand, especially one at the request of the president.

Harriman had a powerful start in life that provided him with key contacts and supporters in his business and public affairs. But it seems to me that he was a self-made man in the sense that he had to remake himself for each phase of his life. He had to struggle to be accepted for his own acquired abilities in big business, international polo, diplomacy, and politics—all hard-nosed, competitive arenas where a name will carry a person only so far and so long. Throughout *Spanning the Century*, Abramson describes Harriman as pushing his way into the action where he wasn't wanted in each of these fields, especially toward the end of his public service in the Kennedy and Johnson period. Probably so, but a driving quest for power and reputation doesn't surprise in Washington. We who watched him at first hand were more impressed with his steady dedication to public service and his determined loyalty to President Kennedy (and later, President Johnson, despite differences on Vietnam), overcoming his disappointment in not finally being chosen secretary of state, eagerly working long past the retirement age for Foreign Service officers, and over such a basically losing proposition as Laos.

KENNEDY ON GROUND TROOPS IN LAOS

An exhausting complication in the life of a desk officer is possessing a piece of information vital to a rapidly moving decision-making process and being unable to get it to the high officials who need it. This happens when he or she is excluded from key meetings or can't get in to see these officials and is forced to compete for attention in the long chain of command. Even victory there doesn't mean that the right conclusions (as the desk officer sees it) will be drawn from the information or, indeed, whether it will be relied upon at all.

In the fall of 1961, Harriman twice came back to Washington from Geneva for special instructions on what to do about the conference on Laos. He saw President Kennedy at the end of his two- or three-day stays, afterwards going straight from the White House to the airport. I had the duty of driving out with him in his chauffeured black Checkers cab, whose astonishingly durable engine he insisted was guaranteed for 400,000 miles. I liked this task because it gave me a chance to brief him on the latest messages from Geneva and Vientiane. Also, mixed in with his often bewildering instructions about his travel, dinner engagements in New York, and the like, would be some clues as to possible new policy directions. Harriman was discreet about presidential discussions, but he also had confidence in the career Foreign Service people who worked for him. I always thought that, one way or another, he told us what we needed to know and assumed we'd take it from there.

Often big news came without build-up or warning. Once as we were crossing Memorial Bridge, five minutes from National Airport, Harriman directed a string of orders to the chauffeur, abruptly closed the glass partition, and said firmly, "The president will not put ground troops into Laos." Harriman had assumed that all along, but this meant that he had just confirmed it in some way with Kennedy. He didn't need to add that the implications were clear for the tactics at the conference. Harriman should push as far as he could to get the North Vietnamese to withdraw from Laos but not put us into a situation where Laos would be seized unless U.S. ground forces intervened. That could happen if, by our actions, it would appear to the Soviets, who were thought to be a light—but only light—brake on the North Vietnamese, that the United States was stringing the conference along and did not intend to reach an agreement of some sort. At the same time, the threat of a full-scale use of force was about the only leverage the United States had on our British co-chairman allies, who wished to keep the conference alive as an alternative to an active military effort by the United States. The credibility of this threat had to be sustained. President Kennedy's real position was extremely sensitive.

We arrived at the airport a few moments later and Harriman instructed briskly in his cryptic way, "They should know—only the department— Walter (Walter P. McConaughy, the assistant secretary for East Asian affairs) and Alex" (U. Alexis Johnson—at that time the deputy undersecretary for political affairs). Typically, Harriman didn't elaborate and quickly grabbed his briefcase out of my hands, greeted a smiling New York politician who would fly to New York with him, and left. I got in the front seat of the Checkers beside the driver and returned to the State Department.

Back in my office, I hurriedly dictated a short word-for-word memorandum of exactly what Harriman said without adding my interpretation and addressed it to McConaughy and Johnson. State Department procedures and ordinary good manners would have had me at least show the memorandum to my immediate boss, the director of the Office for Southeast Asian Affairs, but I reasoned that I was just passing a message for Harriman and one he expected to be carefully protected. I took the memorandum to McConaughy's office myself and left it with his secretary, saying that I would be glad to discuss it.

The State Department is not the worst of bureaucracies. In fact, considering the volume and import of the matters it handles, it can often move quite efficiently. Still, it is highly conscious of levels, and because the hierarchy among career officers is loosely built on merit and experience, there are sometimes penalties for not playing by the rules.

In this case there were none, but the response from on high was odd. A few days after my ride to the airport with Harriman, the office director, Daniel Anderson, a kindly, soft-spoken Marylander, walked into my room holding my memorandum. He wasn't disturbed at my leaving him out earlier but instead was rather surprised that Harriman had entrusted such a vital piece of information to someone so junior. Apparently McConaughy and Johnson thought so too, because one had written on the memo, "I don't think we should be hearing this sort of thing from Chuck." And the other said, " I agree."

I had carried out Harriman's instructions, but I was never sure that his message had gotten through. At the bottom of the chain, I began to firm up my views on the connections between the threat of ground forces and the influencing of events—subjective feelings that have stayed with me.

During the full year of the Laos conference from the opening in May 1961 to the final signing of the agreements in July 1962, much of official Washington doubted that we would succeed in using the ups and downs of the conference to impede the North Vietnamese–supported Pathet Lao. What should we do about Laos if the North Vietnamese broke the cease-fire? Worries kept each other company: What would happen in Thailand and South Vietnam if the United States, by not responding with force, "allowed" the North Vietnamese to seize all of Laos, and—most unpalatable of all—with help from the Soviet Union and China?

Thailand was an ally in the Southeast Asia Treaty Organization covered by the Manila Treaty of 1954, and the military who ran the country were receiving massive amounts of American military aid. It was formally anti-communist, but those who knew the country accepted that that could change quickly if the United States looked like it would be ineffective in keeping the communists from the Thai borders. Ngo Dinh Diem in South Vietnam might be cranked up to more effective counterinsurgency efforts through augmented American advice and assistance, but that was far from certain, and would be more so if we were wobbly on Laos. It was weakly assumed that the United States would have to intervene if the conference failed to stabilize the situation, but no one dared to say how.

We on the aptly termed "lower working level," far below where such transcendent issues would be decided but still responsible for thinking hard about them, heatedly "trying on for size" numerous schemes for "handling the Laos problem." The popularity of debates on Laos, already assured by President Eisenhower's attention, grew during 1961—the first feverish year of the New Frontier. Action officers from all over the government flocked like pigeons—often on the weekends—to the offices of our superiors to present conflicting views. To my mind, possible courses of action depended upon the fundamental decision on using American ground forces inside Laos. I knew that President Kennedy had decided against their direct employment and so felt that much of our talk was "fighting the problem"—hand-wringing about whether to use them rather than what to do instead. However, I recognized that this profound issue would come up constantly to torture policymakers in the future. Laos would be a model for debates to come.

Both pros and cons read the situation the same way: the Pathet Lao would not be able to capture the populated areas of Western Laos from their noncommunist compatriots unless they were reinforced by North Vietnamese troops; then they could do so easily—the North Vietnamese being regarded as invincible by all the Lao, or so we assumed. The Royal Lao government (RLG) would do better when substantially assisted by Thai forces, but Thailand would not intervene effectively without clear evidence of American resolve.

What American "resolve"—always an important word in policy discussions during the Cold War—would look like was the permanent question. Here the military branches differed. Classically, the Air Force touted the psychological effects on both sides of bombing troop concentrations and built-up areas under Pathet Lao control. If this didn't deter the North Vietnamese and Pathet Lao, American planes could provide air support for RLG ground combat operations, which could go forward under the guidance of significant numbers of American military advisors. Some of us felt that neither the Thais nor the RLG would be emboldened by these kinds of gestures and would need a more substantial commitment— meaning American forces on the ground in Laos.

Kennedy did take a partial step in that direction in 1962 when he placed Marines along the Laos border in Thailand in response to ceasefire violations by the Pathet Lao. The Thais took the Marines as credible evidence that the United States would intervene in a decisive way should the communists threaten Thailand, even though it was clear that the Marines would not be employed deeply in Laos itself. I remember being tense as we drafted the orders, wondering what our next step would be if the NVN went after the whole of Laos—which they didn't do until 1975—but I was pleased as to the effect in Thailand. A well-publicized appearance of troops *on the ground* seemingly could deter.

In the end, the United States did fight a long "secret" war on the ground in Laos—using others, the Meo (now usually called Hmong) tribesmen, and much American bombing from bases in Thailand.

HARRIMAN THE NEGOTIATOR

Abramson quotes Isaiah Berlin, a distinguished British philosopher, political scientist, and historian, on Harriman. "He had the uncanny sense as a negotiator of what would work and what would not. He sized up people, situations and the nature of contending forces as art experts determine the authorship, date and earliest significance of a piece of art."[5]

I'm not sure how Harriman would have reacted to such a high-flown description, but his ability to strike right through to the heart of matters as he did in the Laos conference fascinated me. First, he took on board that the United States would not fight on the ground in Laos, thereby dictating a bluffing strategy. Then, as a part of that strategy, he insisted that the communist forces follow through on a cease-fire and freeze on their movements before and during the conference—in effect, stopping them from seizing Western Laos diplomatically rather than by fighting them.

When the Pathet Lao seemed in place, Harriman changed gears and concentrated on producing a "neutralist" government for Laos under Prince Souvanna Phouma that would be acceptable to all of Laos's neighbors and thus create a vested interest in its continued existence. Back in Washington after the summer of 1961 at the conference in Geneva, I drafted masses of high-priority cables to Bangkok and Vientiane as Harriman pursued an intricate balancing process that involved cajoling and arm-twisting those elements in Laos whom the United States had formerly supported into giving up their positions of power—and some of their American financial support.

Throughout, Harriman labored with the Indian and Canadian members of the International Control Commission and the British and Soviet co-chairmen of the conference to establish an international system for superintending the agreements and providing for continuity. Nothing in these kinds of negotiations really goes well, but Harriman doggedly pressed on for over a year until the Laos agreements were signed in Geneva in July 1962.

The agreements failed to save Laos from being partitioned because the North Vietnamese would not abide by its undertakings to remove its forces from Laos and to stop using Laos as a corridor into South Vietnam for its troops and supplies. Harriman knew that they would probably behave this way; otherwise they could not seize South Vietnam by force, and the American strengthening of South Vietnam then underway precluded other alternatives for them. However, he based his tactics on the hope—and it was always only a hope—that the international community could help hold back North Vietnam. He thought there might be a formal role for this in the vague supervisory responsibilities over "their side" given to the Soviet Union. As an official co-chairman of the conference, the Soviets could bring pressure to bear on North Vietnam to curtail its activities in Laos and also direct the Polish member of the International Control Commission to join honestly in investigations of North Vietnamese violations of the agreements. The United Kingdom was the other co-chairman of the conference and would presumably look after "our side." The interplay between the co-chairmen later formed a key angle in the behind-the-scenes negotiating strategy in U.S. efforts toward ending the war in Vietnam, as I was to learn a few years later in London.

Harriman was severely criticized by some of his State Department colleagues for relying too much on occasional appearances of Soviet cooperation. John Steeves, Harriman's original deputy in Geneva, remarked at one point, when Harriman had urged a compromise based on a Soviet position, that he supposed the next cable from Geneva would be signed "Pushkin"(the head of the Soviet delegation).[6]

In Geneva, it seemed different to us as we watched Harriman work on G. M. Pushkin, developing easy professional give-and-take dealings between them. Pushkin would say things like, "All the North Vietnamese forces which are NOT in Laos will be withdrawn in 90 days" (that is, according to the terms of the agreements), and Harriman would take that as a Soviet intention. It wasn't just on faith that Pushkin, a descendant of the great nineteenth-century Russian poet, could deliver on such vagaries. Harriman saw events—and himself—in a big-picture context. Used to the worldwide implications of negotiations with the Soviet Union, he seized on the fact that the only agreement between Khrushchev and Kennedy in their painful 1961 meeting in Vienna, so full otherwise of threats and dangers, had been the mutual acceptance of the neutrality of Laos. "They (the Soviet Union) have to be held to that," he would say, believing that possibly Khrushchev, trying to force action in Berlin his way, would like to reduce tensions with the United States in at least one area of the world.

Whether or not the Soviets really tried to carry out their implied commitments to cool off their fellow communists is hard to say from this distance in time. There were signs in 1962–1963 that they curtailed their military assistance to the Pathet Lao, and they joined in an international assistance program to the neutral government of Souvanna Phouma—although to the Pathet Lao elements in it. However, they did not force their wholly owned Polish third of the International Control Commission to cooperate with the Canadians and Indians in investigating and reporting on violations. Nor, more significantly for the future, did they obtain North Vietnamese adherence to the agreements, thereby facilitating NVN incursions in the South.

I have just described a classic Cold War miscalculation by both the American and Soviet "sides" of the other's capacity to "deliver" their Vietnamese "clients." The Laos agreements, if observed, would not assure the North Vietnamese that they could take over the South, so they broke them selectively; the South Vietnamese regarded negotiations of any kind with the North as illusory and blocked them whenever they could. Both sets of Vietnamese depended on foreign support for their war, but both were Vietnamese nationalists inside. Both Americans and Russians misunderstood them in the same way.[7]

The Soviet Union was also inhibited in the pressure it could exert on North Vietnam by its recurring difficulties with the PRC. Harriman put the superpower dilemma succinctly to Anastas Mikoyan one late November afternoon in 1962. That shrewd survivor and still-powerful holdover from the Stalin era had come to see Harriman about some details of the arms test agreement that would be signed in Moscow the following summer. I had unexpectedly been asked to go with John Guthrie, the salty officer in charge of Soviet affairs, to Harriman's house in Georgetown to take notes—no one was sure about what—but "please hurry."

I sat, curious but silent, for an hour in Harriman's smallish study while he and Mikoyan talked easily through Soviet Ambassador Anatoly Dobrynin about significant matters, and Guthrie filled his yellow pad. Just as his guests were leaving, Harriman tried to make a quick point about an obscure problem in Laos to an uncomprehending Mikoyan and an only slightly more informed Dobrynin. He explained to the already overcoated Russians that there weren't any Chinese Nationalist troops in Northwest Laos as the Soviets were claiming in their co-chairman role. His sudden plunge into this insider's subject came from the implication in communist propaganda, brought to his attention that morning, that the United States was allegedly still supporting these forces—a violation of the Laos agreements—when, in fact, we had been urging Taipei to withdraw them from Southeast Asia for several years. Harriman's vehement clincher: "And anyway, Chiang Kai-shek (the president of the Republic of China on Taiwan) doesn't do what we tell him anymore than Mao Zedong does what you tell him to do!" Dobrynin gasped, "Oh, Governor!" Mikoyan smiled weakly. We never heard anything more on this issue.

DRAFTING FOR HARRIMAN

The procedures for preparing messages for Harriman's approval were both casual and tense in those precomputer days. Casual because Harriman found the State Department's clearance system cumbersome and restrictive, which it was, and liked to avoid it; tense because time-consuming though clearance was, many high-ranking voices throughout the government wanted to be heard on Laos matters or at minimum be registered on important messages as having been consulted. For me this meant tiresome arguments with desk officers in other State Department bureaus and other departments and agencies over words, and sometimes even substance, while the evening deadlines for sending out the messages relentlessly approached. Harriman issued an extraordinary number of instructions.

Every morning orders came down through my several bosses or were passed to me directly at meetings in Harriman's office on the floor above. During the day we drafted and cleared, sending the product in draft upstairs to Harriman's accomplished assistant, Hildy Shishkin, who would have them lined up in order of Harriman's priorities, which she often knew better than he did. He was, after all, dealing with many countries besides Laos. Down in my office we would spread copies out on the desk awaiting the usual after-hours call. Suddenly, without introduction and rapid fire, "I don't think you should say 'understandable'" (as in "the embassy's views are understandable"); "Why did you say 'understandable'?" "Do you think we should say that?" "What do you mean?" A squeaky "Understandable, Governor?" as I desperately searched through the half-dozen drafts for the word, "Oh, that was to let Win Brown (the tall, soft-voiced, undeviatingly honest, New Englander ambassador to Laos) know that you had carefully gone over his suggestion." "OK" and he would hang up. After a couple more such calls, Hildy would send down the approved drafts, the duty secretary in the office typed them up, and out they would go.

Harriman usually allowed disagreement, as he did in this case, and the longer I did this kind of work for him, the more of my ideas he would accept. The biggest practical problem arose when he scribbled in changes giving an entirely new meaning, sometimes conflicting with something in another message, or even more troublesome, producing a new message of his own, necessitating a race upstairs to argue in person. This was tough to do at the end of Harriman's long day at the department, when he had many other matters on his mind. He was always engaged in the evening, so key issues were sometimes put on hold until later at night. Often accompanied by Shirley, I would go to the Harriman house on N Street in Georgetown, sit under the Van Goghs and Cezannes, and struggle with the still alert seventy-plus-year-old over a whole new draft. Then I would go back to the semi-darkened department, type up the message myself "in green" (the color of the top sheet of the message form), and cross paths on the way to the message center with other weary desk officers who were dealing with Berlin and the Middle East.

Harriman didn't have many rules except a preference for short to-the-point messages covering a single subject—not always the practice in the department. Once, when changing at his last minute request a flat instruction to Win Brown in Vientiane—from "Tell Phoumi (the right-wing leader in Laos who was resisting American pressure on some issue) soonest that American patience (that is, Harriman's) is running out. Unless etc. etc. happens . . ." to a gentler "Phoumi should understand that there are limits on American patience . . ."—Harriman rather pleasantly ordered, "Don't try to be a British admiral!" He had somehow picked up the thought during his time in London during World War II that the admiralty liked to superintend the Royal Navy's battles minutely from afar. Whether the British sea-dogs had actually behaved that way was unclear but I took the lesson seriously, even, though very rarely, interjecting, "Wouldn't that be like a British admiral, Governor?" There are limits to the consistency of great men and I always lost. Mysteriously, because neither word was in the paper we were discussing, he once announced without warning or explanation that henceforth he never wanted to see either "fruitful" or "delicate" used to describe anything in any draft.

In August 1963, I started a year at the National War College in Fort McNair. Harriman, who had become the undersecretary for political affairs and was leaving for Moscow to sew up the Test Ban Treaty, wrote me a kind note. He said something I had not observed: "I have found that your knowledge and sound judgment have frequently compelled me to reverse positions I have taken." He added an interesting warning: "Don't let your increased knowledge blunt your determination to get action. I find that frequently the more knowledge people get, the more ineffective they become." I was to see him again on business and socially in the next couple of decades, but it wasn't the same.

NOTES

1. Lucian W. Pye, *Politics and Nation Building* (New Haven, Conn.: Yale University Press, 1962).

2. Before I came to the desk in 1959, the United States had publicized an offer of $20 million to build a road for Ne Win. This bold entirely politically motivated generosity had not been checked out with the foreign aid bureaucracy, who insisted during drawn-out technical meetings that the sum was inadequate for anything like the grandiose scheme of our propaganda. They had "development" projects in mind for the money anyway. The Burmese professed dismay at their share of the local costs, which had not been stressed early on. The issues were not resolved on my watch, and a much shorter road was finally completed much later for little political advantage to the United States. Meanwhile, Ne Win came to the United States in 1960 for some medical exams at U.S. government expense cum high-level talks about the road. He was enraged when his well-known American private physician confided to him that the CIA had asked for detailed reports and records on his condition. Ne Win was pleasant to me personally, but his subordinates, having no one else to complain to, lumped the difficulties over the road and CIA prying together, not as inept and gauche American behavior but as signs that the United States looked down on Burmese.

3. Also known as the International Conference on the Settlement of the Laotian Question. The participants: United States, United Kingdom, France, USSR, PRC,

North Vietnam, South Vietnam, Cambodia, Thailand, Burma, Canada, India, Poland, and Laos.

4. Rudy Abramson, *Spanning the Century* (New York: William Morrow, 1992).

5. Abramson, 17.

6. Abramson, 587.

7. Philip Manhard, who will come up in my account of the NVN Tet Offensive in 1968 (chapter 14), illustrated the single-minded stubbornness of the NVN for me during a debriefing of his experiences as their prisoner. Phil had been captured at Hue and held in solitary confinement in a camp in North Vietnam for five years. His only news of the outside world came—usually months after the events—in occasional talks with a Vietnamese civilian interrogator whom Phil called "Cronkite" after the leading American television anchor of that time. (For example, "Cronkite" asked Phil in the fall of 1968 about the significance of Lyndon Johnson's decision not to run for a second term, announced six months earlier.) Phil was coolly able to recall these conversations in exceptional detail, even for a professional Foreign Service officer, especially remarkable because he had no way of making notes.

In the fall of 1972, Phil developed a dangerously large carbuncle on his back and was taken to a hospital in Hanoi and put up at a hotel during treatment. On the last evening before being returned to his camp he was "invited" to dine with a Vietnamese official, who Phil later figured to be a vice–foreign minister, although they were not really introduced.

The NVN obviously assumed that the public and secret negotiations led by Henry Kissinger then underway in Paris would lead to peace and quickly thereafter to diplomatic relations with the United States because their questions were mostly practical ones about embassies in Washington, size, costs of living, and so on. At the end of the dinner, however, the Vietnamese host mentioned that they had been under pressure from their Soviet ally to retreat on an issue of sovereignty in the hope of stopping the war. The Soviets had even sent President Nicolai Podgorny to Hanoi to urge restraint. The Vietnamese had responded that if Podgorny continued to insist on Vietnam giving up its war aims, not only would he lose the respect of Vietnam but of the whole socialist world! Phil asked about the Chinese. "They sent Zhou Enlai and we told him the same thing," was the proud reply.

Chapter 12

London—1966–1967

In 1966, after serving as deputy chief of mission in Nicosia, Cyprus, we were assigned to the American Embassy in London where I had the much-prized slot in the Political Section dealing with East Asia. The family was not delighted to exchange the excitement—even danger—of life at a small post in an island country in perpetual crisis for the restrictions and anonymity of a large embassy. However, London is London and we made our adjustments.

I had been led to believe that part of the reason for our assignment was to help out on the British end of negotiations with the Soviet Union over Vietnam. Such negotiations seemed possible because the United Kingdom and the Soviet Union had been co-chairmen of the 1954 Geneva Conference on Indo-China and of the Geneva Conference on Laos (1961–62) and in both cases had some residual responsibilities. These theoretically gave both powers an unobjectionable pretext to intervene indirectly by exerting influence on the two sides—the British on us, and the Soviet Union on North Vietnam. Practically speaking, it meant that the British could forward American proposals to the Soviets, who could then give them to the North Vietnamese and report back reactions. Thus, through these intermediaries the United States could maintain another, albeit long-range, channel to Hanoi. Harriman, who was in general charge of the project, also hoped that for broader reasons of their relationship to the United States, the Soviets would put pressure on the North Vietnamese to stop the fighting and bring about a negotiated end to the war. Naturally, if the British were to be helpful, they had to be kept fully in the picture, not only about our own conflicts with the Soviets but about the Johnson administration's policy thinking on Vietnam. Occasionally that could be used by the Labour government to deflect the hammering it was receiving from its own back benches over its refusal to condemn the United States outright for Vietnam. I expected to play a small, but necessary, liaison role.

DEFENDING THE WAR

Instead, given the importance President Johnson attached to Great Britain's qualified support of, at least not open opposition to, his policies on Vietnam, my real Vietnam work was mainly public relations. Ambassador David Bruce, experienced and old-school, was discreet even with his senior staff, but I gathered from my first talk with him immediately after Shirley and I arrived in London that he thought Vietnam was taking American attention away from Europe and that he was, therefore, dubious about our policies. Of course, on the other hand, there was no question that he would scrupulously carry out instructions to have his embassy garner support for the administration's positions wherever it could.

For officers in the Political Section, this meant many off-the-record background talks with journalists to present less blatant arguments than were coming out of official Washington at the time and the quiet cultivation of selected Labour, Tory, and Liberal politicians. For me it meant providing background information and the "party line" to the others in the embassy besides preparing myself for the almost daily lunches and dinners where I knew that Vietnam would be the only subject discussed—at least with me. Concurrently, of course, I had the usual reporting responsibilities covering all of East Asia and sought out British experts on Southeast Asia, such as Patrick Honey of London University, Sir Robert Thompson, one of the world's recognized experts on counterinsurgency, and British reporters who had come back from assignments to Vietnam: Mark Frankland of the *Observer* and Ken McKenzie of the *Economist*, whom we had first met in Cyprus.

There was always much ado over Vietnam at the Foreign Office, especially the day before the prime minister's question time in the House of Commons. This institution of British parliamentary democracy allows members of Parliament to question ministers of the government in power, upon adequate notice—usually the day before—on almost any issue, and depending on the political import, to receive an oral answer from the minister concerned or, when big matters were involved, from the prime minister—all MPs themselves. The inevitable follow-up questions habitually generated some active give and take, and Prime Minister Harold Wilson had to look informed in great depth so that he would not be caught off guard. Often someone from the parliamentary secretary's office (a Labour MP working in the Foreign Office) called in the late afternoon asking a specific question of fact like the number of bombing missions to North Vietnam in the past week or, more provocatively, the number of refugees created by South Vietnamese/American military operations.

The friendly British voices conveyed a tinge of urgency, and I would immediately send off a message to Washington. I hoped for some coordination there because I knew the British embassy in Washington would be responding to the same queries, as would its counterpart in Saigon. It was useful to have a single authoritative statement. In the brisk political atmosphere on both sides of the Atlantic, discrepancies between different parts of the American government were exaggerated by the Labour Left and its supporting press.

The next morning I would pass Washington's reply to the Foreign Office (despite occasional doubts as to content—realizing it was what Washington WANTED to say). In the afternoon I would take the embassy pass and sit in the Strangers' Gallery of the House to hear how our information was used. That was usually in abbreviated form, but then the questioners weren't really interested in the facts and the Labour government tried to confine themselves to straight, unadorned answers—"We have checked with the State Department and the numbers are such and such." It was sometimes difficult for an outsider to assess the ensuing rapid-fire debate in varieties of British English (visitors were not allowed to take notes), and I would arrange to be invited to take tea at the House of Commons with an MP sympathetic to our positions on Vietnam. As a consequence, I spent several evenings with Tory and Labour politicians drinking beer with their constituents at pubs in the Greater London area, listening to authentic British opinions (generally, in those groups, not strongly opposed to our war in Vietnam and warmly pro-American otherwise) rather than giving my own.

There were many questions the United States wanted to ask the British or drafts of diplomatic notes that needed prior discussion and often on nice days I would walk from Grosvenor Square to Whitehall via St. James Park. The uniformed "messengers" at the Foreign Office greeted me by name after a couple of visits and, if I timed it right, I would arrive for one of the two daily teatimes.

The most time-consuming and often nerve-wracking job was defending our Vietnam policy before groups all over the country. I spoke about Vietnam some twenty times in the ten months I served at the embassy. With the exceptions of an afternoon appearance before the Lady Conservatives of Godalming (sort of the Greenwich, Connecticut, of London) and an after-dinner talk to a somnolent Army/Navy Club in London, the audiences were at the least mildly or, more often, aggressively hostile. The out-of-London appearances were often wearying, requiring me to leave London by train in the morning for a "red brick" university in say, Birmingham (two hours away) or one at industrial cities even farther out, like Leeds or Sheffield, locate my host (usually the secretary of the school's Socialist Club), eat a hasty lunch at a student cafeteria, followed by a jam-packed two-hour meeting attended by people who noisily came and went, then a train back to London. Both Cambridge and Oxford were able to be more welcoming and at each of them I was put up at one of the colleges for a couple of nights, argued comfortably with my firmly opposed audiences, and in the late evening sipped straight un-iced whiskey out of an ordinary drinking glass with one of the Fellows—like a British movie.

The format was almost always the same, whether at a university, church, or a city public affairs group, although students were the most combative, as they were all over the world at that time. I spoke for fifteen or twenty minutes, interrupted by heckling, and was followed by an opponent who challenged, to applause, everything I had said. Then we had questions, the fun part for the audience. These were rarely devised to elicit information, but often were undergraduate cagey. "Can you tell us how many children were killed by your planes last month?" "What do you personally think of using napalm on civilians?" Or, at a slightly more sophisticated level, "How much does it cost the United States to keep the corrupt South Vietnamese government in power?" "Why don't the South Vietnamese people fight for themselves?"

In answering questions such as these I tried to color my arguments with some idealism—not too much, because doing good for others is a private matter in Great Britain and boasting about it is very much out. So was helping small, poor, newly independent countries to resist communism because most of the audience thought that American anti-communism was overblown and that, anyway, the Vietnamese variety as described in most of the newspapers they read was probably a good thing—way out there in Asia. It was also ineffective to attempt to balance the stream of wild accusations of American atrocities with documented accounts of North Vietnamese and Viet Cong misdeeds; everybody understood that "war is hell." The miseries the communists created didn't turn up on television every day. I eventually accepted the reality that large public gatherings were not places to win acceptance but rather occasions to show steadiness; the American representative might not expect to win supporters at the meeting, but the powerful reliable country behind him was firm in its commitments.

And then there was the China connection to what was going on in Vietnam. In the eyes of many Americans, including policymakers, the most persuasive rationale for our decades-long concern with Indo-China was essentially the negative one of preventing the spread of Chinese communist power. In the late 1940s, the concept was simple enough: the "communist side" led by Stalin's Soviet Union, soon to be joined by a new, united China under Mao Zedong's highly ideological Chinese Communist Party, and bringing along a less clearly defined guerrilla movement in the French Indo-China colonies led by a known communist revolutionary, Ho Chi Minh, was linked in its basic objectives of seizing control wherever it could. It would do this by supporting each other wherever possible by propaganda, subversion, and armed force. The proof of this unity seemed to lie in the whole "communist side" singling out for its enemy the only country able to support serious worldwide resistance to it, the United States. "Monolithic communism," as it came to be called, simplified the work of American policymakers for twenty years, even after the fundamental rift between Mao Zedong and the leaders of the Soviet Union became noticeable at the end of the 1950s.

I tried to establish the China connection with Vietnam by referring to a 1965 essay on "People's War" by Lin Biao, a hero of the Long March and one of China's top generals. Lin was defense minister of the People's Republic of China when he wrote the essay and was shortly to become Mao Zedong's "closest comrade in arms" and designated successor. Lin was killed in a mysterious plane crash in 1971 after incurring Mao's enmity, but in 1966 his ideas were those of Mao. "People's War" was a flat, simplified description of the Chinese Communist strategy of surrounding the cities and towns with the "people" of the "countryside" in fighting the Japanese during World War II and the Nationalists in the civil war in China. Lin Biao extended this revolutionary strategy by calling on the "countryside" of the Third World to rise up against the "urban" West, implying that the proving ground for People's War was Vietnam. China appeared to have gone mad in the Cultural Revolution, and it didn't seem all that far-fetched then that China's leaders would be expounding worldwide violent revolution.

So I argued in public. I saved for private talks a more sophisticated and accurate line that Lin was only portraying a successful revolutionary theory that combined the complete control and organization of the rural population with a single political/military strategy. This was, indeed, being applied in Vietnam, aimed at an eventual communist, but not necessarily Chinese, takeover of the independent countries of Southeast Asia. I must admit that in keeping with the mood of the times, many in my student audiences joyfully applauded my eloquent references to Lin Biao's theory, believing that, somehow, I was perversely arguing the Vietnamese communists' cause. I changed few minds.

BRIGHTON

In the still cold, early spring of 1967, I spoke at an evening meeting sponsored by a peace group at Sussex University in Brighton-by-the-Sea. By this time I felt I had acquired some virtuosity in British-style public meetings. I had grown used to the constant interruptions and to identifying those in the audience who, whatever their feelings on Vietnam, might sympathize with my isolated position and in the spirit of fair play listen to what I was trying to say. They were often, but not always, older than the others and to my desperate eye seemed less gleefully confrontational.

I discovered that humor, hard to come by in any case considering the subject, would only help if directed at oneself, and knew that it was imperative to keep my temper. I actually found this easy to do, perhaps because my experience had taught me to separate my government's views from my own, and I was able to argue relatively dispassionately, at least compared to my usually young opponents. So, although the anti-Vietnam movement was especially well organized at Sussex University, and despite a busy day going back and forth to the Foreign Office by cab and foot, I got off the train at Brighton, having missed my dinner, resigned to a long, hard night but fairly sure of myself. Brighton turned out to be the toughest of all the meetings I had starred in.

I was met by the chairman of the group, a young man who was able to spot me immediately as an American, even though my sufficiently old British raincoat, my perfectly furled umbrella of which I was terribly proud, and my battered black briefcase all seemed to me to be identical to those of any tired commuter from London. He introduced me to the lady who would preside over the meeting and added by way of reassurance that as a Quaker, she would add "some balance" to the discussions. I was unsure about this because he went on to say that "the other side" would be taken by a Lord something-or-other, who was said to be the only communist in the House of Lords, and John Mendelssohn, an MP from the extreme left of the Labour Party, who I knew from the newspapers was not only opposed to United States policy in Vietnam, but was virulently against all things American.

The three of us walked the few blocks from the station in the usual drizzle. I could see from the posters, "American Embassy Debates the Peace Movement, Your Chance to Stop the War," "Let Them Hear Us," "Why is America in Vietnam?" that the meeting had been heavily advertised; so much so that there was an unruly crowd on the steps of the meeting place, and a way had to be cleared for us by the police. The lecture hall was an amphitheater with sharply banked rows of seats reaching to the high ceiling, all filled, as was the stage itself, with maybe 400 people altogether.

The communist lord and Mendelssohn were already on the platform, and once we picked and stumbled our way through the crowd on the stage, we were introduced. The peer seemed oddly diffident and polite, given his politics. I don't recall Mendelssohn saying anything at all, distantly shaking hands.

During our walk to the hall, I had told the Quaker lady of my concerns over the posters, especially the ones that advertised a debate. Ambassador Bruce, quite rightly from the point of view of the embassy, had forbidden direct debates between embassy officers and members of Parliament in order to avoid looking like we were engaged in any British political process. Consequently, I told her that I would only be able to make a presentation and could not respond in debate fashion to arguments made by others. I asked her to bring out this distinction in her introduction at the meeting. She said—as moderators invariably did—that I should then speak first. The other two naturally agreed when she politely suggested that "As our visitor, perhaps Mr. Cross should start," ostensibly giving them the last word.

The Quaker lady tried to call for silence, but as usual at these gatherings in the United Kingdom, the public address system needed to be adjusted and volunteers hurried up to stifle its shrieks and yowls while organizers struggled ineffectively to move people off the stage or at least to give us enough room to stand and talk. In the middle of the uproar the Brighton Fire Department came in and cleared some of the aisles. All of this took some time, and there was an uneasy rowdy atmosphere with cheering and little pre-speech speeches from various people in the audience.

The Quaker lady was introduced by the now scared-looking student chairman. She presented me courteously as "one who has come all this way from London to present the American side of their intervention in Vietnam," neglecting any mention of my not being able to debate. I gave my standard speech, coming down dramatically—I thought—on the Lin Biao aspect. The communist lord, who spoke after me, talked mostly about his several trips to North Vietnam—the "lovely spirit of comradeship with peace-loving friends in Britain and around the world" of the Vietnamese people and the great courage they had shown in the face of wanton attacks by the United States. He spent several minutes on the whole question of social justice in Southeast Asia and how the Democratic Republic of Vietnam was leading the search for a better life for the peasants and "other common people" of Asia. Mendelssohn, as I had expected, attacked American imperialism everywhere, widening the range beyond Southeast Asia to cover our sins in Europe. Neither responded to what I had said about Lin Biao.

I could sense that the audience was only half-attentive during the speeches. Our Quaker leader had silenced most interruptions during my talk and there was only mild applause for the others. The active members of the crowd, especially those right on the platform itself, were waiting for the question period, which would allow them to make their own points. All the questions came directly at me, not really questions at all but impassioned speeches, with perhaps the demanding, "Does the

American have any comment on what I have just said?" kind of question. I fielded most of these as well as I could since I had heard them all before, but it got wilder and wilder as people began to crowd up onto the platform waving their arms for attention and interrupting each other. The Quaker lady kept shooing them off and gaveling for silence, saying, "Please let the speakers (that is, Cross) respond," trying desperately to keep control.

I watched two people during the commotion. One was an older man in his proper suit, jammed in among the students wearing what, even in those days, were pretty messy clothes. The other person was a sad-faced African sitting in one of the middle rows, showing no sign of interest. Suddenly, the older chap stood up and in a loud, parade-ground voice, and in an unmistakable upper-class accent, said, "We have listened to this for over an hour now, and I don't believe that we have been able to hear the American gentleman present his views for even a few sentences. I suggest that he be given five minutes to talk without interruption." The Quaker lady, thus put on the spot, somehow got everyone to shut up, and I was asked to talk.

I started by saying that it was sad to hear these unfair things said in England about America, and although I was not free to engage in a debate with the other speakers, I would like to make a few comments. I said that there had been a lot of talk about social justice, but social justice in Southeast Asia was not earned in the halls of Westminster but in the paddy fields of Asia, and that was where we were. I made a few more such brave remarks and then turned to something that seemed to be nearer the basic parts of the discussion: United States commitments to go to the aid of countries all around the world. We had always lived up to these commitments, as the people in Great Britain well knew, and we were going to continue living up to them. Many of these commitments were to non-European countries and, I challenged ringingly, "We will live up to these commitments to our Asian friends the same way we will live up to them with you white Europeans."

There were gasps and nervous giggles throughout the audience because, of course, no one had raised this kind of issue with such racial overtones. The African, who had been looking at the ceiling, suddenly stood up and began clapping. He was joined heartily by several people scattered around the hall. This brought the whole affair to a close because the mood was gone. The Quaker lady thanked the audience and the speakers. The communist lord and I shook hands; Mendelssohn walked off without a word to any of us; everyone began to file out.

The British have a practice similar to ours of talking briefly to the speakers after an event. Not very many came up to me; most headed to the communist lord. No British congratulated me or indicated any agreement, but would look me sternly in the eye and growl ambiguously, "You're wrong, but I now understand better why you're wrong," or unequivocally, "Really you're a bloody fascist!" Among the group crowding onto my end of the platform was a rather wild-looking girl in a long gray RAF surplus overcoat much affected by the younger students of both sexes. Plain and pale, she was part of the crowd; but when she got close she half-smiled, took my hand and whispered, "I'm an American, and I'm very proud," and slipped off. Thus heartened, I rode back to London on the train with the charming Quaker lady and the friendly communist lord. British amenities were observed and none of us mentioned Vietnam at all.

Speaking publicly about American policies in Vietnam was always hard work and occasionally absorbing, but it caused more internal turmoil than I could admit to anyone. This came from a disturbed conscience built up from different directions by my parents and by the Marine Corps, both teaching that it was hypocritical to advocate participating in a war while far removed from its effects oneself. At the same time, deep down I felt that Harriman and others in Washington were right from the standpoint of American interests—if not from those of the Vietnamese—to try to extricate us from Vietnam. But then again, nothing was happening on that front in London—at least where I was concerned.

Probably the right thing would have been to volunteer forthrightly to go to Vietnam, but the embassy in Saigon was huge and clumsy. The Political Section was a large collection of sharp, younger Vietnamese-speaking officers and one or two high-ranking ones who, although experienced, were essentially overseers. I would have been in the latter group, where my contribution would have been confined and channeled. As usual, I tried to find a compromise between myself and the system. I told William P. Bundy, assistant secretary for East Asian affairs, during one of his stopovers in London that I was not interested in serving in the embassy, but if there were a job somewhere else in Vietnam, preferably connected with counterinsurgency where I could be "really useful," I would take it.

This kind of nonvolunteering volunteering had its risks, because at any sign of willingness to go to Vietnam one became fair game for the personnel managers of many programs, including those who could send me to the embassy in Saigon, whatever I had said. Thus, I was relieved to receive a personal message from Bundy in June 1967. "We need you right away for deputy regional director job in I Corps. Are there any personal factors that would preclude your getting to Vietnam within the next 30 days?" This was in fact an order, and although Ambassador Bruce offered to object to the assignment on my behalf, I knew that I should reply that I would be glad to go.

I was used to making that kind of decision without too much consultation with others. I see now—but took for granted then—that our family was run on the "What's good for General Motors (me) is good for the country (family)" principle, and although going to Vietnam wouldn't necessarily push my career (the department often has a short memory span on sacrifice), refusing or being ungracious about going could hurt it. Consequently, the family meeting that night was only how to deal with the problems that my early departure would cause. Ann had just arrived in London after a strenuous junior year at Carleton, and we had planned a relaxing summer for her. Kathy, now a junior in high school at the Marymount Academy near London, had a summer job in the Visa Section of the embassy, and Richard, soon to be freed for the summer from his grim London grammar school, and I were looking at boats and moorings near Portsmouth on the Channel for possible sailing weekends.

The basic issue turned on whether the family would go back to Washington, stay in London, or move to one of the cities nearer Vietnam such as Bangkok—which were dramatically called "safe havens," and where I could have had what were spookily known as "visitations." Staying in London meant leaving our embassy apartment and finding an affordable private rental, but otherwise seemed the least disruptive. The consensus was for London. In early July 1967, feeling lonely already, I was seen off at Heathrow by a solemn family, bound for Washington and Honolulu for consultations, and thence to Vietnam.

Chapter 13

Vietnam

"We will pay any price, bear any burden, meet any hardship, support any friend, oppose any foe, to assure the success and survival of liberty."— John F. Kennedy, Inaugural Address, January 20, 1961.

These inspiring words were not taken literally by either foreign friend or foe but they reassured or warned both. They initially thrilled Americans without being precise enough to raise questions of sacrifice, so the thoughts were admired without analysis. I heard them in the nearly empty State Department that day, and assumed only that they promised excitement and action for our country without knowing what. Looking back they seem to have set a policy mood for our war in Vietnam.

It seems that I have always heard of Indo-China. Among the foreign troops in the Legation Quarter in Peking was a contingent of what were called French Annamites, the term of the day for Vietnamese. They were nearly Chinese-looking men in drab brown uniforms, puttees and boots, and too-large droopy black berets, who stood between the male and female stone lions, or inside the red-, white-, and blue-striped sentry box at the gate of the French Legation. They were small; their rifles, with the long French bayonets fixed on them, stood taller than they. The Annamites were colonial soldiers like the huge Sikh policemen brought in by the British from India and thus, in our missionary family, regarded as victims of colonialism rather than one of its instruments.

We had a sort of hierarchy of colonialism, arrived at by innumerable dinner table discussions. The Japanese, because we saw the misery they were daily inflicting on the Chinese, were by our calculations much the worst. By the mid-thirties, they were followed closely by the Italians of Mussolini because of Ethiopia. But after these two came the French. This, I was taught, was mainly because the colonial government in French Indo-China held monopolies on alcohol and used forced labor. The British, who earlier had been the chief targets of Chinese anti-imperialism demonstrations in Peking and throughout China, were further down on our lists, possibly because of the close collaboration and friendship between the nonfundamentalist British and American missionaries.

I retained these distinctions in my mind for many years. When I returned to Carleton after World War II, I wrote several papers on Vietnam for my international relations courses. I fiercely criticized French behavior during the early postwar years—unscholarly and bitter that it was the Vichy French who had supinely surrendered Indo-China to the Japanese in 1940 and that the same sort of Frenchmen were being returned there by the other allies who had actually fought and won the Pacific War. I read what little there was available at Carleton at the time about Ho Chi Minh, and these romanticized accounts of the Viet Minh independence struggle combined somehow with several re-readings of Andre Malraux's *Man's Fate* (really about China, not Vietnam) to cast the revolutionary Vietnamese in a heroic mold. None of this meant that I tried to study Vietnam itself then or later, but I became fascinated with the mystique of Asian revolutions, and did try to learn about them—especially their connection with China. During our first fourteen years in the Foreign Service I was concerned in various ways with America's responses to the changes roiling Southeast Asia. There actually seemed to be some logic in my being sent to the war in Vietnam.

THE THEORY OF CORDS

I left London knowing that I had been assigned to something called CORDS, another new organization in a war already overloaded with acronyms. But I didn't know what CORDS stood for and the London embassy was not a place where one readily admitted ignorance of anything, so I didn't ask there (I was the only one supposed to know anyway). It wasn't until I got to Danang that I saw it spelled out. CORDS stood for Civil Operations and Revolutionary Development Support. It represented a belated organizational recognition by the United States that there was only one war in Vietnam, that like our enemy we and the South Vietnamese single-mindedly had to combine our political, social, economic, and military efforts into one sustained and coordinated program that was described as "pacification."

To me "pacification" was an unlikable term for the CORDS work, sounding like what Americans did to the Native Americans on our western frontiers or the French did in Vietnam. Nobody else made the connection, but I remembered how the Japanese used "peace preservation units" of Chinese puppets to maintain their control over large areas of

China. Nevertheless, "pacification" was an easier term to handle conceptually than "civil operations" or "revolutionary development support" because it described more accurately the combination of military measures to provide security and thus control of the rural population, and the essentially political programs to gain the support of the people for the South Vietnamese government.

In mid-April 1967, the veteran diplomat Ellsworth Bunker stopped in London on his way to Saigon to replace Henry Cabot Lodge as the American ambassador. I arranged a hurried meeting at the embassy for him with Sir Robert Thompson, who was one of the imaginative organizers of the British success against the communists in Malaysia, where I had first met him. He had since become recognized as the top British authority on counterinsurgency. President Johnson avidly sought his advice on Vietnam while not always taking it, and Bobby had spent many months in Vietnam working to vitalize the American advisory effort. Thompson unselfishly made himself available at all hours and places to give us the benefit of his experience. Once I took another traveler from Washington, Eugene Locke, a Texas political protégé of Lyndon Johnson, to the Channel Island of Jersey for an hour's talk with Thompson, during which jet lag got to Locke, who fell asleep. Bobby good-naturedly continued the briefing to me.

Bunker, who then was already 73, took a catnap in the car to the embassy from Heathrow but otherwise seemed unaffected by his overnight flight from Washington. Thompson had prepared his presentation carefully. That night after Bunker had renewed his journey, I summarized Thompson's views for him in a personal letter because he was cautious about using more official channels for this kind of information, with its frank criticisms of American operations and individuals.

As I had expected, Thompson's overall argument on the basis of his Malaysian experience was that there was no "other war" in Vietnam. To make a distinction between military operations and everything else could lead to the delusion that because we might be doing well militarily, a claim that was made regularly by military PR officers, we were half succeeding. In reality, Thompson maintained, we might not be succeeding at all in terms of the paramount purpose of preventing the communists from taking over South Vietnam.

Thompson attached importance to getting both Vietnamese and Americans to understand their instructions from above in the same way, not just in the translation from one language to the other, but in an identical appreciation of the objectives involved and the underlying concepts. Thompson perceived the subtle interaction between Americans and Vietnamese and took into account the inevitability of cultural clashes.

Thompson pressed Bunker at some length on the necessity for the United States military to switch the emphasis in its operations. Thompson's disagreement with the prevailing strategy was fundamental: he felt that the thrust of the combined military effort should be toward containment of the communist military forces rather than their destruction. Thus, operations should be different in style and tactics from the standard large-scale "search and destroy" operations stressed by General Westmoreland.

Bunker had expressed the usual high-level interest in the effect of our bombing in North Vietnam and how it affected the rate of infiltration of forces from the north. Thompson again came up with a central counterinsurgency concept: "The rate of infiltration depends upon the ability of the organization to absorb it. Unless you break up the organization, they will try to bring in all they can use as reinforcements. They will not bring in more than they can handle."

Thompson felt that after all our long experience in Vietnam, there continued to be poor coordination among the various American and Vietnamese intelligence agencies. These were "very weak" compared to our heavy concentration on information about the communist military forces. Again, there could be no hope of ultimate success in Vietnam unless we could disrupt the basic political organization; we could not do that unless we knew more about it. This hardly original thought applied to strengthening the usually maligned Phoenix program that became one of my important concerns.

An even broader criticism was that despite—or quite possibly because of—crushing numbers of American advisors in all South Vietnamese government agencies, there was still no Vietnamese civil administration worthy of the name. Thompson spoke sharply against the many crash programs in all fields that the United States had started but not always completed, and that had Americans doing all the essential work without leaving Vietnamese to carry on. Others simply sidetracked Vietnamese programs and officials for supposedly more efficient American efforts. He advocated slow systematic retraining of Vietnamese at all levels of the Vietnamese civil administration in an attempt to recover the many skills that were lost to the South Vietnamese government through the successive coups of 1963 through 1965. More attention should be given to timing; measures simply could not be put into effect simultaneously on a nationwide or even provincewide basis. Writing it down now doesn't seem to make this comment seem very profound, but I found almost immediately in Vietnam that in our drive for quick statistical results to encourage support for the whole effort at home or to satisfy higher authorities in Washington and Saigon, we tried to get everything moving at once. We established short time limits for programs, listed exaggerated but specific goals, *and* demanded statistics to show results—the tools of modern business management. Some of this worked but much didn't and, insidiously, fakery slipped in.

There was no talk of the crucial differences between Malaysia, where Thompson's ideas originated, and Vietnam, where they were to be carried out. The British were in complete charge of the military, the police, and the civil services in Malaysia. They had a cadre of experienced lifetime colonial officials, speaking the languages of the country, who could in quiet, disciplined ways maneuver the political process toward clear, unambiguous goals of eliminating the communists and establishing self-government. Moreover, the war in Malaysia had been smaller, with only 8,000 to 10,000 armed guerrillas in the whole country at the height of the Emergency. Single provinces in South Vietnam at times had that many or more, counting the North Vietnamese in regular conventional units. Our own political aims for South Vietnam were as confused as those of the South Vietnamese themselves, agreeing between us only on opposition to North Vietnam.

I'm not sure that CORDS wasn't already in the works when Bunker went through London, but organizationally it certainly grew out of both the One War concept and the need for one director of such a war. True, combined United States/South Vietnamese central direction of the kind Thompson envisaged would remain a not-quite-achieved goal throughout our involvement in Vietnam, but CORDS did become an essential element of what was called in Americanese, "the single manager approach" to working with the Vietnamese.

The formal American chain of command ran from the ambassador through the commander of the Military Assistance Command Vietnam (Westmoreland), through his deputy for CORDS (thus the acronym DEP-CORDS), to the four American commanders in the four corps areas in South Vietnam, to each corps deputy for CORDS, to the province senior advisor in each province, and then to the district senior advisor. The alternating military-civilian arrangement within CORDS was maintained throughout the system; Westmoreland's deputy for CORDS most of the time I was in Vietnam was Robert Komer. In I Corps, the Third Marine Amphibious Force commander, Lieutenant General Robert E. Cushman, had his own deputy for CORDS, Henry L. T. Koren, whom I later replaced, through to the five province senior advisors in I Corps, with the wrinkle that if the province senior advisor was a military officer, usually a colonel or lieutenant colonel, his deputy would be a civilian and vice versa, and so on down into the forty-two districts in I Corps.

On paper, CORDS was part of the military command and could call on the resources of the military. CORDS military officers had responsibility for advising the South Vietnamese army on its military operations—which were deemed to be in support of pacification (that is, almost all)—and for all the operations of the regional forces and popular forces, the local "ruff puffs," of which there were 50,000 in I Corps at one time. The

American military also provided logistic support and personnel for other CORDS operations.

I reread the letter to Bunker a few hours before I left London for Vietnam. That was about the only thing I did to prepare myself, aside from looking through an outdated French guidebook on Tourane, their name for Danang. Far out over the Atlantic, I thought about how hard it would be to focus the efforts of the hundreds of Americans piling into I Corps. Most would be well intentioned but as unfamiliar with Vietnam as I was. We would have to tie in with the American military so that, on the U.S. side at least, we approached Thompson's fundamental concept of the One War. It would not be another Foreign Service assignment with the established precedents and expected roles that had been my working life. Strangely, I was not apprehensive. I was even strangely confident, possibly because I had been looking at Vietnam from the outside for so long that ideas similar to those of Thompson's kept crowding into my mind.

My experience in Vietnam is largely recorded in letters from Danang to my family "Gang," because letters best convey what I thought and felt THEN—on the ground and often late at night. They are presented chronologically for that reason. The letters could stand by themselves, but Vietnam is no longer on American television screens and I have added explanations to many of them. They represent about 10 percent of the total and I have cut out the hairy air experiences encountered by everyone in CORDS. (I averaged some three hours a day flying in something.) Excerpts from these letters in italics and the explanatory comments following them are the record of my service in the Vietnam War. (Unless headed otherwise they are all "Dear Gang" letters and are sent from Danang.)

Francis Scott Key Hotel
Washington DC
15 July 1967

Last night I went over to the Korens' for dinner and a long talk about the job. Barney was naturally somewhat depressed because we had been getting the news about the latest attack on Danang airfield. He said that he had asked for me—way back last May—or even April—but there was no answer. Then Komer telephoned to Washington and said that unless he got action, he was going to go to the President! I think that Barney made it up to help my morale . . .

I have, of course, been spending a lot of time hearing and reading about the pacification program. There are a lot more things right with it than I had thought. One of the best things is the high caliber of the young guys who are going to do the work out there in the provinces. I have met several who have just come back, and I would say they are as good as any I have seen anywhere—articulate, steady, self-effacing and extremely well-informed.

Barney was Ambassador Henry L. T. Koren, who was back home in Washington on a brief leave to receive some medical attention, which he couldn't get in Vietnam. Barney had been my boss in Washington during the wild Laos desk days and had left the Office of Southeast Asian Affairs to become ambassador to Brazzaville, capital of what was then called Congo (Brazzaville). Initially, he had come to Vietnam to be the number two in the predecessor organization to CORDS so was present during the metamorphosis. He knew and was respected by all the players—a big advantage to us in CORDS as we struggled to make the pacification system work in I Corps. Tall, aristocratic in bearing, deeply religious, Barney had been in the Regular Army for a number of years before he transferred to the Foreign Service. He tried constantly to produce a sense of cohesion and professionalism among the diverse staff of CORDS. His leadership style was cool, somewhat reserved; yet he was unswervingly conscientious about his subordinates' welfare and needs.

Robert Komer was a different character entirely. He came from the big-time Washington bureaucracy to be General Westmoreland's first deputy for CORDS, having been largely responsible for ramming the single manager concept through the Washington leadership and the American hierarchy in Vietnam. Armed with an ambassadorial title and consequently four-star status, he fought for CORDS relentlessly against the rest of the brass. I felt that no other individual could have succeeded as well against the reluctant, overblown American military establishment in Saigon. Unfortunately, his personal style was loud and abrasive, and his treatment of subordinates—although not of me— was arbitrary and selfish. I ended up thinking that his wish to control everything from headquarters in Saigon and his unrealistic dependence on statistics were actually impeding pacification, and I was almost glad to see him go.

One of the young Foreign Service officers was Richard Holbrooke, who arranged my Washington briefings. Holbrooke later left the Foreign Service, reportedly because of his opposition to the war. However, through vigorous maneuvering he became in time assistant secretary of state for East Asian affairs in the Carter administration. Later, during the Republican years from 1981 to 1993, he was a successful New York investment banker and in his spare time collaborated with Clark Clifford, the perennial advisor to Democratic presidents, on the latter's highly readable autobiography *Counsel to the President*. President Clinton appointed Holbrooke to be ambassador to Germany instead of Japan, his first choice, but after a short tour in Bonn, he became assistant secretary for European affairs "to improve the department"! He was the forceful American negotiator of the Bosnian peace accords in 1995, and President Clinton nominated him to be ambassador to the UN in 1999. He was especially helpful to me in July 1967 because he squeezed in time for me to talk to Frank Scotton, a very effective United States Information Agency officer who also had just returned from Vietnam.

Scotton and I met in a small park in front of the World Bank headquarters on Pennsylvania Avenue because Holbrooke, who was then serving as a staff aide in the Office of the Assistant to the President for Vietnam, thought that a routine office briefing of a newly appointed CORDS officer by a known critic of the conduct of the war would either arouse suspicions in high places or be uselessly anodyne. I was grateful for his discretion.

Scotton, husky and dark, was in his late twenties and wary on this first meeting. His message was clear enough though, and, in a sense, I had already been converted to it: that there were fatal dangers to pacification if CORDS allowed its programs to become "too military," by which he meant overly controlled, not aimed at winning over the population but only at killing communists—inflexible and too American in style.

Scotton had developed this advice under fire in Quang Ngai Province, the southernmost province in I Corps, where he had organized some paramilitary/political action groups in 1965. These five-man armed propaganda teams had worked effectively under dangerous conditions with the local militia, helping the farmers, setting up ambushes—more or less paralleling what the communists themselves were doing. There were too few teams to make much difference and the scheme foundered in the United States military, CIA, and other American government bureaucratic feuds, in effect making Scotton's point for him by the time we talked. Sitting uncomfortably outside at noon in summertime Washington, I listened carefully to this serious young man. I felt that his words were true and his approach right. But deep down I already knew that the Americanization tide was flowing too strongly in South Vietnam, that I would be too much part of it to resist it, and that whatever contribution I might make would have to be within the rules of the American bureaucratic game. Self-confident, this seemed discouraging but not hopeless.

DANANG

6 August 1967

I have already called on General Lam the Corps commander and the top Vietnamese here. He struck me as a rather decent chap, but hard to tell at first encounter.

Lieutenant General Hoang Xuan Lam was the I Corps commander for the entire time I was in Vietnam and I saw him one way or another almost every day. A small roly-poly man in his late thirties, he was thought to be reasonably honest although he apparently owed his position to being on the successful side during the internecine struggles in the Vietnamese military following the coup against Diem in 1963. He was subject to much prodding by us Americans, especially in pacification matters about which we thought he could be awfully slow. His support was crucial because he was really the South Vietnamese ruler in that part of South Vietnam. The Vietnamese civilian bureaucrats, especially, froze in place without his say so. Naturally, he wouldn't refuse to act. In fact, he would respond with a "no problem" or "pas problème" to pacification suggestions routinely put forward by Koren or me through Lieutenant General Cushman, acting in his capacity as the senior advisor in I Corps as well as the commander of all the American military in the area. But often, despite Lam's crisp instructions in front of us to his starched and alert appearing staff, things didn't happen. We would return to the subject in different ways until we or he finally gave in. Lam had an odd shouting, nervous laugh. His "ho-ho-ho" was occasionally imitated by the American generals in the helicopter taking us back to Marine Amphibious Force (III MAF) headquarters after our meetings each morning.

The meetings themselves fascinated me because they involved some intricate military-style play-acting all around. The American group of Cushman, his chief of staff, several other Marine staff officers, the salty, old-line U.S. infantry colonel who ran the advisory effort with the ARVN, plus Koren and me from CORDS would arrive at I Corps in a thudding of helicopters after less than a minute's ride across the beautiful Danang River from Marine headquarters. We would all trot briskly across the street while the heavy traffic was stopped by white-helmeted ARVN military police and would hurry purposefully into a large briefing room, which was only slightly less elaborate than the one at III MAF—lighted lecterns, two plush arm chairs for Generals Cushman and Lam, rows of chairs lined up by rank with our names on the backs, slide projectors, and the like. The briefings were conducted in English or tediously translated. The I Corps briefing didn't tell the Marine contingent anything it didn't know already because everything about the ARVN and local forces had already been passed up through the advisory channel.

I Corps was already being called the area of the "Big War" when I arrived in 1967 because several divisions of North Vietnamese regulars operated in it. They were opposed by two South Vietnamese divisions, two Marine divisions, one U.S. Army division, a Republic of Korea Marine Brigade, and dozens of auxiliary elements—Navy, Air Force, Marine Air—to say nothing of the 50,000 or so militia forces and police field units, which were constantly involved in combat operations. From time to time both sides added forces so military activity was intense and continuous. Consequently, the briefings on both sides of the river were filled with reports of big clashes, large troop movements, enormous expenditures of ammunition, and inevitably, high casualty figures.

War is always distorted at headquarters, more so than ever in Vietnam where there were no front lines and where enemy forces skillfully shifted from direct confrontation, falling back to defend specially fortified and mined areas, then slipping away to come back around or through our forces to ambush or attack weak points. Enemies killed became the chief accepted criterion of military success on our side.

Even at my first briefings I sensed unreality when the Vietnamese and American briefers in their identical military monotones rolled out the daily tolls. I didn't feel that anyone was cooking the figures at the higher echelons, but enemy casualties—as briefed—were almost always many times ours, raising questions of what kinds of pressures were being put on the combat units to show statistical winnings. Typical of the cynicism inspired by the attrition approach to war was the comment by an experienced U.S. Army lieutenant colonel advisor when I raised the ticklish question of differing enemy casualty figures. He claimed that whereas American forces frequently counted dead noncombatants in their scores, the South Vietnamese often merely made up enemy casualties. He went on to say that this habit put the latter at a disadvantage because enemy casualties were also reported up through the advisory channels by American advisors who observed the action and the discrepancies were noted as evidence that the South Vietnamese commanders were covering up "lack of aggressiveness." The Vietnamese could have argued, but didn't, that listing killed civilians as enemy was actually the same thing and had no direct effect on the enemy either—except perhaps to help him by alienating the population.

By 1967 the business of "advising" the corps-level Vietnamese had become exceedingly complicated. The Vietnamese generals had been around a long time, even the young ones like General Lam; they knew a lot about what to do in combat situations—or had staffs who did—so they didn't really need much "advice." What the term really meant was the process of urging the South Vietnamese to fit in with American plans, often worked out at the huge American headquarters in Saigon with a chain of command running back to Washington. This had to be done while maintaining the illusion of Vietnamese autonomy and equality within the alliance, a politically essential aspect of the entire American effort. Consequently, although oral instructions from above to us in CORDS often were full of "put the heat on," "push for," "motivate to," and other exhortations to exhort, the actual practice was to be uniformly courteous, paying elaborate attention to Vietnamese ranks and personal prestige, "face" in Chinese terms.

I thought Cushman, who could be a bluff Marine with his American subordinates, played this game as well as it could be done. I noticed especially that when pressing Lam to act, to issue the appropriate orders and to follow through on them, he skipped the false joviality common among many American generals, seen through by the Vietnamese and resented. Rather, he was cool and steady in tone, treating Lam as a fellow professional. Lam learned over time that Cushman would return tirelessly to the same subject and that sooner or later it would have to be faced.

8 August 1967

In general Danang is quiet (except for the noise), a rather attractive town with a corniche along the river in the faintly French look of Vietnam, and nothing but the immense number of troops and the sounds of war outside to make one feel uneasy— which I don't.

When I arrived in Danang, there were brilliant flame trees all along the river, tropical gentleness masking the barbed wire and sandbags at the cluttered roadblocks, civilian touches against the light-brown ARVN jeeps and trucks growling and honking their way down the street. Six months later the trees had begun to thin out and fade—in a year they were gone. There, far away from the target areas, on the banks of a river, less than a mile from the open sea, they had been defoliated. The cause was simple enough: aircraft returning from defoliating missions had not closed their spray cocks after they had completed their runs—or worse, were still dumping Agent Orange so they would appear to have used their quota by the time they had landed. Bitter complaints by the Danang Vietnamese authorities through CORDS finally got the planes rerouted, but by then it was too late for the flame trees. The U.S. Army defoliation units even tried to blame the disaster on the Vietnamese scrap metal dealers who, the Army claimed, had not washed the Agent Orange containers properly before driving their trucks with the open containers under the flame trees, bouncing along the corniche on the way to a Korean junkyard. It was an odd, silly excuse and not accepted by the Vietnamese.

Much has been written about defoliation because, aside from the health hazards it posed, which were suspected from the beginning, the ugly scars it left everywhere inevitably drew the attention of the press to the practice. There were two general kinds: the removal of vegetation to eliminate ambush sites, provide fields of fire, and open spaces around inhabited areas, which was done mostly by hand spraying, and the use of herbicides by planes to destroy crops that could feed enemy forces, usually in remote upland areas. Both clearly had valuable military purposes and, because they were effective, they became increasingly popular with small unit commanders and local officials, especially in the populated areas heavily infiltrated by the VC and the North Vietnamese. There were strict procedures for avoiding cultivated fields, and the final decisions on using defoliants were made at the province or district level by the Vietnamese; but the dangers of overuse were not really understood, lay in the future anyway, and thus couldn't compare with the threat of enemy attack. There were always overwhelming reasons to defoliate. Carelessness of the kind I have described was common as technology forced itself over long-range caution—a feature of the Vietnam War.

16 August 1967

I've been rather lonesome without any of the great flow of guests from the States I had been led to expect. Last night, I went to another Korean party (their Independence Day). Quite obviously, they can afford it because of their stevedoring contracts.

The Korean presence in South Vietnam resulted from a sustained campaign by the Johnson administration to draw as many allies into the war as openly and substantially as possible, even though practically speaking, at American expense. I've heard that the two Republic of Korea Army divisions performed well in other corps areas where they were stationed, but the Korean Marine Brigade in I Corps did not. It operated aggressively when it was attacked directly, but it was rough on the civilian non-enemy Vietnamese in the area it was supposed to defend. General Cushman, always careful about openly criticizing an ally (as were all American commanders), issued several quiet warnings about indiscriminate shooting. Toward the end of my stay in Vietnam I brought to his attention reports of atrocities committed over a long period, which I had received through CORDS channels, meaning that they were originally from the Vietnamese. These were investigated by III MAF and were found to be substantiated, but I never heard what happened to the actual perpetrators, if anything. By brutally protecting only themselves in their own enclaves, rapaciously exploiting the American Post Exchange system in the black market, and obviously overprofiting from their stevedoring and construction activities, the Koreans were a heavy drag on pacification in I Corps.

19 August 1967

Yesterday I made my first trip to the provinces, to Hoi An, the provincial capital of Quang Nam. It's about 20 miles or so south from Danang. I went by helicopter and was given a seat on the open side. In fact, both sides were open because the back part of the seating space was taken up by two 50-caliber machine guns, manned by American soldiers in helmets and flak jackets. The flight down lasted about 15 minutes. We went down the coast a bit along miles of beautiful beach, just inland of which were pretty battered areas with green fields spotted here and there—heavy VC area. When we turned inland, it all became green and deceptively peaceful looking with people working in the fields and an occasional vehicle on the famous North-South Route Number One. (We say it's "open" but actually there are daily mining incidents on it.)

I was taken on a V.I.P. tour of the town and shown, among other things, the jail from which the VC had sprung some 1,400 prisoners a few weeks back. Another interesting feature of the town itself was a covered bridge, very ornate with Vietnamese decorations but built by the Japanese as some sort of gesture to the town during their occupation of it. Otherwise, the place is dusty, drab, full of sand bags, pillboxes, barbed wire, and Vietnamese soldiers. In the town, we have only the CORDS advisory group and some German and other medical people. The general impression is that the VC/North Vietnamese could easily overrun it if they wanted to. And like everyone else in I Corps they were expecting a major attack before election day September 3rd.

We ate a standard lunch in the MACV (Military Assistance Command, Vietnam) compound which is completely dug in and defended by a system of bunkers, barbed wire, booby traps, etc. They all sleep right next to places where they can dive if they get an attack. After lunch I went to the CORDS compound, which is quite different. Only one of their houses has sand bags around it, and the compound itself is half taken up with banana trees. They have seven Nung guards—a hill people of Chinese descent (in fact, they seem almost to understand my Mandarin)—who are fairly reliable. The houses are pre-fab and are attractive and comfortable, being air-conditioned.

On the way back, we stopped at a district headquarters. It all looked pretty grim—heavy fortifications—radios crackling away—a sort of military purposefulness about everything. This area had been one of the more fought over in Vietnam and looked like it. There were several villages which had been abandoned and their inhabitants had moved, or were moved, to new camps. In fact, there were New Villages just like Malaya with much the same purpose: to remove the villagers from communist domination and put them under South Vietnamese control. Here and there were the encampments of the famous regiments of Marines, like the First Battalion, First Marines, dusty rows of tents and aluminum roofs. Typically, a few minutes afterwards I was back in the air-conditioned offices of Danang and shuffling papers again.

As in all wars, there was a huge difference between the life of headquarters types like myself in Danang and that of a CORDS officer on the front line in the provinces. Had I spent more nights with the province advisory teams when they were more relaxed or not under attack, I could have had a better grasp of the military situation than I got from their formal briefings.

25 August 1967

On Wednesday I went to a "County Fair." This is another Marine invention. What they do is to surround a village before dawn without warning and set up defenses around it. Then the Vietnamese police and Popular Forces (those are the local Vietnamese militia from the area) go in and move everybody into the square except for one person for each house. The village is then very carefully searched by Marines while the population is checked for I.D.s. At the same time the Marines start a dental and medical clinic. The dentists have already pulled 169 teeth in two days! They also provide treats for the kids and a band which plays for hours in the hot sun. The Marines have learned how to make some vaguely Vietnamese-type sounds and the village elders sing. I don't know what lasting effect a County Fair has, but everybody, especially the kids, seems to have a good time.

County Fairs were not all fun as I might have implied. The searches were thorough and the Marines were by this time very experienced. They included probes with steel rods for tunnels, and there were always questions about identification documents if the villagers even had them. The very few young men around were naturally regarded with suspicion—not so much as possible VC—but as ARVN deserters, the assumption at that time being that one was either in the ARVN or the VC. Real VC would likely be hidden someplace or supplied with acceptable identities. There was often confusion between the Vietnamese attached to the Marines as interpreters and the interrogators provided by the police, and between the Vietnamese local forces and the Marines.

The villagers were cautious about giving information anyway, knowing that the Marines would pull out in a couple of days again leaving them vulnerable to the VC. Differences arose as to how pressure could be applied to them. It boiled down to how much rough stuff the Marine commander would allow the accompanying Vietnamese. I suppose Marine officers varied on that, but in the six or seven County Fairs I went to, I didn't see anything that looked like coercion—certainly no mistreatment. On balance, the County Fairs probably did slightly more good than harm for pacification—if only because they differed from the harshness of a sweep as part of a "search and destroy" mission. But the reality was that the cooperation the rural people would give in response to kind gestures of medical care and so forth, depended on whether the Marines stayed and provided genuine security—the *sine qua non* of pacification.

The Marines also introduced a more sustained and therefore more effective pacification operation—the protection of the rice harvest—called Golden Fleece. From its first test in the Hao Vang District near Danang in 1965, Golden Fleece had expanded throughout the I Corps area by 1967.

There are two rice harvests each year in this part of South Vietnam: February and September in the north around Hue, May and October around Danang and further south. Before Golden Fleece, VC tax collectors would move quietly through the hamlets levying a tax on the upcoming harvest, ranging from 25 percent of the crop to as high as 90 percent, depending on the needs of the North Vietnamese who would be coming in and out of the area. In other words, the local VC would confiscate food from the farmers to feed the North Vietnamese regular forces, the main fighting units in I Corps. For the farmers, the tax also included the dangerous labor of carrying the rice to caches back in the hills. The communists were ruthless in enforcing the tax because their remarkable mobility depended on the prepositioning of their supplies so that their units could travel quickly, unhindered by baggage and without waiting for their supplies to catch up with them as more conventional armies had to do. For this strategy to succeed, they had to get their rice from the farmers or bring it down all the way from North Vietnam. Recalcitrant hamlet chiefs were killed, and the houses in hamlets that had failed to deliver were burned by VC hit squads.

Golden Fleece, in the areas where it was applied effectively, could turn the situation around. The five provinces of I Corps were not like those of the Mekong Delta far to the south, which had paddy fields spread out everywhere. Rice growing was limited to patches usually less than ten miles across between the South China Sea and the foothills, so it was possible to saturate the area with troops during the actual harvest, removing the entire crop (except small amounts for the immediate use of the people) to large well-guarded warehouses. Then each farmer could draw on his crop when he wished to sell, pay his not so heavy South Vietnamese taxes, or to eat. Golden Fleece thus served another aspect of pacification, because the hamlet leaders could credibly claim to the VC that they had no choice but to give up their rice in this way.

Golden Fleece didn't always work. Some ARVN unit commanders took a rakeoff, others were lax and let the rice get away. American Army commanders didn't like to be seen by Saigon headquarters as committing the large numbers of troops needed to such relatively passive, low-body-count operations as guarding paddy fields and sometimes pulled their troops out before the rice was completely stored. Heavy fighting turned farmers into refugees and entire harvests had to be skipped while the fields were fought over. Nevertheless, evidence of success came from the increasingly heavy attacks by the VC/NVA on storage facilities and the discovery by search and destroy operations far back in the mountains by special force units of rice that had obviously been brought down from North Vietnam.

Somewhere, early in the game, what was called Civic Action unfortunately got mixed in with pacification, even in the minds of experienced commanders. Civic Action—good works by the American forces—building schools, conducting clinics in outlying areas, distributing toys sent out from the United States and a hundred other kinds of decent, friendly gestures, were very much part of the Marine routine in areas where they were concentrated. They were appreciated by the Vietnamese and served to alleviate some of the harshness of the war for many young Americans. Higher-ups described Civic Action as "Winning the Hearts and Minds"— a slogan I had first heard in Malaysia and not totally subscribed to by the combat units. A hard-bitten Marine colonel new to Vietnam put it: "All that stuff is nonsense, grab 'em by the balls and their hearts and minds will follow." Both Civic Action and "Hearts and Minds" were beside the point for pacification: the American objective was not to be liked or appreciated but to build strength among the South Vietnamese people.

August 27, 1967

Today is Dick's birthday, and I'm terribly homesick for him and all of you just now, at about 9:00 in the evening. The town is quieting down while the planes and artillery are picking up. I'm all alone in the house, my last visitor having left this afternoon and have only today's hectic activities to think about, trips by helicopter to Hoi An, meeting the CORDS types who fought off a VC attack last night, the 80 or so dead VCs stretched out on the ground around the hospital compound (some are so small and young, much the same size and build as Dick is now [a slight thirteen-year-old]); the also young, dead Marine; the older "spook" [C.I.A. officer] whose last post was Mexico City and who spent the night in combat in the sandbag bunkers and this morning, only a few hours later, calmly, in a cultured way, showed me the course of the action. He's a Province Senior Advisor and was in charge of the whole show. Then in the afternoon my weekly time-off at the beach, a little Vietnamese boy, about 7 or 8—hard to tell—asked me to take him into the water. He just came up and grabbed my hand—he sat on my shoulders and screamed happily as the breakers knocked us about. When I got tired I led him ashore and without a word, but a gentle smile, he ran off.

10 September 1967

Dear Mom and Dad,

Now we are wondering what the elections will mean. There has been a slight decline in VC terror activities, but that is only because they are recouping and there has been no reduction in what is called the main force effort. The Vietnamese are rather proud of themselves and are surprised that they haven't received as much credit in the eyes of the world as they should. Some of the voting was accomplished against great odds. Some towns were mortared during voting hours, and the people just waited patiently until it was over and went back to voting. Just a sense of accomplishment and resistance in the face of the VC terror must mean something.

You don't hear much about peace negotiations as a result of the elections because up here they can't see the VC and North Vietnamese just stopping the war, especially when the American people are publicly showing signs of wanting to quit. The more we look like that, the more the North Vietnamese (which predominate in I Corps) will pour on the force and the more they do that the more the South Vietnamese will begin to worry about our leaving and begin to make adjustments. Obviously, nobody wants peace more than the South Vietnamese but they are really afraid of peace on VC terms, which is what many Americans are advocating. What is painful is that by having gotten through the elections and having convinced many Vietnamese that the VC will not be the winning side, and having therefore begun to move forward on many of our programs, even up here where the fighting is the heaviest, we might throw it away by looking as if we wanted out at any price.

These elections in September 1967 confirmed the choice by the insiders in the South Vietnamese military of Nguyen Van Thieu as the president of the Republic of Vietnam. It was not an exercise in democracy as the Johnson administration would have liked because the choices were limited. However, voting itself was significant because there was a large turnout despite threats by the communists. It was indicated that most of the population in South Vietnam at that time was hedging its bets on the government side. Carrying out elections at all was thus a setback for the North Vietnamese.

17 September 1967

We've had info that some "sapper" or demolition type VCs are loose in town and nobody knows what they have in mind. At the same time, we are approaching Children's Tet—some sort of special celebration for them, and the streets are full of kids of all sizes doing rather good dragon dances with torches. . . . They've got all the grown-up cymbals and drums and they "dat dat dung, dat dung, dat dat dung, dat dung dung" bang through the streets until curfew. Tomorrow is the big day and I've got a couple of boxes of hard candy for the little ones who live here.

24 September 1967

At the Senior Province Advisors meeting yesterday we discussed RD, or Revolutionary Development (read "pacification"). We have discovered—or rather knew all along—that because of the heavy fighting and the tough security situation we face in I Corps, we are having less success than in other areas of Vietnam. We also found that, despite our difficulties, we are making progress in some of the worst districts. There are two reasons for this: even in the roughest areas, but where we can provide some security, the people respond well to the 50 person RD teams as long as the VC/NVA don't physically come in; that is, they can mortar or shell the area and the people go about their business, but everything collapses when the communists get into the villages even secretly. The people become afraid, intelligence dries up, proj-

ects dwindle, and the RD teams begin to spend their time looking after their own security.

The other reason for success is simply a matter of good Vietnamese leadership. We discussed cases where there was a relative degree of security but because the local district chief (always an ARVN officer) didn't have any guts, was dishonest, or couldn't administer, the situation deteriorated. And then there were places with bad security where a vigorous officer, without help, kept up the morale of the people so that when the VC hit, the RD team and the [Popular Forces] fought back and drove them off. That gave everyone confidence and things went ahead.

From what I can gather, we are in for a tough time here for the next few months. The monsoon has begun. It rains several times a day, and the roads are flooded. Our supply system takes to the air, and that means less of everything. Meanwhile, the North Vietnamese are bringing in more rockets, which make the airfields more vulnerable, require more troops to stop them (nearly impossible) and raise tensions all around. Every place is fortified, but the VC/NVA army have switched to demolition squads, firing very powerful bazooka-like Chinese and Russian rockets which destroy bunkers.

The tactics they use are surprisingly effective. They start by dropping mortars and rockets all over the place which gets everybody into the bunkers. Under cover of that, they bring up the sapper teams of about 30 men, each carrying explosive charges. And, while the mortars are falling, they blow the wire at strategic places and come into the perimeter, attacking the bunkers from behind, killing the defenders in the bunkers with satchel charges, and the like. The local Vietnamese forces (the ones CORDS has responsibility for) have a hard time because the NVA units are so much better equipped for what they are trying to do than our side in trying to defend against it.

One of the things we have done is to form CAPs (Combined Action Platoons). One squad of Marines plus 35 or so of the Popular Forces. The Marines live right in the hamlets all the time. They get to know the people—who's a stranger and who isn't—and they keep the Popular Forces from doping off and give them some courage which God knows they need for the dangers facing them every day.

The CAPs were another Marine invention. They enhanced security because the Marines in the CAPs could call for support from designated Marine Corps units, which had well-rehearsed means for aiding CAPs under attack. They brought with them heavy firepower, and continuous inspections by Marine CAP officers ensured that the hamlet defenses were kept up. The Marines became part of hamlet life—repairing damaged houses, finding medical assistance and even providing some themselves, methodically training the PF, and playing with the children, gradually building up the trust of the people. The Marines were all volunteers, spoke a little Vietnamese, and were specially trained. Above all, the CAPs stayed for long periods and tried not to leave until the whole area was secured or the PF were able to protect the hamlet on their own with the extra confidence the Marines had given them. I visited dozens of CAPs, some several times, and was always slightly surprised by the maturity of the young sergeant commanders.

Such an obviously successful pacification program was not popular in the command circles of the Military Assistance Command, Vietnam (MACV). It was not regarded as efficient use of American manpower, because it required a special support system for the scattered small units. The American Army leadership felt that American forces should be devoted to fighting the enemy main force units rather than in the static defense of population. The CAPs statistics for body counts and enemy unit contacts were not as spectacular as some of those claimed for other types of American forces, although they were superior in providing security. The argument went on that better training for the Popular Forces would accomplish the same purpose. I didn't agree. The absolutely essential element of pacification was visible, reliable security for the population, and until the PF could be better trained and equipped—both being done by CORDS—the CAPs made a great difference.

I often wondered why the ARVN didn't form up CAPs of its own and concluded that they didn't like to break up their regular units for control reasons. ARVN reaction forces never were very reliable, villagers were suspicious of Vietnamese from other areas, and, perhaps most significantly, there was no real acceptance or understanding of pacification at high levels of the ARVN due to their American training. In fact, the ARVN tendency ran the *other* way, which was to incorporate the militia units into the ARVN structure whenever they could. We resisted this while I was in Vietnam.

15 October 1967

Dear Mom and Dad,

The rains are really upon us now. We had some 10,000 temporary refugees the other day to add to the 570,000 we already have for I Corps as a result of the war. Everything for these people had to be moved by air, but we were able to get in enough food and shelter to take care of them until the water went down. It looks as if we will be faced with this same problem every few weeks until January or February.

We read every day of the heavy debate on Vietnam. From here, it sounds very discouraging. No one has really come up with any alternative to what we are doing and yet, I'm afraid, those who want to step things up will force Johnson's hand, mainly because the moderate line people are deserting him on the basic issue of continuing the war as it is. The sad fact is that if we could convince the North Vietnamese we were going to keep on this course, come what may, for as long as necessary, we would have the peace we are looking for. Except in I Corps, and to some degree even here where the fighting is the heaviest, we are steadily, if unspectacularly, reducing the VC. In I Corps, their forces are mainly North Vietnamese, and they consistently suffer fantastic losses.

This letter was written only a few months before the Tet Offensive. Many of us in CORDS felt that the appearance of American steadiness and continuity was more critical to success than the actual numbers of military forces or the quantities of aid we were sending. It would be more discouraging to the North Vietnamese than their own frightful casualties. Sometimes, sitting by myself with the war booming around me I became almost obsessed with the need for America to endure the "long twilight struggle," as President Kennedy had called it. The conviction that peace would only come if the United States looked as if it would stay the course alienated me from some friends in and out of the Foreign Service for awhile—at least I thought so—until we did indeed achieve a different peace simply by slowly quitting.

8 October 1967

The monsoons are really on us now, nearly 24 hours a day of steady rain. The air is strangely silent because only the helicopters and the big jets bound for the States can take off. Even the artillery has a muffled sound that makes it barely audible above the rain on the tin roof of my house.

Yesterday, the Helgoland, a German hospital ship, tied up just down the street. She is gleaming white with bright Red Crosses, has a 150-bed capacity, and will stay in Danang for a year if all goes well. The captain and chief surgeon called on me this morning and we had a good chat. I've been paying quite a bit of attention to our medical program because it has been going well despite some tremendous obstacles. The pace of the war up here is such that there is an endless stream of casualties. The day before yesterday, for example, the VC blew up two buses near Danang killing 18 people in one and 20 in the other. There were a corresponding number of wounded, all of whom found their way to the civilian hospital here in Danang.

CORDS had medical advisory teams in each of the five provincial hospitals in I Corps and in the two big civilian hospitals in Danang. The teams were a mixture of young Navy doctors doing their national service, experienced American civilian physicians on contract to the Agency for International Development, young and older American nurses. They were almost continually reinforced by volunteers, usually surgeons, from organizations such as Physicians for Vietnam. Theoretically, they were in Vietnam to "advise" the Vietnamese, but the loads were so heavy that they simply shared the work or even took over in the continual emergency situations. I admired them immensely and because, quite properly, they cared nothing about the hierarchies of bureaucracy, I became close friends with several of them.

During my first visit to Danang Hospital #1, I saw a battered military ambulance pull up at the front door, already jammed with relatives and sponsors of the wounded and sick trying to crowd into the emergency room—really the receiving room for the hospital. While the husky Navy medical corpsmen briskly lifted off the stretchers holding the silent, staring Vietnamese civilians and pushed their way through the mob, my American nurse guides and I picked up two badly hurt, quietly whimpering children and carried them into the hospital.

I asked where the children had come from and was told that no one knew; they had been brought by helicopter with wounded Marines and the adult Vietnamese to the U.S. Naval Hospital near China Beach several miles away across the river. There, triage procedures automatically put them last in line until all the Marines had been attended to. Then, after a cursory inspection, those who could stand the bumpy journey and the traffic delays on the bridge over the river were put into the ambulance, real care having been postponed for hours. Because there was no landing pad for helicopters near the hospital, even evacuation flights loaded only with Vietnamese—which often occurred—had to go all the way out to China Beach.

It turned out to be easy to build a pad on a large, partially used dirt parking lot adjacent to the hospital. I mentioned the problem to the Seabee admiral who rode over on the launch every morning to the III MAF meeting with Barney and me; and one afternoon, big trucks, heavy rollers, cement mixers, and their Seabee crews showed up to lay down a fine landing zone. Marines provided a radio for the emergency room to alert the hospital of incoming flights.

There was no ceremony, but in the early evening of that day a small gathering of Vietnamese and I stood beside the hospital as two dusty helicopters with their large red crosses and tired but smiling crews came clattering in. Hospital workers, including some off-duty American military volunteers, rushed over and unloaded the Vietnamese. In less than a minute the helicopters were off into the tropical dusk, slanted slightly for takeoff, lights blinking triumphantly—at least it seemed so to me.

(Letter of 8 October 1967 continued)

The other day, 300 of our Revolutionary Development cadres in Quang Ngai Province apparently decided to take their work seriously. The second or third of their stated objectives in moving into a village is to "remove corrupt elements." As they explained later, they were having a hard time with the people who kept pointing to the corrupt provincial officials. Finally, the RD folks had had enough and they went to the province headquarters and "arrested" the finance chief and economic chief and shaved their heads. They then went back to their work. There was a great flurry of excitement on the part of various generals American and Vietnamese, but the damage (or good) was done. Actually, General Lam then replaced the province chief and a couple of other officials. Some of the top Vietnamese seem secretly pleased that the RD cadres had the guts to do something. It is the kind of thing that gives you some hope for the country.

The subject of corruption will turn up constantly in my account of the war. As the example of the Quang Ngai RD team indicates, there were plenty of Vietnamese who understood what corruption was doing to them and their cause. CORDS's job was to find these people and reinforce them against the others.

10 October 1967

Dick, I get called in the middle of the night a lot. Maybe it's because my telephone number is near to some very busy numbers, but probably it's because I am the Number Two and just as in Cyprus, everyone calls me first.

Later a CB-type radio added to the nighttime disturbances because it was supposed to be monitored all the time and ceaselessly crackled away until I finally mastered the art of hearing only messages meant for me. I've forgotten my call sign but it was mixed in with Cougars, Lions, Tigers, Eagles, and such courageous beasts. I thought Chicken 7 would be adequately descriptive but was told one didn't "play around with the airwaves."

16 October 1967

Dear Dick,

This afternoon I went on a visit to the surgical hospital where they treat the wounded civilians. There was a boy there with a badly wounded foot from a VC mine. His father, or maybe grandfather, sat right beside him and sort of held his head. The man seemed so worried and the boy was in such pain, I felt tears in my eyes and thought how I would feel if you were there and a lot of strangers were around not telling me anything. It's been years since I thought of being a doctor, but I really wished I were one just to be able to take care of that one boy.

19 November 1967

Last night's big blast [seems an odd choice of word for that time and place!] *for Ky* [Nguyen Cao Ky—then vice president of the Republic of South Vietnam] *took place in the ARVN officers' club only a block from my house, but the security arrangements were such that I had to take the car.*

We ate Vietnamese food at round tables while Ky and the assorted dignitaries sat with their backs to us at a long table. They faced a stage on which performed various groups of Vietnamese, climaxed by one of those fabulously beautiful young Vietnamese girl singers who sang a sad song; they all sound sad. However, after the Vietnamese portion, the Koreans were invited to perform and they put on a perfectly ghastly show complete with a striptease. The Vietnamese all sat in cold embarrassment as did most of the Americans, although we clapped to be polite. The most avid audience were the hard-faced Vietnamese soldiers and guards who were looking in the windows. I doubt if the scene did much for Ky's image with his own people.

I really did not deal directly with Ky but saw him in action quite often when he came up from Saigon to attend one of the innumerable conferences. He was a hard man to figure out. Was he just the mustachioed "flyboy" he looked or a shrewd Vietnamese-style politician? Probably a combination of both.

Americans found that he could be harshly frank at times. At lunch in Danang a year or so after this miserable party, Ky coolly looked General Cushman and me in the eyes—the only Americans in a gathering of Vietnamese generals—and told us that he and the other generals believed that the United States was unreliable and would eventually abandon South Vietnam. It was irritating to hear that, given the heavy fighting we were doing, but we only put up the usual pro forma arguments—"No we won't, we've gone too far with you to quit now." Then, as always, we felt the conflict between efforts to succeed in Vietnam and efforts to get out by the people at home.

3 December 1967

Dear Mom and Dad,

We are suffering a deluge of VIPs. They must all be briefed, fed, shown things, and moved around by air. Last week we had three eminent ladies who were sent here by President Johnson: Ambassador Eugenie Anderson, Mrs. Chandler, owner of the Los Angeles Times, and Mrs. Robert Strauss whose husband is a big wheel in the Democratic Party from Texas—where else. They were particularly interested in refugees and civilian casualties. Evidently, these two subjects have become a political problem in the States. Senator Edward Kennedy is holding hearings and is opening an attack on A.I.D. and the way these colossal problems are being handled. My theory is that Kennedy has found the one safe way to criticize the Administration on Vietnam. He doesn't have to talk about the bombing of the North or negotiations, or even the whys and wherefores of the war itself. He can concentrate on the humanitarian aspects and only complain about how we are not doing enough. With that approach, we won't be doing a thing right.

I had talked at length with Kennedy's supercilious staff member, a Mr. DeHaan, and tried to argue for what I thought was a better approach to the massive refugee problem in I Corps. The refugees made up nearly 20 percent of the population, not counting the tens of thousands who had moved to the cities and therefore were not technically refugees. DeHaan, whom I never saw again, deliberately misinterpreted my comments about refugees and "nation building"—the catch phrase of the day. After all these years it still makes me angry, but it illustrates how difficult it was to handle professional, politically motivated opponents of the war, or to discuss important matters frankly with the waves of visitors thrust upon us by Washington. Candor and honesty have to go both ways.

What I tried to say was that I didn't believe that the emergency care of refugees was an important nation-building activity, meaning simply that it wouldn't make much difference to a future peaceful Vietnam if, after great difficulty, we were able to produce some Vietnamese qualified in providing emergency shelter and food distribution. Of all the burdens on the government of Vietnam resulting from the American heavy-firepower way of fighting the war, this was the one I thought the United States could relieve to the greatest extent. On the other hand, we could not succeed in the war unless the relentlessly growing number of refugees were provided shelter and food more efficiently than we had been doing. Thus, I felt that the Americans should take on directly more of these emergency tasks, even to the point of constructing refugee camps and facilities ourselves using our own ample military resources.

However, I thought that other aspects of the refugee problem such as education for the thousands upon thousands of children in the camps, police, relief payments, health, the whole range of government concerns, were nation-building projects. That is why I maintained to DeHaan that direct American participation (as differentiated from material assistance and advice) should not go beyond providing shelter, transportation, and food.

Later, with more daily experience, I began to see that I was wrong. Care of refugees couldn't be divided neatly between providing essential food and shelter and the myriad other services that the refugees needed. A South Vietnamese government presence from the very beginning of a refugee movement was politically necessary to soften the effects of what too often was the result of an American military activity. By the time I left in 1969, CORDS had developed a cadre of conscientious and efficient Vietnamese refugee officials (several of whom died with their American advisors in plane accidents or mine incidents) who could be the "good guys" in the incessant tragedies being played out in I Corps. The American role was still critical because we provided the building materials, tents, and rations, but by doing so through capable Vietnamese we strengthened their ties with the people.

Other CORDS officials and I spent over half our time on the refugees because they touched on all CORDS programs. We had to force our way into planning for all the big, long drawn-out operations, because these invariably drove people from their homes even though the original intent had not been to attack through populated areas. That always happened unless CORDS intervened.

Chapter 14

The Tet Offensive

The Tet Offensive by the VC main forces, and in I Corps, mostly North Vietnamese regular divisions, which began the night of January 30, 1968, raged across the entire country, and has been covered in detail in numerous books and articles. The next few letters give my reaction to it as a headquarters officer. But not all my reactions because in the third day after the offensive began I looked at the battlefields outside Danang and Tamky, the capital of Quang Tin Province, where I saw the almost orderly rows of hundreds of black pajama-ed North Vietnamese who had been caught in the open by American gunships and our mopping up forces. I understood them to be the enemy, but they seemed too young. I respected their courage but couldn't understand the purpose of their commanders in wasting them. I agreed with General Cushman, who maintained from the first moment that the communists had been crushingly defeated in battle; but deep in my heart I sensed the same fanaticism I had seen in the Japanese long before and knew that the North Vietnamese would keep coming. I felt the war would go on and on. It didn't seem right to share these thoughts with my worrying family.

Danang
25 January 1968

Arrived here the afternoon, 24th, but have been so busy I haven't had time until now to get this off. Things here are very tense. There was a bomb placed near the office, but it didn't go off; and there have been several grenade incidents in town. The war is stepping up also.

I'd been on a ten-day round-trip leave in London to see my family and returned to find a charged atmosphere. Intelligence officers at III MAF headquarters were already convinced that the NVA/VC would not observe the truce they themselves had proposed. On the other hand, General Lam and the other ARVN commanders argued that Tet, the equivalent of Chinese New Year, with nearly identical family-based observances, was so Vietnamese—in fact, the only undisputed national holiday—that for propaganda reasons the communists would not wish to disrupt it.

In I Corps, the South Vietnamese military had sadly abandoned this wishful thinking by January 26 or 27 in the face of concrete evidence of an enemy buildup in the nearby mountains. Sightings of moving troops confirmed what had already been sensed for weeks through electronic means. The problem was that the South Vietnamese command didn't want to be the first to cancel the truce, fearing a bitter reaction from the people and accusations in the American press that they were responsible for starting the fighting. It wasn't until the afternoon of the 28th that the Tet leaves were officially repealed and a formal alert called; even so, many ARVN troops were not ready for the attacks.

From Danang we warned the various province advisory teams. Characteristically, we worried less about the team in Hue because there were heavy concentrations of ARVN troops and Marines in the vicinity. We did, however, ask the Hue team under Philip Manhard, a hard-working Foreign Service officer friend and fellow Marine Corps graduate of the Navy Japanese Language School in Boulder (see chapter 11, note 7), to take some precautions. He had only been on the job a few weeks but was firmly in charge of the biggest advisory team next to that in Danang. In the late afternoon of the 29th I talked with Phil on the phone after some difficulties in getting through. Phil said he was concentrating his people in a few places rather than leaving them scattered around town. It was the last contact I had with him for five years and two months.

31 January 1968

Last night was probably the noisiest that I've ever experienced, at least since the war. [World War II—always THE war to my generation.] *The firecrackers of the Vietnamese are so big, so ferocious, so endless that when midnight came, it sounded like the battle for Hill 500 on Saipan. Then I had scarcely returned from a dinner given by two of the American nurses at the hospital when the place began to shake as the rockets came into the air base. But even before I had left the nurses' apartment, Tet midnight passed; and it was absolutely inconceivable. Danang sounded like one great big explosion: flares of red, green, blue floating out into the night, tracers in every direction. Tet firecrackers mixed in at first, then gradually stopping; nothing but heavy firing of all kinds from then on.*

When I got home, duty officers were calling from every direction because there was fighting in every part of town with grenades, rifles, etc. (Barney Koren spent three hours on his porch looking out over the lonely streets while the old mortars banged away.) Anyway, one of the rockets hit a flare dump about 4 a.m., with the result that the whole sky lit up in the most spectacular way—red there, pink here, and the crash and bang was magnificent—great huge orange sky. Meanwhile, small arms fire without ceasing.

The day has been sad though. One of my good friends, a Lieutenant Colonel Tom Jenkins on the Hoi An Advisory Team, was shot through the chest and is fighting for his life at this moment. [He recovered and later returned to his job.] *All day long I sat at the phone hearing of difficulties.*

Anyway now there's a new 7 p.m. curfew, and the whole house shakes as the bombs and artillery boom and the planes come right over the house.... The cook (he of the Foreign Legion) tells me that last night there were "beaucoup morts" in his neighborhood from the shelling and fighting. What a way to start their new year. Right now the town is being hit again. Great shocking explosions. Ten p.m., absolute silence except some barking dogs, then sirens, warning about what? It's weird because there really are no sounds or lights on the streets, but in the background, great crashes and the house sways. Just now an MP jeep goes by with a rattle of "Roger, over." And those hostesses of last night sent me a note saying that after I had dutifully washed the dishes, they had had to go to the hospital and before noon had 100 casualties.

I just got a call. Big noises were new rockets on the airfield so here we go again. Flares are up all over the sky and everything is orange.

1 February 1968

The most worrisome [area] as of now is in Hue where the NVA have been getting control of most of the city since early morning yesterday. We haven't been in contact with our CORDS people since then although we know that some are safe. I'm worried about Phil Manhard. We don't know who is out (i.e. safe) and who isn't.

We've been under a 24-hour curfew, which is a real blessing. Except for the guns and the military traffic, the town is quiet. There's supposed to be an internal effort but no one knows what direction it is coming from, probably all or none. I'm moving from the street side of the house to the other side (guest room—no guest) to sleep. I ran around the corner earlier this evening to where three of our nurses live and told them if they wanted, they could spend the night here but they decided to stay put. They're actually better off where they are because they have some Koreans on one side and some Special Forces across the street. They are awfully tired besides and didn't need the trouble of moving. 480 casualties since early morning of the 30th, 200 in the last 24 hours. I don't know how they do it.

The American civilian medical people in I Corps were not given enough credit for their courage and dedication at the time and now seem almost forgotten. The visiting opponents of the war looked only at the casualties themselves and recorded their misery, which they usually ascribed to the American/South Vietnamese side. The supporters we saw thought more should be done, and they were right. But they had no real suggestions on how to cope better with the seemingly endless waves of civilian wounded. Meanwhile, the staffs of the hospitals, Vietnamese and

Americans, just struggled on. I remember all the faces as they were during those desperate days but not all their names; because I don't want to leave anyone out of the list of honor, I won't name any. They know who they are and that I think of them often.

4 February 1968

The air is hideous with jets taking off. Apparently, the wind direction makes them come right over this area. Then there is the steady rumble of artillery with house-shaking thumps every once in awhile. Meanwhile, the kids and their parents are chattering pleasantly in the sort-of basement. The streets are absolutely deserted except for the patrols—two Vietnamese, three Marines in a jeep, two looking forward, three back, their weapons pointing in the air.

Each evening when I get back from work at about 1900, I go around the corner to the nurses and tell them the latest situation, give them unneeded advice and then come home, have my drinks and a nice dinner although now we are running out of meat. The markets are open only a few minutes each day during the day-long curfew and, of course, the prices are fantastic. Then I get about 15 phone calls, real DCM-type calls: little problems, reports, shooting here or there, but it all shades off at about 9 (right now). I take my shower and assemble all my armament. It gives me confidence even though I'm not sure exactly what I ought to do about an attack. I think it's being alone without being able to talk to the guard which bugs me. Then I go to bed. Ten minutes later, phone. Then I sleep for a couple of hours. Then too much noise; then phone. I sneak out on the porch and look at the silent streets and the lit-up sky. Then sleep; then more noise; then phone, etc.

10 February 1968

The situation in Hue is still bad, but bit by bit people are coming out—usually after the most hair-raising escapes—or their bodies are found—nothing on Phil or about ten other people in CORDS in Hue.

On February 5, we were expecting a major attack on the city so we concentrated people, about 60 Americans and 117 Filipinos and Koreans, in a half-finished apartment building, set up gun positions, and organized our defenses. I'm the overall commander of this operation and sleep on a cot (as does everyone else) up in our command post, which is a bricked in, unfinished room on the roof. We can watch the firing from the sea with flares and see the gun flashes. Nothing has happened in Danang yet, although last night we manned the parapets on the chance that a group of sappers would actually come our way. They didn't. [There was only a slim possibility that the sappers could have penetrated into our area, but it is indicative of our nervous state that we thought we should take precautions. The first few times we gathered were rather fun, but later this became a resented chore.]

There is a 22-hour curfew in Danang which makes life quite comfortable for us Americans but is becoming a real problem for the Vietnamese. The servants sneak out and buy vegetables and stuff in little clandestine markets near the house.

One of the hopeful things that has happened is that, far from rallying to the communists, the Vietnamese have been notably active in trying to resist them and to help the other Vietnamese victims, e.g. the Danang hospital usually can get Vietnamese to give only about ten pints of blood a month. Last week they had nearly 300 pints. The fact that Tet, like Chinese New Year's, is the only real holiday the Vietnamese have all year to relax with their families has led to real hatred of the VC for violating the truce they, themselves, proposed. How does the British press play that?

15 February 1968

Dear Mom and Dad,

The morale of the population in the cities of I Corps, except for Hue, seems to be fairly good. This is because none of the other cities were actually penetrated for long, and the ghastly enemy casualties were here for all to see. In the countryside, it may be different. The VC and the North Vietnamese have had a couple of weeks now in some areas to undo all our work of last year. Nevertheless, we aren't too discouraged, mainly because, as I said, we just don't know what the situation is.

In I Corps the situation in the countryside turned out better than we had feared. The VC/NVA had gone around the villages to get at the provincial capitals and larger district headquarters. They had suffered such heavy casualties that most of the remnants pulled way back to the mountains, leaving the rural areas better off than they had been for many months.

17 February 1968

The battle for Hue is still going on. We have heard that Phil Manhard has been captured although we don't know exactly when or how. Since I talked him into this, you can imagine how hard a time I have in writing to Peg. So far, we know for sure that seven of our CORDS people were killed, but there are many others missing, presumed captured although some of those are probably actually dead.

I'm really touched that people have been so thoughtful to you. It's another reason London was a good idea.

Phil was captured the morning of January 30 emerging from his prearranged secret hiding place in his large house, formerly the residence of the American consul in Hue, at the pleas of the servants, who told him in French that they would be killed if he didn't surrender. A few weeks before he had told me of his plans to defend himself. Knowing how tough he was, I'm sure he would have tried—or at least stayed hidden—if he had been on his own. After being tortured for several days at an assembly area near Hue, he was taken into North Vietnam with some twenty other CORDS personnel. He was held in solitary confinement for almost exactly five years, then taken to the "Hanoi Hilton" to join the rest of the POWs in early January 1973.

In March 1973, the State Department, at Peg Manhard's request, asked me to go to Clark Field in the Philippines to meet Phil when he was repatriated with the other POWs and to accompany him home. I was honored to share in the joy of that brave family.

It was all extraordinarily moving: the arrival of the POW repatriation plane, the first glimpse of Phil in his North Vietnamese–donated clean gray uniform, the long trip home in an Air Force evacuation plane, the stops at Hickam Field in Honolulu, where friends had gathered in the early morning to meet the POWs, the final arrival at Andrews Field met by a high-ranking State Department group including Barney Koren, the ride by helicopter to the Naval Hospital at Bethesda, and the private reunion with Peg and the children—all links in my memories of the Vietnam War.

21 February 1968

We are still having a rather strict curfew which has eliminated all social life, such as it was. It is a typical Danang night, almost country-like silence with just the sound of the little kids of my family fussing away in the yard or in their rooms— then the thunder of one of the jets as it turns on its afterburner—then silence again—then a house-shaking bang of naval gunfire—then silence—then a couple of shots way off—then a couple nearer—and then quiet. The people aren't working very hard these days, but they sure go to bed early. Most of us Americans are enjoying the respite from visitors.

There are many disturbing things going on in the US military bureaucracy that give me the feeling that we are losing sight of the main aims of the war in favor of getting back at the VC/NVA, something we are doing with a vengeance everywhere but in Saigon and Hue. I have a feeling that in I Corps we have settled for the Big War, and pacification, which I believe is the only real war, will take a back seat.

The disturbing things I was talking about were the creation of the new Twenty-fourth Corps headquarters led by an Army general and the assignment of two big U.S. Army divisions, the First Air Cavalry and 101st Airborne, to the northern I Corps area. Thus, concentrated in I Corps would be five American divisions, two South Vietnamese divisions, one Korean Marine Corps brigade, plus the Marine Air Wing and the U.S. Navy offshore.

The reason for these movements was the battle for Khesanh, which went on for weeks and was the main subject for the morning briefings at III MAF. Khesanh itself was originally a small Special Forces camp atop one of the pleasantly green, rolling hills near the border with Laos in Quang Tri Province. The base had been gradually reinforced during the latter part of 1967 to around 8,000 U.S. Marines and South Vietnamese Rangers in response to a methodical buildup by the NVA in the area surrounding it—variously estimated by our intelligence to number as many as 40,000.

The situation at Khesanh in February and March 1968 was roughly analogous to that faced by the French in 1954 at their base in Dienbienphu, a couple of hundred miles to the northwest. The total French defeat at Dienbienphu led to their withdrawal from Vietnam. The certainty that the loss of Khesanh, by now under siege by well-equipped communist forces, would cause American public opinion—already in shock from Tet—to abandon the war gave the battle supreme symbolic importance to President Johnson, who ordered the base held at all costs. The costs were high for Americans—almost 500 Marines killed—but infinitely higher for the NVA, which probably lost at least 10,000 to the nonstop saturation bombing with which we defended the base.

Khesanh was Westmoreland's attrition strategy at its peak. It consisted of attracting communist forces to gather in areas vulnerable to our bombing and to the rapid deployment of our firepower and then piling on with our unlimited resources. The strategy worked in that we killed many times more enemy than they did us. It can also be said to have failed, because it drew Marines away from support of pacification and began the concentration in I Corps of 40 percent of the "maneuver battalions"—the American ground combat units in Vietnam.

25 February 1968

Last Friday, we had a meeting of all the province senior advisors less Phil, of course. The purpose was to assess the situation and to see where we go from here. Surprisingly—to me at any rate—the consensus was, that with the exception of Hue, and although we had taken a tremendous setback, things were far from hopeless. In fact, Komer, who was attending, claimed that we had entered the climactic period of the war and that six months from now would see us very much on the way to finishing it. He was incredibly optimistic, of course, and probably totally wrong; but he did give us the feeling that we had a fighting chance for pacification.

After the meeting, Komer asked me to go out to the airport with him, which I did by car, boat, and helicopter, taking ten minutes in all. During the trip he told me I was going to take over when Barney leaves sometime before the middle of March. So that's that.

Chapter 15

DEPCORDS

3 March 1968

Barney and I have been traveling all over, from way up by the DMZ to southern Quang Ngai Province, as he said good-bye to all the generals on the I Corps and the CORDS staffs.

We have many thousands more American troops here, and it looks as if we are getting into the Big War.

Perhaps the most dispiriting aspect of CORDS was that once we became part of a major headquarters, we became participants in military protocol. There was much confusion because it was difficult to equate Foreign Service ranks with CIA ranks, which were unknown or could be anything, AID ranks, which seemed awfully high to everyone else, and all these with each other and with military ranks. No one was ever pompous or rude, but stupidly, these things mattered in the many bloodless but painful battles to keep CORDS concerns up front. I had to spend much time trying to maintain our position by attending exclusively American ceremonies or Vietnamese affairs featuring Americans, by entertaining the brass, and so on. I used as my excuse that, even though my presence at these affairs had no rational connection with the war (nor did the affairs themselves), it somehow helped CORDS. Pomp and circumstance was one of the recognized weaknesses of the American effort.

13 March 1968

. . . I was in Hue the other day. It was really battered. We went all over the citadel and into the great throne rooms, etc. (kid stuff compared to China but mostly destroyed anyway). There were a lot of Marines wandering around just looking, too. One of the things I noticed was how the fighting types look so much like we did in the War, the same tired, tough, and very dirty faces. The only Vietnamese they seem to notice are the kids who are everywhere, usually chewing gum and just standing

185

close to the men or holding some piece of equipment or even hands. They get growled at or roughhoused (something no Asian seems to do), but they don't seem to mind. When the shooting starts, the kids just get into a ditch or foxhole and sit quietly without showing any particular fear. Marine policy discourages too much buddy-buddy stuff with the kids because they are often spies, or worse, for the VC. Most Marines appear to be willing to take their chances rather than be really tough or rude to the kids.

This sounds different from other accounts of Marine behavior, but it is what I saw.

19 March 1968

Today I went to Quang Tri, the province just under the DMZ. It was a heart-breaking trip in a way because there were literally dozens of hamlets that had been wiped out because of the heavy fighting—some by the enemy but most by our side because our troops didn't want to take chances, and much of it inexcusable or hope-lessly careless. The poor, brave people of Vietnam—they will end by being the heroes of this generation. How can they keep going in all this? But the bravest resisters were the little ragged, awfully under-armed PFs (Popular Forces) who stood up to the North Vietnamese Army and succeeded. What makes the ordinary Vietnamese so courageous and the leaders, in many cases, so poor? What makes the children laugh and the others so courteous? Why don't they quit when it is all so horrible? It all adds up to people who are really worth saving. Not the so-called elite, but the peo-ple. We and the communists are on the same track there.

There were often fundamental differences in I Corps between CORDS and the military over fighting tactics. These were difficult to resolve because many of us in CORDS were serving military officers or had seen plenty of war, like Barney and me or Phil Manhard, and knew the pressures on unit commanders to reduce American and ARVN casualties and to add to the enemy killed by using our heavy firepower.

Furthermore, we in CORDS often had no useful alternatives. In the villages I was talking about, the North Vietnamese had slipped through or around the American and South Vietnamese forces, had entered some of the villages in collaboration with the villagers after only token resistance, and had fortified themselves knowing that they could only be dislodged by direct attacks. The longer the NVA stayed, the more neighboring villages and communication lines were threatened, stay-behind cadres recruited, and the VC infrastructure established. Straight military logic dictated going after them as soon and as hard as possible, meaning artillery, napalm, tanks that destroyed the rice paddy, and the rest. It was hard under these circumstances, which existed throughout I Corps, to argue pacification that emphasized protecting the population instead of killing off the enemy. Occasionally, when the time seemed right, we could point out that the large "search and destroy" operations encouraged by MACV were seldom effective, because the enemy was usually forewarned and the way the operations themselves were carried out often alienated the population and undid months of CORDS work. These arguments began to be listened to by General Creighton Abrams when he took command later in 1968.

27 March 1968

Here it is Saturday night—the only shootout so far is in English on TV which Gao, the maid's 7-year-old, watches all day. He has stayed out of sight most of the time, but tonight when I came home from the office, he yelled a real "Boo" and I jumped so satisfactorily that he rolled on the tiled floor with joy. Gunny Hollis has got a blackboard for him and he has the two of us Americans, his sweet, widowed mother, the policeman off duty (part of my bodyguard), and the gardener watching him write his lessons. His words are very clear, much better than you could do at this age; but otherwise I didn't understand a thing. Anyway he is a thoroughly satisfactory child and shows that, despite all the pain and strain of being a human being in Vietnam, most of these great people are normal and balanced.

Today we had a morning meeting followed by a lunch for 25 at which I had Generals Walt and Cushman. Walt, you know was the previous Marine commander here. I asked him to say a few words and he made a fighting speech on how, despite what we read in the press, the American people are behind us, although uninformed. It wasn't all that well formulated but most of the guys thought it was great.

I admired General Lewis W. Walt, who had an instinctive understanding of the needs of pacification. Most of the Marine Corps innovations in pacification, such as the CAPs, County Fairs, and Golden Fleece, were introduced during his time in command of III MAF, 1965–1967. A big, tough, total Marine, he had the special presence and style of a combat infantry leader, which he had been in World War II and Korea. Genial and friendly most of the time, it was said that he only had to fix the "Twin Blues" of his eyes on someone to obtain instantaneous results. His book, *Strange War, Strange Strategy*, was mostly about pacification and movingly portrayed his respect for the rural people of South Vietnam.[1] In retrospect, Walt's statement that the American people were behind the war seems odd, so soon after the psychological blow of Tet at home. I think he said it because that was what he was supposed to say; no combat Marine commander would say discouraging things to his troops about something they couldn't change. Also, and this sense lasted throughout the war among high-ranking Marines: if the American people knew the truth, they would support "their own." The opposition especially was dismissed as biased, unfair, or self-serving—the same criticisms that were applied to the military in the field by journalists.

28 April 1968

SPOT REPORT FROM I CORPS G-2

Possibility of rocket attack on the Danang area higher than usual tonight. Also increased possibility of terrorism for the next few days.

Such messages came in like weather reports, and individuals were supposed to take precautions "to the extent they didn't detract from the performance of normal duties," meaning there really wasn't much one could do. First Lieutenant Michael Gilman, my Marine aide-de-camp, routinely urged more alertness on the Marine and Vietnamese guards, who would briefly appear inspired. My own security wasn't the problem; I had the huge CORDS staff to worry about and had to consider whether to order the American staff to assemble in specific areas or not bother them at all. I usually didn't err on the side of caution and often paid no attention—but we came out all right in Danang anyway.

12 May 1968

During the week I visited all the provinces. In Quang Tri, the furthest north, I spent several hours in two hamlets which showed both the terrible problems and misery of this war and its gripping, hopeful side.

One of these hamlets is about 5 kilometers northeast of Quang Tri town (we actually were able to go by jeep). It has been one of our model Revolutionary Development hamlets and considered pro-GVN [government of South Vietnam]. They had built their own meeting house, their own maternity dispensary, and dozens of other worthwhile things. During the Tet Offensive they had been successful in holding off the North Vietnamese; however, a week ago a North Vietnamese force got in and actually occupied one little area of the hamlet. The ARVN came out to take it back and after drawing some fire, pulled back and called in air strikes, which completely obliterated the whole place. Fortunately, most of the people got out but they're now wearily putting their homes back together again, and the pro-GVN flavor of the village and all our work (or rather, their work), has been lost—for awhile anyway.

The other hamlet was quite different. We went to see it because it had a remarkably successful self-defense force. In fact, during the Tet offensive, they had held off a North Vietnamese battalion all by themselves, killing over 50 of the enemy. I've never seen a place with so much barbed wire. They had it strung in dozens of clever ways; and I was told the place was totally booby-trapped with only the villagers knowing where they were. The center of all the defense activity was a Catholic chapel built about 1850 and the burial site of 2,500 people (I was told), killed by their Buddhist fellow Vietnamese some 100 years ago. The chapel is surrounded by sandbags and bunkers with tunnels leading all over—just as good as anything the VC could do.

It was the people that I found most fascinating—all the boys from 13 or 14 up were armed and had regular assignments. They didn't line up for us but just seemed to be standing around to show us what a ready-for-anything force they were. They'd even captured a North Vietnamese scout just outside the village just an hour before. They all had that gentle Vietnamese smile; and although they were proud of being considered Vietnamese men, they were also shy. The young Vietnamese district chief who took us around was obviously respected by them and you could see how hopeful the people were about the future. We must never desert these people!

29 June 1968

Last night, at the same time as a farewell party for Cliff Nelson [then my deputy, a highly motivated and experienced Foreign Service officer] *and typical of the unreality and contradictions of my life here, we had one of those disasters that make this war so horrible. There was a resettlement village called Son Tra* [My Lai hamlet was in that area, but I didn't know about the massacre there several months earlier] *in Quang Ngai Province, made up of people from the neighboring areas—many of whom didn't want to move but had been told that by concentrating this way they could have better security because American troops were nearby. Well, last night the VC mortared the village and also attacked it on the ground. Over 60% of the village was destroyed, 71 civilians were killed (most of them burned to death because the wind fanned flames over their little shelters), and several hundred wounded. The American forces came, all right, but they were too late. There wasn't anything CORDS could do for them the next day either when I went down to see. I stood around feeling incompetent and somehow responsible for them and, of course, bitter and sad.*

7 July 1968

This week I have been taking trips with Lieutenant-General William B. Rosson, an Army general who is the acting commander of III MAF for the month of July while General Cushman is away. We really have an interesting situation—a Marine Amphibious Force with only two Marine divisions but three Army divisions in it, now commanded by an Army general.

These inspection visits are valuable because General Rosson takes action on the spot and gets things done that would take days—or weeks—for me to ram through the staff. He is personally very interested in pacification, and I'm going to take advantage of it.

The Province Chief, a Colonel Tin [of Quang Nam Province], *is perhaps the best Vietnamese I've met. He is ex-Viet Minh and fought against the French. He has been at our staff colleges and is really a good administrator. He gets out among the people and shows his concern for them. He visits each one of the 30 Revolutionary Development cadre teams, 150 armed men in each, in the province at least once a month. If anything happens in the province he goes right out there the first thing in the morning. It's the genuine nationalists like Tin who give me some hope for Vietnam. I would say that two of the five province chiefs are in this category now.*

Tuesday, Rosson and I went to Quang Tin Province. It was a good trip too, especially at the end when we went to the embattled district headquarters of Thang Binh and talked to the district chief, a Major Dang. He's a sort of chubby Vietnamese with rather expressive English. Unlike everyone else official or military, he wears the black pajamas of the peasant; however, with a serviceable—and used—pistol at his belt. He has a legend in Vietnamese and English outside his office, saying the number of VC killed this year in his district—376—number of weapons, etc., and then the casualties on our side. Every night he sleeps in the district out among the people, organizing ambushes, patrols, and just showing himself unafraid of the VC. People apparently love him. He has a moving way of talking, even in English. "High cadres (VC), they hate me because I kill—low cadres no hate—they understand— many 'ralliers' because Vietnamese I tell them if you stay VC I kill you always, but I cry because you Vietnamese. People they know me—kill but cry." He's very proud. "What I control by day; I control by night. That's only way." An advisory effort for someone like that is sort of nonsense and the youthful US Army CORDS advisor has sense enough to stand back and arrange supplies, etc., because there is almost nothing he can advise on.

The last stop yesterday was a place called Duc Tho in Quang Ngai Province. We were met by the slick looking District Chief and his beautiful wife, a real Madame Nhu,[2] complete with earrings. General Rosson had been there over a year ago, and we had finally established some security for the people. We had a meeting with their advisory team, which got somewhat confused because the two hard-bitten but young US majors were coolly upstaged by the equally tough Vietnamese, and General Rosson got mad at the Americans' rather scrambling presentation—redundancy— leaving stuff out.

After inspecting the quarters, we went out into the familiar dusty courtyard amid all the sandbags. There all the town officials were drawn up in a straight line and behind them some 40 men, women, boys and girls, rather battered and sullen, squatting on the ground. There was a long speech in Vietnamese, then repeated in horrible English. Then two thin Vietnamese girls put a garland around General Rosson's neck. Then a speech by him about people who fight for their freedom. Finally, the piece de resistance, the district chief announced that all the squatting VCS (VC suspects) were to be freed in honor of the occasion. No change of expression. The affair broke up and the general, district chief, wife and I walked through the deep dust of the cleared streets while the freed prisoners moved quickly but uncertainly off in the other direction.

I was gratified at Rosson's obviously sincere interest in CORDS and pacification but did not find him terribly revealing, and I never found out what he thought of this disquieting ceremony. To me it epitomized much that was wrong with the American effort in Vietnam. Duc Tho had been one of the most penetrated districts in I Corps. And although there had been some improvement in security, the atmosphere was far from relaxed, so a ceremony to celebrate anything was premature. The district was also poor and the hard-eyed, city-dressed, district chief's wife— astonishingly beautiful as she was—must have reinforced the suspicions of Duc Tho's population about the district chief while he flaunted his prosperity. We big-shot Americans, self-conscious but polite to South Vietnamese officials as always in public, silently accepted being made the centerpiece of the sordid, hypocritical show and Americans the objects of hatred. The few "VC suspects" who were not VC already had undoubtedly joined up after being mistreated for days or weeks.

21 July 1968

On Wednesday we had a visit by the Secretary of Defense Clark Clifford. He got a very smart briefing by General Rosson and later we had lunch. Clifford seemed pretty easy going and asked a few good questions. Those who know say that it was nothing like a McNamara appearance. [Robert McNamara was Clifford's predecessor as defense secretary.] *The latter constantly interrupted with hard, penetrating questions, drew conclusions out loud, and forced the briefer to dispute them. At lunch I sat beside the new Assistant Secretary of Defense for Public Affairs, a youngish man by the name of Goulding. He told me he was actually doing very little in the way of explaining the war to the American people anymore. I guess the implication was that there was almost nothing left to be said. He characterized Senator Eugene McCarthy* [a candidate for the Democratic nomination] *as the laziest man in Washington, with only the war as an issue—what an idea!*

Perhaps Rosson knew that Clifford had already given up on the war—the high-ranking military have ways of reading the secretary of defense and they tell each other. But I didn't realize that the inevitable had indeed happened and that we were actually beginning the process of withdrawing from Vietnam. I had not shared in the generals' dismay that President Johnson had turned down General Westmoreland's request for 200,000 more troops, figuring that would mean more efficient use of the ones already in Vietnam. I thought that the leveling out of American forces would be a net gain for pacification—especially as the wise and tough General Abrams had taken over from Westmoreland. So, along with everyone else, I played the briefing for real, and because of Clifford's easy manner I thought we had received a fair hearing.

The nuances of the conversation with Goulding—if I had paid attention to them—would have provided all the clues I needed. I reflect now that I never would have missed them had he been a foreign diplomat. Philip Goulding talked frankly about his role as a Pentagon spokesman in *Confirm or Deny: Informing the People on National Security*.[3] He said that he had relayed incomplete and inaccurate information obtained through reports "deliberately falsified at lower levels" (as quoted in his obituary in the *New York Times*, Sept. 10, 1998).

The big briefings for American civilian VIPs varied little in style and approach no matter who the briefee was. The briefings started with a short review of the military situation in the area and then went immediately to the subjects of special interest to the visitor, which he had made known in advance. If he hadn't expressed any preference, he was told about things he SHOULD be interested in. Briefings were often carefully rehearsed, especially for known critics of the war, and the answers to probable questions were gone over in detail so that everyone from top to bottom—at least for that particular briefing—used the same arguments in the same way. Statistics dominated because they were instantly available on almost any conceivable subject, sometimes ranging startlingly in the same briefing from how many Vietnamese children were actually in school full time to how much JP-4 aviation fuel was needed to be imported each week in Danang; from the ratio of patients in the CORDS-assisted Vietnamese hospitals with war-related injuries to those who were just plain sick or hurt by car accidents, stove explosions, or boiling water, to name a few of the most common "ordinary" disasters, to the number of houses (called "hootches" by salty briefers for air power admirers) damaged by air strikes in the mountains west of Danang. The real preparations, however, centered on how the multitude of statistics were to be interpreted either in the presentation or in answers to questions.

Here there were problems, as interpretations naturally differed. For example, we were once expected to brief a congressman known to be interested in the refugee situation about a military sweep then underway that had already created some 500 refugees. That this many new refugees were quickly taken care of adequately could be presented as encouraging evidence of superior organization and energy by the Vietnamese refugee officials and their CORDS advisors—which it was. But 500 more refugees was a blow to pacification far outweighing in my mind any military gain from that operation—a truth difficult to express to our visitor in front of the commander. This was why just touching-down visits to Danang of the Clifford type were useless for acquiring information helpful to making major policy decisions. I've forgotten what I ended up saying to the congressman, but the increasing number of critics of the war who appeared after Tet just to say they had been to Vietnam, and the pressures to be as optimistic as the top brass wanted, created credibility gaps and became increasingly wearing on all of us—even the top brass.

21 July 1968

Yesterday I went to Quang Tin to the opening of Ky My village. I think I wrote about this village some time ago—the one from which the VC had chased the people about three years ago. It has since been recaptured, and for the past three or four months the people have been rebuilding their homes. Yesterday we had the ceremony—I helped cut the ribbon with the ARVN Second Division commander and sat on the dais in the little square and listened to a couple of hours of speeches. Then back by jeep through a blazing hot but tranquil countryside.

Also in the week I went up to Quang Tri to attend the long-awaited opening of the Cam Lo water supply system. Cam Lo is a refugee area just south of the DMZ and it is pitifully short of water. We had been working for many months to build a reservoir and a pipe system so that people didn't have to carry water a couple of miles from the river. The North Vietnamese had tried to disrupt the work, and several Marines were killed or wounded in the process. Water for about 10,000 people.

The same afternoon we went to a place called Cua Valley. This area had long been dominated by the enemy, but in late May and June, clearing operations were run in it; and about three months ago we moved some 5,000 Bru Montagnards there from Cam Lo. These Bru were originally from the Khesanh area and when the fighting got too heavy, they walked out of Cam Lo where they were unhappy and getting sick. The Bru have to live at a certain altitude and climate or they suffer. Cam Lo is at sea level and hot, dry, and horribly dusty. Now the Bru have cool hills and fresh streams of running water. In fact, literally hundreds of little brown bodies were splashing around in the dammed up irrigation stream.

The CORDS advisors there are a young Foreign Service officer, Class 7 (equivalent to a first lieutenant), on his first Foreign Service assignment, more or less assisted by an odd, but effective, chap who somehow got to Vietnam by himself and was working for CORDS as a local employee. He wears a camouflage suit and lives either with the US Special Forces or right in with the Bru themselves. Anyway, these advisors say that the bad skin infections the Bru had are almost gone now because they're getting their daily baths. It was very peaceful despite the occasional crackle of shots nearby and the heavy rumble of artillery and bombs up on the DMZ.

My only other trip this week was to Quang Ngai and Quang Tin to look at the Chieu Hoi Centers. These are the places where the Hoi Chanh, or ralliers to the GVN from the VC, are kept for 45 to 60 days while adjusting to life on the government's side. The centers are not all that nice, but they are adequate. At one of the centers, the Hoi Chanh are learning to be barbers, and the men in the neighborhood come in for free haircuts. The women Hoi Chanh were learning to sew and some were making clothes for their families. The Hoi Chanh have to be handled very carefully because they are prime targets for the VC, and they usually move from their old homes. In both Quang Ngai Town and Tamky, they're building their own hamlets and will start a new life of their own. They also have to contend with the suspicion of their neighbors, which dies hard among people who have suffered at VC hands for so long.

Some of the Hoi Chanh volunteer to become Kit Carson Scouts which are attached to, in fact become part of, a US military unit. They have saved countless American lives by recognizing mine fields, booby traps and the like, and also have killed large numbers of their former comrades. They obviously don't need much military training but learn the American military system, some English, and the US weapons. One Marine is assigned as a buddy and the two eat, sleep, and fight together from then on. Other Hoi Chanh become members of Armed Propaganda Teams which go into contested areas and speak to the people about Chieu Hoi and try to talk other VC into it. They are armed for obvious reasons.

3 August 1968

Memo from my secretary

Re Hoi An incident. Duane [Puckett, my deputy] *said an estimated platoon hit the RD compound 0215 this morning. RF/Sector* [province headquarters] *reacted very rapidly. 8 KIA* [killed in action]. *Rest cornered and they hope to get those. Seven Nung guards wounded. No KIA. Four or five B40 rounds* [a hand-held rocket similar to a bazooka with enormous explosive power]. *House where Puckett formerly lived took some small arms fire. No American casualties.*

This was one of the innumerable small engagements of pacification. The NVA/VC regularly hit the provincial capitals in I Corps just to show that they could, and here eight of their young men died to make the gesture.

3 August 1968

We are on our way back from Saigon; we, that is, Lieutenant General Rosson, Bill Colby and a couple of colonels from I Corps. Went down yesterday afternoon for dinner with General Abrams. Were met at the VIP strip and driven at frightening speed through Saigon's awful traffic to a place improbably called Blair House, really luxurious accommodations, private bath, air conditioning, etc.

Everyone wore sport shirts to dinner and all the brass was there, Abrams, Andrew Goodpaster (Deputy MACV), a General Corcoran the Chief of Staff, Komer and the I Corps delegation. The after dinner talk turned into a shambles. Abrams and Komer got into a big row about the management of CORDS, chains of command, etc. with Abrams criticizing Komer for his efforts to centralize everything (my criticism too), and Komer getting mad, his point being pacification has no precedents; therefore, he had to run things from Saigon or nothing would get done. At the end, Komer abruptly got up and broke up the party.

I was encouraged by this socially exciting incident. This was the first time I had seen Abrams in action, and I felt an immediate surge of confidence in him. He showed he had a sophisticated understanding of pacification; Komer was partially tamed in front of my eyes, assuring that CORDS I Corps would henceforth be given more latitude.

11 August 1968

I had dinner with Francois Sully and Gerald Blocker of Newsweek *and Johnny Rich.* [John, my old Marine Corps comrade from Boulder days, was a well-known NBC reporter who covered East Asia from Japan. He was visiting me but making it legal with NBC by doing some of his dangerous work.] *I made some very frank comments about the conduct of the war and the overwhelming emphasis of the military on purely military action rather than pacification, which woke me up in a cold sweat at 3:00 a.m. worrying about the consequences if they should appear in print. Komer watches these things like a hawk and he will have no trouble tracing them back to me.*

Actually, Komer believed the same things about the conduct of the war but wouldn't have wanted his subordinates quoted because it would only irritate MACV and Washington.

23 August 1968

Dear Dad,

. . . I suppose that you have been glued to the TV with the conventions. It doesn't sound very exciting from this distance—at least the Republicans didn't—now the Democrats are going to have quite a time on their platform. I can't help but believe that anything other than a statement of objectives on Vietnam could be helpful at this stage. Telling an elected Vietnamese government what they must accept in the way of an unelected government, a coalition of their enemies, would be tantamount to telling them we want them to fold. . . . I have been saying that if we could have a continuation of security and lack of enemy initiative for the next three or four months, we would have established a trend in pacification that I don't think the communists would be able to reverse. I'm not sure that the current activity isn't a reaction to this probability. If so, the certain failure of their action may actually speed things up a bit in Paris.

27 August 1968

The week has been filled with emergencies brought about by the increase of enemy activity up here. We don't know yet whether this is the long-awaited third offensive, the beginning of it, all there is to it, or what. They are suffering frightful casualties: over 1,600 NVA killed in I Corps during the past 72 hours. I wonder if you are get-ting very much news of Vietnam what with Czechoslovakia [where Soviet troops crushed a brief effort at liberalization] *and the Democratic Convention. The fact that these two things are preempting the headlines is itself a big setback for the com-munists who are hoping to influence US opinion with another offensive.*

Later [flying north to Quang Tri] *—This is the part of I Corps I really hate to see as I fly over it. It's the "Street Without Joy" area (so-called by the French who suffered heavily in trying to control it. The "street" refers to Route Nationale Une, which ran from Saigon to Hanoi) and most of the villages are destroyed and replaced by the tin-roofed refugee camps. The area was always desolate, but it really looks grim now. I can see North Vietnam easily from here and the Benhai River, which divides the country, as a blue ribbon with puffs of white smoke from the artillery on either side of it.*

Even later, back in Danang. I have a humdinger of a family row going on at home here. It seems that Sergeant McGee had given the maid some PX things to take to her sister on the other side of town, apples, some Coke. I don't know how many times he has done this, but I doubt if it has been very much. Anyway McGee says it hasn't. Well, the police at the gate, of course, see this as a beginning of a black-market operation in which they have no cut. So they give Momma San a bad time. She calls on McGee who has words with the police. They are making a report therefore. The English in the report is being supplied by Oanh the driver who has been trying to get the maid fired for months. McGee finds this out and in typical USMC fashion tells Oanh that he'll kill him at the front gate if there is any more of this. Now all factions are appealing to me.

22 September 1968

In I Corps we are embarking on one of the most hopeful things I have been in on since I've come here: We have begun a fairly extensive program of resettling the refugees back in their original hamlets. There have been a lot of schemes which involve moving refugees from insecure areas to secure ones; but because of the heavy fighting in this corps area, we haven't been able to get many people back to their homes, where, of course, they really only want to go. Since most refugees in I Corps have just moved a few kilometers at most from their homes, security has been the only reason why they couldn't go home.

We have set up a package operation. First we go into the area to be resettled, clear it of the VC, the only people who would be in it since the inhabitants abandoned it. The second step is to provide some good permanent security. Then we would assemble all the people from the hamlet—they usually stick together in their refugee shack areas anyway—and screen them for VC infrastructure and help them with some of the Revolutionary Development type projects such as schools, wells, etc. The villagers continue to live in their refugee camp, or whatever, and go back and forth to their old hamlet, rebuilding their homes and sometimes planting their old fields. We help with rebuilding the bigger things like schools, dispensaries, etc., through civic action by US or ARVN units. The hamlet is laid out in a more defensible configuration, but the villagers have the same neighbors as before and farm the same land. Finally, when everything is ready, everybody moves back at once, and we have a ceremony. We have done this twice already, moving back 4,000 to 5,000 in Quang Tin and have just started on 13,000 in Thua Thien Province.

29 September 1968

The presents to the maid and Gao were accepted in the proper Vietnamese fashion—a slight nod, a faint smile, and nothing more said. Gao and I have been working on the paint-by-numbers ever since, but he has been in real trouble with his mother because he got number 14, bright yellow, all over the coffee table in my room where we located the project. I am in trouble too, but this is expressed in rather cold silence. Anyway, he is a wonderful kid . . . long division at 7, etc., and an incipient artist, too. Tootsie toy cars would be OK, but Sergeant McGee has loaded him with fire engines, etc.

I had just returned from four days in the United States to attend the memorial service for my mother, who had died after a long illness. She disapproved of our actions in Vietnam and had prayed that I wouldn't be called "to be in another war," but was brave about it when I was.

5 October 1968

We are on the point—or think we are—of a real breakthrough in pacification. There is going to be—or we hope there is going to be—a shift in emphasis to the political and other aspects of the war away from the "Big War." We're going on a real drive to recover several hundred hamlets which are in VC hands or severely contested before the next Tet. It is a tall order and involves the coordination and utilization of all our forces and resources. The most encouraging aspect is that the Vietnamese themselves want this, have done a lot of planning on it and are putting their hearts in it. Well, so far at least.

The Accelerated Pacification Campaign (APC) was a genuinely hopeful development because the Vietnamese began to see themselves succeeding. It grew out of their own assessment of the situation six months after Tet and the fact that the North Vietnamese had not been able to enlist any wide support among the rural South Vietnamese for the Tet Offensive. It always happened; the more confidence they gained in their own abilities and their security, the more they tried. The impetus came from Komer, who applied his driving style to getting the ambitious overall plan accepted at MACV (which would have to devote extra American forces to helping out). More important, the top-level Vietnamese showed more than perfunctory interest.

The APC dominated my work for the rest of the time I was in Vietnam. Within a few days after I wrote this letter, everything began moving at once. We started distributing M-16 rifles to the 25,000 Popular Forces in I Corps so that for the first time they would not be outgunned by the communists. Simultaneously, we dispatched three-man ARVN and U.S. military training teams to teach them how to use these weapons. I spent hours watching the training process, from the initial weapons familiarization and marksmanship to follow-up exercises by the PF platoons in their own hamlets, choosing to inspect those that the Vietnamese district chiefs thought were the most vulnerable. Predictably, as the security improved in these wobbly hamlets, schools began to be rebuilt in the neighboring areas and throughout I Corps; young women teachers (special targets of the VC assassination squads) returned to their villages. With less mining of the roads, market activity began to pick up. CORDS medical advisors had more opportunities to open public health and immunization programs as the numbers of wounded decreased.

The hamlets that were selected for concentration in the APC were identified by CORDS and the South Vietnamese government in Saigon. Specific instructions were sent down through both channels listing identical objectives and schedules in the way that Bobby Thompson, the British expert, had outlined to Ambassador Bunker in London a year and a half earlier. The statistics governing the choices came from the much-ridiculed Hamlet Evaluation System, a computerized, tiresome means of judging the pacification status of the thousands of hamlets in South Vietnam.

HES depended on the integrity and accuracy of the American senior district advisors, who filled out a monthly form answering a series of direct questions designed to measure the political, economic, and especially the security situation in each hamlet—usually thirty to fifty hamlets in each district. Had there been an enemy attack during the month? Was the attack successful—did the VC enter the hamlet? Were there mining incidents? Did the hamlet chief sleep in the hamlet or slip away to the district headquarters at night? Was the school functioning? Could the hamlet people safely use the local market? The questions were designed to be as objective as possible to shift the burden of actually determining the status of a hamlet from the district advisors to the impersonal machine.

The questions were weighted in ways that were changed as the system was refined. When aggregated, the responses determined the pacification status of every hamlet in South Vietnam, at least as far as the Saigon planners were concerned. To be fair, no one connected with HES ever claimed total accuracy but the ratings, which ranged from A to E, were used to determine trends, up or down.

An A rating, of which there were not many, indicated that there was no noticeable communist activity, officials were present and working, a local self-defense unit was active and reliable, the school was going well, and the people were confident. B hamlets were almost as good but regarded as slightly more vulnerable. C hamlets were supposed to be relatively secure, with most of the community development projects progressing slowly, but where the communists were able occasionally to make their presence felt, at least nearby. D hamlets were under heavier pressure to the point where their populations were up for grabs—largely dependent on the security situation. E hamlets were dominated by the enemy but not totally controlled by them. They were not entirely lost, but if some effort was not made to help them, they would fall into the V category and be assumed to be under VC control.

I had reacted negatively to the whole HES process when I first heard about it. One of my jobs as Barney's deputy in 1967 had been to urge the province senior advisors to harass the district advisors to get the reports in, to listen to their bitter complaints about losing man-days of pacification effort on forms, and listen to their uncomfortable confessions that much in their reports was guesswork. The morning briefings at III MAF and I Corps headquarters had early made me uneasy about quantifying this kind of war, especially by such flagrantly abused means as "body counts." HES seemed like another misguided report imposed by Saigon, which in turn was responding to Washington's unslakable thirst for information—any information. I was not impressed by an intense Army colonel from MACV, who spent nearly two hours lauding the advanced computer techniques the HES had adopted, because it seemed to me that Saigon and Washington would just be getting bum dope faster.

In the aftermath of the Tet Offensive, though, I began to see HES differently. There was a need for the Vietnamese to establish priorities, and the HES showed in a general way which districts in I Corps were recovering from Tet faster than others. But more than anything else, HES— because it was prepared by Americans—was valuable in showing the Vietnamese leadership at the national and corps level where we thought pacification was going badly or well. It made it possible to approach General Lam about incompetent or corrupt provincial or district officials—often those he had a personal interest in—while pointing out those who were doing well—not always his favorites.

There were tricky techniques for doing this. Once, I used my briefing on the I Corps HES results to urge General Cushman to face Lam directly with our objections to an individual, the province chief in Quang Tri, a Colonel Anh. The colonel had retreated into a bunker in the provincial headquarters when the NVA attacked the town and didn't emerge for several days until the NVA had been driven off by the local troops he was supposed to have commanded.

In the end, our efforts could be rated successful in I Corps. In July 1967 when I arrived in Danang, four of the five province chiefs were noticeably bad, that is, corrupt, weak, unresponsive to their peoples' needs; of the forty district chiefs at least thirty were very bad. When I left two years later we Americans rated all five province chiefs as good and three of these were counted as superior. As leaders those three would stand out in any country. Only ten of the district chiefs were classified as poor. The standards were also raised during this period as part of the APC, but ten were judged to be really superior. These changes mean that at one time some provinces in South Vietnam had fairly good government and were psychologically resistant to the communists, whatever the leaders in Saigon were doing.[4]

31 October 1968

There has been a lot of talk about possible peace, but nobody is actually saying very much. . . . Most people around don't think we ought to try right now because

we are rapidly moving so far ahead—on the military front. We are actually moving
ahead on all fronts, and I think we could continue to do so even if we had negotia-
tions. We aren't in a bad position to "fight/talk" any more than they are.

Being in favor of any kind of negotiations at all at this stage would
have been tantamount to being a quitter in the eyes of most senior officers in III MAF.

Six months after I wrote this letter I had returned to Washington and
talked with Averell Harriman about this period, when he had headed the
American delegation at the peace conference in Paris. Neither of us had
any formal connection with Vietnam anymore, but Harriman was carrying around some crippling disappointment. After a sustained effort for so
long, the peace conference he had engineered had not progressed, and
peace in Vietnam was in the hands of President Nixon.

I knew very little of what had gone on in Washington and Paris, but my
experience in London made me sure that Harriman had urged halts in the
bombing of North Vietnam and that President Johnson had not concurred
at crucial times. I sensed that the exhausted subject of bombing would
not come up, certainly no criticism of President Johnson, because Harriman was always scrupulously loyal to the presidents he served in front
of subordinates like me. However, I was not quite prepared for Harriman's bitterness over South Vietnamese President Nguyen Van Thieu,
whom he characterized as the greatest obstructer of the peace process,
whose failure to "understand his own dangerous situation" was due to
his determination "to save his own skin," "keep us in Vietnam forever."

I set Harriman off on a different tack when I remonstrated that I
thought the South Vietnamese under Thieu were actually making slow
but real progress against the VC, citing the modest gains of the APC and
the campaigns against corruption. Harriman growled that the announcement of the APC just as the Paris Conference was convening "couldn't
have come at a worse time," that its very success—which he doubted
anyway—gave the other side the prospect that the Americans were bent
on preventing a peaceful, political option for the Vietnamese communists, and without that they would not agree to anything.

There was little more to our conversation, which turned agreeably to
my future plans. When I was leaving he thanked me for "your frankness," which he occasionally had done in the past, and for "listening to
me," which he had never needed to mention before.

10 November 1968

Last night, in fact all day yesterday, we celebrated the 193rd Birthday of the
Marine Corps. Today is the real day but it being Sunday they moved it to Saturday
to avoid any conflict with anyone's indiscernible religious scruples. Christian that

*is. We had lunch for "foreign" brass such as the Vietnamese and the US Army. . . .
I am at home so can't remember whether I have written since our elections. I guess
the less said the better. Did I write, as I have said so many times to visitors, the Vietnamese I deal with are ecstatic? Humphrey's statements towards the end of the campaign have convinced them that we would sell them out if the Democrats stayed on.
It's ironic, but most Vietnamese feel they couldn't trust Johnson either.*

I felt that despite all that Johnson had done to help, the Vietnamese
were suspicious of anyone who talked negotiations.

3 December 1968

*Later on this afternoon, I'm going down to Binh Son in Quang Ngai Province
where there was a battle and the place was overrun last night. . . . 4 December—
Binh Son was a real mess. The VC had gone right through the district headquarters
which looks like a big school house, or did. We walked around the battlefield. There
were about 100 people killed on both sides, and we were told not to go close to some
of the smoldering ruins. About five minutes after we had moved over and were
standing behind a truck 100 feet away, there was a huge explosion and brick and
metal came flying all over the place. If we had stayed, we'd have been hit for sure.*

8 December 1968

*Tomorrow will be the political meeting, an innovation of mine which has been
copied (by order) in the other three corps areas. It is a group which plans and exe-
cutes political action as well as deals in political reporting.*

The Political Committee (the American Consul in Danang, Spence
Richardson, fluent in Vietnamese and a thoughtful observer, military intelligence types, and CIA officers) never did anything. Electoral politics in
Vietnam were an illusion anyway. We knew that the real politics in I Corps
were within the South Vietnamese military, and the few civilian Vietnamese politicians I met seemed ineffectual and diffident. Possibly the
younger ones could have played an influential role in time; but when I was
there, they were regarded with great suspicion by the Vietnamese military,
and their contacts with CORDS were monitored. However, our aim was to
begin to develop a few potential nonmilitary leaders who could help rally
the population in future peaceful confrontations with the communists. It
was an intelligent, long-range approach for a situation that never occurred
but seemed logical to expect while the APC was going fairly well.

Really, everything that CORDS did was politically motivated because
we were concerned with all aspects of the lives of the South Vietnamese:
their self-defense and security, their rice crops, their schools, their roads,
their hospitals, their lives as refugees, and on and on. These were programs

of the South Vietnamese government; and even though we were the initiators of most and provided the financial and material support for all, CORDS always tried to ensure that the Vietnamese received credit for the occasional successes. The avowed purpose was to engender support for the South Vietnamese government.

It did not always work that way. A young Army district advisor in CORDS told me that the only people the villagers in his district disliked more than the Saigon government were the North Vietnamese communists. I took this as candid proof that CORDS in I Corps was trying along the right lines, encouraging conscientious, hard-working village chiefs, pressing constantly through the CORDS system to remove weak or corrupt (usually both at once) district chiefs while rewarding the good leaders like Major Dang in Thanh Binh District in Quang Tin Province (chapter 15, p. 189) with extra help of all kinds. This was a subtle political effort; and while not part of an election process, was producing some genuine, noncommunist Vietnamese leadership at the local level where it mattered.

Letters to my family never mentioned another vital aspect of my work: the harsh unceasing struggle with the communist "infrastructure"—their web of intelligence gatherers, propagandists, tax collectors, underground government officials—who in close coordination with the armed guerrilla units tried to establish control over the population. I kept silent because the operation of this absolutely essential part of the One War was directed by the CIA, and my Foreign Service training had put comment of any sort about that agency out of bounds. This was unnecessary discretion on my part because the American press was aware of everything we did in Vietnam, interpreting it as they chose.

My first briefings in Danang about the enemy underground organization were full of thrilling anecdotes about the elimination of the secret enemy. These involved actions of the Provincial Reconnaissance Units (PRUs), which were advised, and often, I'm sure, actually led by CIA or specially trained American and allied (New Zealand and Australian) military officers. The PRUs were nominally under the direction of the province chief, but some of the units, ranging from 15 to 100 in I Corps, were pretty free wheeling. In one case, in Quang Nam Province, the PRU had to be disarmed. It had more or less hired itself out to the local leader of the Dai Viets (originally a secret anti-French revolutionary party), who was targeting noncommunist political opponents and those local Chinese he thought were interfering in the rackets he had going.

The actual disarming procedure, which I witnessed from a distance, was simple but tense. The PRUs were lined up in their combat gear holding their weapons, told they were to be issued even better equipment, ordered to place their old weapons on a long table, and then marched around the corner of the building, where they were arrested by the province chief and his staff. The leader disappeared into prison or worse, and the rest were returned to regular ARVN units or scattered through other PRUs in I Corps.

Busy as the PRUs seemed to be—in the briefings anyway—it was obvious that they sometimes operated with limited information and did not record carefully what they learned about the enemy so it could be codified and followed up. They often had the flimsiest evidence on which to act and they made mistakes—killing or seizing innocent noncommunists. These were atrocities. Although I heard about only one or two questionable cases, I felt that CORDS had to be concerned.

The CIA officers on the CORDS staffs in the provinces were brave, conscientious, and hard working, but I never was confident that they had brought their Vietnamese counterparts around to any kind of reliable intelligence effort. That only began to happen in July 1968 when President Thieu issued orders to implement the Phoenix program—the first step of which was to establish formal intelligence collection centers around the country. To help the centers get started, the CIA and the American military supplied specially trained advisors, initially of quite modest capabilities because it was not an eagerly sought-after, career-enhancing assignment. By the time I left Vietnam the next spring, I sensed that workable intelligence gathering and disseminating machinery was in place.

Phoenix was just the intelligence element in a far wider drive that was part of the Accelerated Pacification Campaign. The intelligence acquired by Phoenix was used to induce defections, to go after identified VC, and to capture or kill them. By breaking up the communist organizations, Phoenix and its collateral operations sought to lift some of the major miseries of the war from the rural population.

I realize that I have just described in a peculiarly bloodless way an intensely violent process. Phoenix became the focus in the pounding criticism of the war after the program began to produce results in late 1969. I believe that it was at the heart of the war effort, was no different from what the communists had been doing for many years, and, brutal as it was, caused much less pain to the suffering villagers than the heavy firepower and bombing by our side's military forces.

12 December 1968

The recent statements by Clifford and Johnson [urging South Vietnam to participate more heartily in the Paris negotiations] *have had less effect on the Vietnamese we deal with than I would have thought, although all Vietnamese, whether they agree with Thieu or not, don't like to have pressure put on them in public and are proud of their independent position. It does seem from what one can gather in the* Stars and Stripes *or the newscasts that we are changing the terms under which the South Vietnamese agreed to go to Paris. Also, both we and the Vietnamese go about our exceedingly absorbing daily business as if the war and our participation in it would go on forever.*

2 February 1969

Although it is hard to judge from day to day, the pace of the war is gradually stepping up, not in the same way it did last year before Tet, but generally. We are finding more and more caches of weapons and rice indicating that the enemy is "preparing the battlefield," which he always does before he starts. We bring our supplies along behind; he gets them there first. Of course, when we find them, he has to postpone things until he can build up again so we guess his effort won't be as great or even comparable to last Tet. We do expect an increase in terrorism and are taking more precautions.

24 February 1969

A week from today I'm scheduled to leave Danang. Saturday night we had a reception here (for me) despite the fact that we had ample intelligence that the long-awaited offensive was to begin, complete with terrorist attacks in this quarter of Danang. About 12:30 we could hear the rockets and mortars hitting the bases near town, and at 0200 or so rockets began to impact about half a mile away across the river. I saw them all hit. One started a fire in an ARVN ammo dump, and for the next six hours we were "treated" to a thundering fireworks display. Between 0600 and 0800, there were five gigantic explosions besides the run-of-the-mill blasts. These knocked out all the plastic windows—thank God no glass—blew down the curtains and lamps and shook the pictures off the wall. For the first time in all these months, the maid, who was in the bunker we'd built under the stairwell, seemed frightened and began to cry. Gao wanted to come up on the balcony with McGee and me. Some of the shells from the ammo dump were blown all the way across the river, and we had one land in the front yard. It didn't go off, obviously!

We expected more last night and again more tonight, but the enemy has been quiet. I hope the play in the States was more reasonable than previously. The enemy didn't get anywhere. Over 1,000 killed in the first 36 hours in I Corps alone. The Vietnamese have reacted very well, government services going full blast, military unflapped. If nothing happens tonight, I'll begin my farewell calls with a trip to Quang Ngai.

My conscience still bothers me for leaving Vietnam just then, after all that talk about staying the course. I knew I could have stayed on, maybe strengthened our CORDS's effort by working with the new and vigorous Vietnamese provincial officials and the competent Vietnamese military in I Corps, and I was sure that with my hard-won experience there wasn't anyone who could do the job as well. I didn't ask and went back to Washington when my tour was up.

Saigon
5 March 1969

I'm just getting ready for my final packing at Bill Colby's and then on my way. Departure from Danang was sad, especially from the maid and Gao. I still can't believe I'm not going back or am no longer responsible for my beloved CORDS I Corps.

I never became so emotionally involved with another country again.

NOTES

1. Lewis W. Walt, *Strange War, Strange Strategy* (New York: Funk and Wagnalls, 1970).

2. The wife of Ngo Dinh Nhu, President Ngo Dinh Diem's brother, who was also killed in the military coup against Diem in 1963. Nhu was Diem's hatchet man, narrow, opinionated, intense, and ruthless. Nhu's resistance to American advice to stop some of the more egregious persecution of the noncommunist opposition to Diem, and the latter's refusal to rein in his brother, motivated the Kennedy administration to support the coup by a coterie of South Vietnamese generals. The flagrantly beautiful Madame Nhu had added to the Ngo brothers' PR problems by cynically referring to the self-immolation by a monk protesting the treatment of Buddhists as a "barbecue," typifying to many Americans the depravity of the Diem regime. I personally had no illusions about the Diem autocracy, but in retrospect—I was at the National War College in November 1963 when the coup occurred—I believe the coup was a mistake because the United States had no one in mind as a capable successor to Diem. (In this letter I was only referring to the ostentatious display of wealth amidst misery by some South Vietnamese officials.)

3. Philip Goulding, *Confirm or Deny: Informing the People on National Security* (New York: Harper and Row, 1970).

4. Concise summaries of Vietnam War statistics can be found in Thomas C. Thayer's *War Without Fronts: The American Experience in Vietnam* (Boulder: Westview, 1985). Part IV is on pacification.

CORDS, Danang. Theoretically grenade-proof because grenades would roll back down the slanted screen. Never tested during my time. (Refers to p. 164.)

The German hospital ship Helgoland *docked to the right. Her patients and staff avoided rocket attacks on the city by sailing out to sea at night. The Germans were especially effective in medical work in I Corps because of their skills and nonpolitical approach to the Vietnamese. (Refers to p. 173.)*

With Colonel (later Brigadier General) Tom Bowen, the superb, charismatic senior province advisor for Thua Thien Province. I wrote after this visit, "What makes the ordinary Vietnamese so courageous and the leaders, in many cases, so poor? What makes the children laugh and the others so courteous? Why don't they quit when it is all so horrible? It all adds up to people who are really worth saving." (Refers to p. 186.)

District headquarters in Binh Son, Quang Ngai, after an attack. We were standing by the truck when the roof blew off the left side of the building. (Refers to p. 201.)

Chapter 16

Looking Back at Vietnam

The lesson of Vietnam is not that we were right or wrong in being there. The lesson of Vietnam is that we do not know which we were. The further lesson of Vietnam is that we cannot now find out. (Terry McDermott, an Air Force veteran, in a travel article, *Seattle Times*, January 9, 1994)

I guess the truth is we all managed to lose the war together, those of us who fought it, those who ran away, those who protested. (Colonel David H. Hackworth, U.S. Army [ret.])[1]

Shirley and I drove down to the southern tip of Florida right after I returned from Vietnam. Still stupid about the sun as late as the spring of 1969, we put the top down on our slick, blue Buick convertible, raced too fast on the interstates, stayed only at large chain motels, reveled in being unnoticed—comfortable American travelers. Shirley says I talked incessantly about Vietnam, the way I had about the other war I had returned to her from almost twenty-five years before; as then, only the good stuff: the CORDS's Vietnamese and Americans, the courage of the Marines, hopes for success; saving the bad for later. Thus began a process of thinking back and forth about Vietnam, which has continued to this day—drawing conclusions and then rejecting them, looking for new and different meanings, finding none, and retreating to revive old emotions.

This has not been an altogether frustrating process. Hundreds of substantive books have been written on the United States and Vietnam. I have read dozens myself in preparing for classes I taught on that subject at the University of Washington and at Carleton College. Everything has been covered by others. My own conclusions are common and controversial, haphazardly presented here as they came to me in the years since I served in Vietnam. I agree with Terry McDermott that probably there are no abiding lessons of Vietnam despite the varying claims of politicians and scholars. Perhaps the only real relevance to a vastly different post–Cold War America lies in the feelings of the Americans who were there—subjective glances at personal events, their meaning to be interpreted by others.[2]

IMAGE AND STYLE

When we returned from Florida I wrote a short informal piece on "Vietnamization" for Bill Sullivan, who headed the governmentwide Vietnam Task Force. I attacked the term, used by the Nixon administration to cover its long, slow policy of quitting Vietnam, as inaccurate and arrogant, because I felt that the Vietnamese had always been fighting the war—certainly suffering its effects. I thought it was also wrong conceptually because "Vietnamization" implied that we would pull our forces out as the Vietnamese showed they were capable of preventing a North Vietnamese takeover by themselves. Whether they really were or not would be hard to determine; in effect, we would be leaving the pace of our withdrawal to American politics rather than to what was actually happening on the ground in Vietnam. I proposed that a more truthful description would be "de-Americanization," which, although it amounted to the same thing, would simply be a listing of American force reductions as determined by us without public, politics-driven judgments on Vietnamese capabilities. It seems a quibble now, but significant to me then, with the war still going on. Nothing came of this suggestion, which was politically incorrect for that time when both hawks and doves blamed the Vietnamese for our failure in Vietnam.

Six months later I was in Singapore as the American ambassador. Vietnam came up again and again in my talks with the island republic's perceptive prime minister, Lee Kuan Yew. What I heard was a reasoned, hard-nosed, undisguisedly self-centered argument for the critical importance to Southeast Asia of the United States handling correctly its withdrawal from Vietnam (which Lee assumed was inevitable even while the war was still raging).

What struck me then and still does decades later was that, while Lee expressed himself brilliantly in sophisticated Western terms, his thinking was Asian in that he put his strongest emphasis on psychological factors when discussing United States policies toward the area. Here he meant how the United States would appear to Asians, which he invariably tied to the style and pace of our winding down in Vietnam.

Lee was always quite clear about his version of the Domino Theory: If the United States left in such a way that the South Vietnamese leadership lost morale and thereby collapsed, the scared Thailand military would fall from the top almost immediately, followed shortly thereafter, if not simultaneously, by Malaysia, with its sizable population of pro-PRC ethnic Chinese. On the other hand, if some American presence remained after the November 1972 American elections (thus showing, he believed, that a complete United States withdrawal was not related to our politics nor voted for by the American people), then the South Vietnamese would have the confidence and therefore the will to carry on alone, and the other dominos would be enheartened. What mattered was how the South Vietnamese felt. We could judge the success or failure of our withdrawal policy by whether or not the Vietnamese leaders and "informed people" fled the country. If these people continued to stay, even as the United States withdrew, then we had succeeded and "by any definition, you have won the war."

We did not succeed in our basic objective of preventing the North Vietnamese Communists from capturing South Vietnam. Maybe we came closer to winning it in the political sense by the definition of the other countries in Southeast Asia—Thailand, Singapore, Malaysia, Indonesia, and the Philippines—who were encouraged by our continuing presence to form their own grouping by the early 1970s, the Association of South East Asian Nations (ASEAN).

The urgency of Lee's words has long passed. The more enduring aspect of his argument was his repeated emphasis on "morale" and "guts," both leading to his key to the future for Southeast Asia: "confidence." In several well-thought-out private lectures to me, his focus was not on how *much* the United States might be doing with the countries in Southeast Asia, but on our style, particularly in showing "consistency" and "coolness," qualities he professed to admire in the British (when talking to this American anyway!). Our task as Lee would have liked us to see it was to provide the confidence that was absolutely essential if the governments in the area were to deal effectively with their own threatened communist insurgencies and the massive problems of modernization. We would succeed in that by the way we behaved, doing what we said we would, staying when we said we would, showing self-confidence ourselves.

HOW WE BEGAN THE WAR

The Kennedy administration encouraged thinking about the graduated uses of military power as alternatives to Eisenhower's cataclysmic doctrine of "massive retaliation" in the less than all-out war situations typical of most areas of the world. It was assumed that the most immediate application of these theories would be in Indo-China, and the arguments centered on what stage in the process the United States should begin bombing North Vietnam. Easy to figure out were the first possible moves to meet the accepted objective of preventing South Vietnam from being seized by North Vietnam. We would first increase the military advisors, then increase the size of the ARVN and give them more modern weapons for mobility and firepower. These steps would go along with encouraging better handling of the strategic hamlets (the Malayan new villages scheme transferred to Vietnam by one of its originators, Sir Robert Thompson), and other counterinsurgency and "nation-building" measures. If these efforts, taken together and done well by the South Vietnamese government, were not enough to reduce infiltration and VC activity, then everyone accepted that the direct introduction of American military power would have to be considered. The issue of whether or not we would initiate our full military intervention by bombing turned out to be fundamental to our overall approach to the war in Vietnam.

The arguments for bombing before introducing numbers of ground troops eventually prevailed and led in 1965 to Rolling Thunder against targets north of the Seventeenth Parallel in North Vietnam.

Bluntly stated, the rationale for bombing first was that systematically increasing the volume and severity of the attacks would "send a message" to the North Vietnamese leadership that the United States had unlimited capacity to inflict damage with low American casualties. Advancing the targets ever closer to Hanoi would provide incentives for the North Vietnamese to curtail their infiltration of South Vietnam via Laos in violation of the 1962 agreements and even, hopefully, to negotiate the future of Vietnam rather than fight over it. Proponents also believed that evidence of serious American purpose on their behalf would motivate the South Vietnamese.

I found these arguments unappealing then and am convinced that initiating our intervention by bombing was one of the causes for our failure in Vietnam.

North Vietnam lacked the industrial targets whereby an old-fashioned strategic bombing campaign might have made a difference. American (and world) public opinion would not accept a war of obliteration, so the frightful potentialities of an all-out air offensive against people were never tested. But more important than these handicaps, the mind-set of trying to avoid American casualties by relying on the mystique of air power showed that our leaders did not understand the war we would be fighting. The airplane is the most spectacular evidence of material power, so the Vietnamese Communists had to prove the ultimate superiority of the human spirit over machines, whether they sincerely believed it or not. Inevitably, they had to increase their efforts on the ground in South Vietnam or give up. In all such situations the leaders themselves seldom run real risks from bombing.

The other side of the same coin was their belief that "imperialists" would not risk their lives for unworthy causes, such as vague political aims in South Vietnam. Thus, they reasoned, by showing that they and their South Vietnamese allies would suffer, the Americans would find ways to quit. Beginning our direct participation with Rolling Thunder locked into place miscalculations on both sides that persisted until the United States finally called the war off. The Vietnamese Communists did not bend to the limited bombing, doggedly pursuing their kind of war in the South; and despite the casualties, the United States sent waves of ground reinforcements to Vietnam.

MY LAI AND GROUND FORCES

A different aspect of Vietnam also came home to me while we were serving in Singapore. In mid-November 1969, the *Straits Times* and other local papers began to carry accounts of a massacre in Quang Ngai Province during March 1968 (when I had just assumed charge of pacification in I Corps) of hundreds of Vietnamese civilians, mostly women, children, and old men, by troops of the United States Army's American Division. The story was so horrible, I briefly doubted its authenticity—at least for the numbers cited. But one evening in the car going home from a dinner party I found myself trying to conceal my anguish from Mohammed, the chauffeur, after an old friend from Kuala Lumpur days, himself an army brigadier general, told me quietly, "Chuck, I'm afraid it is all true—and they knew about it way up the line."

I kept to myself and Shirley for the next couple of days until forced by my job to meet the embassy staff and the Singapore public, ashamed for my country and bitter that a couple of cowardly, poorly trained, ill-disciplined officers should disgrace us all—and have forever. Later, I was asked to testify under oath in Washington to a Commission of Inquiry established under Lieutenant General William Peers. Because of the distances involved, I eventually submitted a notarized statement saying that there were procedures for reporting incidents involving Vietnamese civilians through CORDS channels. These were not followed because I was not informed. The Peers Commission also determined that the sordid betrayal of "duty, honor, country" went high in the regular command channels. The division commander, Major General Samuel Koster, soon thereafter to be promoted and named commandant at West Point to teach those ideals, had covered up the indiscipline of his own command.

The mass murders at My Lai and the light treatment of the platoon commander, Lieutenant Calley (the only person convicted of a crime but who had his life sentence commuted to three years' house arrest by President Nixon), and of those who covered up the crimes reinforced a series of broad-brush subjective judgments I had already made in Vietnam about the way we had conducted the war. These centered on General Westmoreland's (and Secretary of Defense McNamara's) strategy, or non-strategy, of the "war of attrition."

The concept of inducing the North Vietnamese to stop their war by killing enough of them didn't work because most of the time they could choose to initiate contact when they wanted to and avoid it most times when they didn't. In effect the communists determined their own rate of attrition. They even did so when they threw away the lives of their young by the thousands in the Tet Offensive and in the siege of Khesanh—or casually as they did at Hoi An (chapter 15, p. 194).

The standard essential steps in the American war process of FINDing the enemy, FIXing him in one place so that we could FIGHT him with our firepower were nearly impossible for large American units operating in populated areas. Attempts to do so inevitably blurred the distinction between the armed enemy and his unarmed supporters. For example, supporters overwhelmingly predominated in the area of My Lai for many years, all the way back to the war against the French. Firepower was ineffective against mines and booby traps placed by a sullen population in the way of our troops bashing through the neighborhood. Although there can be no possible excuse for the viciousness of Calley and some of his men, their panic and madness came from their impotence in being unable to hit back at other armed men, even while their buddies were being killed. To them the Vietnamese enemy was everywhere and everyone. This could even become accepted as a natural reaction by combat troops in poorly disciplined and low morale divisions as the Americal was at the time.

This phenomenon is tied to another feature of the war, and one that did not receive adequate notice in comment about My Lai. The opposition to the war and the escaping of the draft by America's better-educated potential small unit leaders produced some "bottom of the barrel" unqualified junior officers like Calley. Because these officers were inferior to their own men, they were afraid of them, tolerant of slovenly soldiering, and incapable of dealing with low morale. These are harsh words about young men who often were asked to do too much; but they reveal a depth of feeling about those who avoided the war, which was not uncommon in Vietnam.

The attrition strategy set the tone of the war away from protecting and controlling the population—that is, away from pacification and hopes of a political result. It also set the standards that determined the promotions of senior officers. This led to a premium on the appearance of aggressive leadership, the need for favorable statistics coming up from the echelons below: the body counts, the numbers of patrols per unit, their time in the field, and so on. This in turn, on the part of the less conscientious commanders, led to the inflation of good results, the camouflaging of the bad, and the dereliction of duty by the likes of General Koster.

THE OPPOSITION

My letters from Danang regularly showed our consciousness of the antiwar movement at home, often considering it a cause of actually prolonging the war. But it was not until Shirley and I arrived in Ann Arbor, as diplomat in residence at the University of Michigan in 1972, a few weeks after leaving Singapore, that I began to appreciate the stylized quality and immensity of the opposition.

In Vietnam we seemed to have spent excessive time answering criticisms of specific aspects of war operations such as refugee care; explaining exhaustively for Congress why tents for immediate shelter were slow in arriving where they were needed; why those particular people became refugees in the first place—all backed up by statistics and our own eyewitness accounts. Insatiable Washington was determined to meet every kind of attack on the war head-on, always on the defensive, always cautiously optimistic. We were never asked to falsify or embroider information or to leave out bad news, but we all knew that public disagreement out of command channels with the way the war was being conducted led automatically to loss of influence.

There is a career officer's moral distinction here. I felt that after General "Abe" Abrams succeeded Westmoreland, we were headed in the right direction and that I was able to get my views forward without having to play into the hands of the opponents of the war. Therefore, I conscientiously played my role as spokesman for the pacification effort in I Corps by being carefully upbeat, describing difficulties, but holding out hope—although only for the long haul. It helped that I generally felt that way anyway. I misunderstood the real opposition to the war, which went far beyond the details to the very national objective of preventing the capture of South Vietnam by the North.

There was probably no better place to learn this truth than at one of the greatest American universities. When we reached Ann Arbor in 1972, some of the steam had gone out of the peace movement, mainly because Vietnamization made the draft less threatening for young men who, even if called, were not as likely to go to Vietnam. Demonstrations on the Michigan campus occurred regularly but seemed orderly and rather passionless. What intrigued me were the numbers of National Liberation Front flags of the Viet Cong that appeared and the placards appealing for "solidarity with the Vietnamese people" in "their struggles against American imperialism"—common enough slogans abroad but jarring to me at home. It was the wholesale rejection of American motives, sometimes expressed in affected, self-righteous tones, that I found painful.

During one lunch hour I wandered into a meeting at Lane Hall, which housed the centers for Asian studies of all kinds. The event featured a young, imported British antiwar activist, a self-described student at one of the British "red brick" universities who claimed "study visits" to both North and South Vietnam. Interrupted by laughter and applause from his graduate student audience, crowded up the old-fashioned staircase and into the halls, he condescendingly compared the "plumes and gold braid" of the South Vietnamese generals with the austere black pajamas worn by their Northern counterparts. I had never seen a South Vietnamese of any rank dressed so fancily, and quickly bored, I stumbled over the book bags and blue jeans and left.

Later that afternoon I was called upon in my tiny office by three graduate students in Chinese studies. The first to come in was a quiet person whose impeccable manners and kindly eyes behind her thick glasses established her upper-class Quaker credentials. The other two were a young couple; he was blond and nondescript; she was dark and striking. There were only three chairs in the room so I perched on the small table, leaving the letter I had been writing to my father on the desk for the male openly to shift around for easier reading. His wife waited until he looked up and came smoothly to the point, inviting me to attend a large public meeting the next day where I would debate the visiting Britisher. She put it, "Explain the American government's position."

I replied that there seemed to be little interest at the university in that aspect of the Vietnam situation. "Then give your own views, after all you were there, weren't you?" I said that there was nothing to be learned from a discussion of American policy in Vietnam with a racially arrogant Britisher. The couple looked smugly triumphant, but the Quaker appeared sad, so in the end I agreed to think it over.

That evening I was to give a talk at the Center for Chinese Studies on "Growing Up in China," such a noncontroversial subject of intrinsic interest only to me that I was momentarily surprised at the excited atmosphere in the crowded hall. This was caused by the young couple of the afternoon, who were hurriedly circulating a petition, which they eagerly showed to me after I had taken the speaker's place. The subject was the signers' objection to the "presence on our campus of someone who had been prominent in the Vietnam War" and asked that I personally appear in public to "explain myself." Several of the younger professors had signed the petition along with twenty or so graduate students. They joined with the young couple sponsors to demand that I agree to such a meeting right then and there. This effort was sharply frustrated by the practiced sarcasm of the director of Chinese Studies, Albert Fuerwerker, who argued for my academic freedom. Half of the audience then noisily walked out. "That was nothing compared to what they were doing last year," he told me later. "Then, they really would have nailed you as a war criminal."

The next morning, early enough to be inconvenient, I telephoned the young couple. "Listen," I advised them, "in a political action ploy of the kind you were trying yesterday, the trick is to get the victim to agree before you challenge him publicly; any other way is childish, showing off, and ineffective."

I must comment here lest I be misunderstood. My recounting of this trivial incident doesn't mean that I regard the national opposition to the war as immoral, superficial, or inept. What I am saying is that I feel opposition became an end in itself. Opposition was useful politics for the Kennedys, as an example; it formed the starting blocks for many of the sweeping social changes of the '60s and '70s, and it brought people together the way the war didn't. However, no matter how the antiwar arguments were marshaled, their largely unrecognized, but inescapable purpose was to convince the people of the United States to accept North Vietnam's seizure of South Vietnam.

That final result had enormous long-range implications for the American military because the ultimate decision to abandon the effort in Vietnam was arrived at through democratic processes. Our military leaders could see that despite the high stakes our elected officials had set for the United States in Cold War terms, despite the sacrifices asked of those who served and the casualties they suffered, and despite our widely advertised promises of continuing support to the South Vietnamese, the United States, in response to its own politics, left the field—although it did so over time. This democratic, nationally determined withdrawal was labeled a "defeat" by American and foreign commentators, particularly the communists. The "Lessons of Vietnam" American military planners learned from this bitter experience were not that the Vietnam War had been fought with the wrong methods but that henceforth wars should be short, have clear objectives and predefined endings; that these wars should avoid American casualties by employing high-technology firepower from the air; that, above all, they should have firm support from the public beforehand as protecting, not merely advancing, clear-cut American interests. These are honest requirements in a democratic society, even one with expensively equipped, professional military forces. They may not be those for an activist world leader in an uncertain, nonideological period, because they are isolationist in intent.

TEACHING ON VIETNAM

In 1984 when I began to teach a large heterogeneous class at the University of Washington simply titled "The U.S. and Vietnam," academics were wondering at the revival of student interest in Vietnam. Professors either had been students themselves during the war period or had felt its effects as teachers on the disturbed campuses of the time. They had quietly pushed the whole unhappy subject aside, not in the sense of foreclosing discussion or study but because they personally did not want to get into it. The students themselves were open-minded and serious, but I had the impression that Vietnam was merely history to them—not quite on a par with World War II, but long ago. Saigon had fallen nine years before when the oldest—except for two or three veterans—were just coming into high school. They wanted to know not so much what had happened in Vietnam but why; what the experience showed about ourselves, how our views of the world during those three decades evolved, and above all, what this violent, painful past about which they knew surprisingly little, really, could teach for the future.

I leaned heavily on lessons from personal experiences for many of my lectures, not only from those in Vietnam, but from Hong Kong in the early 1950s, when I studied Chinese Communist propaganda techniques and saw their effectiveness in mobilizing the Chinese people to extraordinary efforts; from Kuala Lumpur in the mid-'50s, when the British methodically crushed a communist insurgency and insured the eventual independence of that country; from the State Department in Washington during the early '60s, when I watched a tentative effort by the Kennedy administration to provide a start on a larger peaceful arrangement covering Indo-China, which failed because our aims were incompatible with the North Vietnamese Communists' unyielding determination to unify Vietnam under its control; and from London, where I learned to organize arguments for our Vietnam policies, which I used when facing hostile audiences throughout England. These exposures to varied, but connected, aspects of our history in East Asia helped me to shape the course.

I was careful to label my own opinions during the strenuous academic quarters when I taught the course, leaving the students to accept or reject or—most often—ignore them on the basis of the heavy reading I assigned or what they had heard elsewhere. It wasn't until the last sentences of the last lecture that I told them what I felt about Vietnam. I said, in an emotional moment for me, "I believe we were right to try to help South Vietnam, and it was probably inevitable. We did it wrong in many crucial ways, and we paid a terrible cost, but we would have been a different kind of America than we actually were then had we not intervened. Our hopes for that country were better than what they have now."

I could see from their final essay exams that few of the students agreed with me. Nor, I think, did most of my friends, who had not been in Vietnam, to whom I expressed these thoughts—certainly not the public at large.

The idealism that had initially inspired the believers in the New Frontier—and by supporting the coup against Ngo Dinh Diem in 1963 it was the Kennedy administration that committed us irrevocably to Vietnam—has been overanalyzed and discounted. But during the long war, that idealism was somewhere there in the field, even among hardened types like myself, cynical about the hypocrisy of political PR at home, suspecting the real motives of many who opposed the war, fatigued by the bureaucratic struggles in our own government and the South Vietnamese hierarchy we were working with, disheartened by Vietnamese and American corruption all around us. Despite all this, we still felt there was a chance to rally the South Vietnamese by providing a hopeful vision of the future; so we kept on trying—most much longer and harder than I or our country's leaders.

There were no emotional rewards at the end because the United States gave up the effort. But twenty years after I left Vietnam, a student at Carleton—himself a Vietnamese who had escaped as a little boy in 1975—spoke to us all in a note he gave me:

> . . . And I would like to thank you for teaching this class, but more so, thank you for going to Vietnam and risking your life to help my country, Vietnam. Vietnam and America owe you their gratitude. Thank you so very much, from the bottom of my heart. Thanks to all the people who gave themselves.

NOTES

1. Colonel David H. Hackworth, *Hazardous Duty* (New York: William Morrow, 1996), 155.

2. Arnold R. Isaacs, *Vietnam Shadows: The War, Its Ghosts, Its Legacy* (Baltimore: Johns Hopkins University Press, 1997). In my opinion this often moving book is the best of the many efforts to explain the lasting effects of Vietnam on all of us. There is a masterful bibliographical essay.

Singapore—Marine Corps birthday, November 10, 1969. Shirley checks the embassy guard receiving line at the residence. (Refers to p. 223.)

Vice-President Spiro Agnew visits a United States/Singapore joint venture printing plant on his first visit to Singapore, January 1970. (Refers to p. 227.)

Missing a 2½ footer to lose the match to Vice-President Agnew and Prime Minister Lee Kuan Yew. (Refers to p. 228.)

Singapore, September 1971. A laid-back, congenial Governor Reagan of California fascinates the wife of President Sheares of Singapore (center). Prime Minister Lee, next to Shirley on the right, didn't really enjoy nonsubstantive lunches but was a good host anyway. (Refers to p. 224)

With chief of the United States Liaison Office George Bush (right) and his deputy, John Holdridge, at the Summer Palace, Beijing, May 1975. They were a good combination for U.S. interests, both savvy about China and internal politics of the United States. (Refers to p. 244.)

Flags at half-mast for Mao Zedong at the American consul general's residence and the house of senior PRC representatives in Hong Kong. The Chinese wondered why the flags flowed in different directions and slyly enjoyed my Mao-like reply, "Politics determines everything." (Refers to p. 243.)

Vice–Foreign Minister Frederick Chien (left) and government spokesman James Soong at Paisawan, Taiwan. They said President Chiang Ching-Kuo believed that President Reagan had assured him Taiwan could purchase advance aircraft from the United States. (Refers to p. 267–68.)

Chapter 17

Singapore

After Vietnam, Shirley and I were restored to the challenges of the more conventional Foreign Service. Our next overseas postings were successively Singapore, Hong Kong, and Taipei—each absorbingly unique in its way. They did have in common ethnic Chinese populations (although Singapore, 70 percent Chinese, was creating a multiracial state). All three, for different reasons, were apprehensive about the Chinese Communists; all three, as competitors and as collaborators, were full-hearted leaders in the phenomenal economic advances in Asia during the last decades of the twentieth century; and all three represented interesting problems in the management of foreign affairs as well as teaching varied lessons in diplomatic style. We headed quite different American establishments in each of these places.

President Nixon appointed me to be the American ambassador to the Republic of Singapore in the spring of 1969, replacing Francis J. Galbraith, an old friend and the Foreign Service's strongest senior expert on Indonesia. Frank was moving, naturally enough, to Jakarta.

Galbraith had established good working relations with the emotionally complex, supremely intelligent, always fascinating prime minister of Singapore, Lee Kuan Yew, and I understood that my job was to build on this productive relationship. In particular, I was to encourage Lee to maintain his cautious support of the United States role in Vietnam, and my background in Vietnam and China was assumed to be helpful in this. I knew that my other concerns would center on the leaping American investment in Singapore (which, indeed, almost tripled during our stay there) and the disparate and fragmented American population pouring into Singapore to support these investments or to live there in preference to Indonesia or Malaysia while exploring for oil in Southeast Asian seas.

Our first twenty months in Singapore were successful, or so many Singaporeans and Americans went out of their way to tell us. I had not

223

expected a close relationship with Lee and didn't have one. I saw him when I felt I really needed to, and he frequently called me in for long talks about developments in Southeast Asia that were bothering him. Our meetings on these subjects were straightforward and professionally friendly, providing the United States with some hard-headed advice and frank assessments of our policies. We also dealt smoothly, if not always agreeably, with a series of complicated issues revolving around the possible use by the United States of the soon to be evacuated, large British naval base. We discussed the purchase by Singapore of high-performance American fighter aircraft, opposed in principle by Malaysia. I grew to appreciate Lee's determined anti-drug policies, and to advise the American community about them.

We had good contacts with other cabinet ministers, and American business and the embassy operated closely together and with the Singapore government to obtain substantial advantages for American investors. Despite our size as the largest non-British foreign community in Singapore—around 8,000—we were doing all this with a low profile. The American presence blended in as Lee had suggested—"prominent but indistinguishable from the others on the horizon"—rather than looking as though we were taking over as had been the American habit in some other places. We maintained this appearance despite a continuous flow of American VIPs and their retinues, culminating (if we're talking about hierarchy) in the visit of Vice-President Spiro Agnew.

PRIME MINISTER AND VICE-PRESIDENT

Singapore was a nice place for American VIPs to visit. It glistened: glass and white skyscrapers rose from the landscaped green. Utterly clean, there simply was no litter. Air-conditioning was everywhere, even slightly chilling the streets in front of department stores and hotels. Members of its superior golf clubs graciously cleared the way for famous visitors to have a round with the prime minister. Security was efficient and experienced in guarding big shots. Vice-President Agnew visited Singapore twice while we were there.

Such visits are a complicating fact of life for Foreign Service posts. It's not that vice-presidents themselves are especially demanding. The three visiting ones in our experience—Richard Nixon to Hong Kong in 1953, Hubert Humphrey to London in 1967, and Spiro Agnew to Singapore in 1970 and 1971—were each personally polite and accommodating. (I'm told that Vice-President Johnson, suffering Kennedy snobbishness at home, was a notorious exception.) But in small- to middle-sized posts like Singapore, these visits tie up the entire staff in servicing and picking up after the crowd accompanying the vice-president on the trip; humoring the numerous advance agents who, sometimes lacking in social skills, expect unearned deference from their fellow government employees; and obeying the Secret Service with its special absolute requirements as to the timing of events, movement routes, and checking on invited guests and servants. These staff people are hardened in the battle for status in Washington. In Agnew's case, they were quite aware they were on the second team and that their man was only given condescension at best from the press and politicians at home. A glitch-free visit where the vice-president could be seen and reported as doing anything at all in foreign affairs would be a powerful achievement. The vice-president's objectives and especially those of his staff do not always coincide with the actual policy needs of the United States at the particular time but such visits usually proceed anyway, driven by the PR requirements of the administration in power.

Agnew faced a separate personal challenge. By the mid-1960s Lee Kuan Yew had become a favorite Asian leader in Washington because he approved of the American effort in Vietnam, despite Singapore's non-aligned policy. More convincingly articulate than either Johnson or Nixon, both of whom listened to him carefully, he provided an Asian voice—in polished expressive English—explaining the war in terms of Southeast Asian security. Moreover, Singapore's exploding economic successes were unarguably due to virtues Americans admire: self-reliance in the midst of potential enemies, an unexcelled capacity for hard work despite being a tropical country without natural resources of any kind, an open, pragmatic approach to foreign investment combined with an unswerving pursuit of their own development plans, and a conscientious effort to create a multicultural meritocracy under an accountable, elected government. All these captured American respect, and all were rightly ascribed to Lee's leadership, not only by those at the very top in Washington, but throughout the bureaucracy, academia, and big business circles as well. The challenge to Agnew was to be allowed into this fast league and, though badly handicapped by inexperience, show that he could stay. At the time I thought he didn't do badly. I helped him vigorously as part of my job—but also because I rather liked him.

I knew almost nothing about Spiro Agnew before he came to Singapore. He hadn't figured in the enthusiasm over Nixon's election at the highest levels of the Marine headquarters in Danang. The politically conscious generals there dismissed Agnew as a correctly thinking lightweight—correctly thinking because he mirrored Nixon's presumed support for the war and lightweight because no one knew of any special accomplishment. Later, when I was working in the State Department while waiting for my appointment to Singapore to come through, he was

not mentioned at all except in casual, disinterested ways. My mostly liberal nongovernment friends disliked him, but their attitudes reflected
their opposition to the war and Richard Nixon; Agnew was just an extra.
Consequently, having nothing for or against him myself, I successfully
carried out my instructions in the fall of 1969—to elicit a warm invitation
for a vice-presidential visit—with ignorant rather than informed dread.

The first informal response to our feelers to the prime minister's office
about the program details of the visit had been calculated and cool, not
implying that it would be an imposition, but hinting that Lee would
involve himself only in the minimum ceremonials of the state dinner and
the ritual round of golf. Lee professed disinterest to his associates in any
real talk with the vice-president. It was hard for us in the embassy to tell
whether or not this was due to prickliness over a time- and resource-
straining event for the Singaporeans—at their expense—or, which was
always quite possible, some unstated irritation with the United States. At
the same time, presumed confidants of the prime minister began to stress
Lee's warm acquaintance with President Nixon and National Security
Advisor Henry Kissinger, implying that his contacts at the top of the
American government were already adequate. We figured that there had
to be some sort of *quid pro quo* clearly tilted in Lee's favor. I knew that
Agnew could not go home without evidence that he had heard some classic Lee, but I also felt Lee would see an advantage to reinforcing his views
with Agnew directly as one more top American notch to his bow.

I arranged a long call on the prime minister on the basis of a carefully
drafted letter referring to the advisability of my seeing him before the
vice-president arrived. During that meeting I stressed that the vice-president was coming at a critical time. The Nixon administration was carefully spelling out its Asia policies and it was seeking advice from Asian
leaders (sort of long-standing State Department instructions). A grand
policy framework, which had already become known as the Nixon Doctrine, had been announced in the summer of 1969 at a press conference on
Guam and had stressed that American assistance would henceforth go to
those countries set on helping themselves in a framework of regional
security. The conclusions reached by Washington would depend in large
part on the reactions of Asians themselves to their own situations, and
now, more than ever, their opinions would get a good hearing. The vice-
president's tour of Asian capitals and especially his visit to Singapore was
to show our interest. Lee had heard it all before, except for the bit about
the vice-president's trip. His response, which took an hour, was also consistent with what he had said previously, emphasizing the importance for
the United States to appear consistent and reliable.

Like so many dreaded events in my life, the first Agnew visit actually
went well. Air Force Two—a shiny 707, an exciting symbol of power and

prestige, the *United States of America* on its sides differentiating it from the Air Force planes that brought cabinet secretaries and other government VIPs to Singapore—inched to a full stop, perfectly in line with the red carpet exactly at 1100 hours January 9, 1970. Shirley and I, along with forty top officials in the Singapore government (except for Lee, who wisely avoided protocol affairs like this), the entire diplomatic corps, and the superbly drilled honor guard had been lined up in the sun for half an hour, so the precision was appreciated. Singapore, having no practical use for a vice-president, was represented by "Punch" Coomaraswamy, a chuckling, friendly judge of Sri Lankan origin, elevated—if that's the word—to the position for the duration of the visit. He was a friend of ours and later was Singapore's ambassador to the United States.

Agnew loomed over Punch and stood—tall, dignified, and emotionless—through the salutes and inspection of the honor guard, both national anthems, and a hand-shaking tour of the Singaporean and diplomatic greeters. Then, urged by the Secret Service and Singapore's suave protocol officers, we moved quickly to our cars for a ceremonial call on the president and the presentation of a few grains of moon rock by Colonel Tom Stafford, a participant in the moon landings. The vice-president and I rode regally in a magnificent olive drab Rolls Royce, loaned for the occasion by Runme Shaw. Runme and his brother Run Run in Hong Kong were the biggest movie producers and theater owners in Asia.

The first day, I accompanied Agnew and his special assistant Kent Crane, an ex-CIA officer, who had some Southeast Asian experience, to our business meeting with Lee in the prime minister's specially chilled reception room (at his order always below 72 degrees Fahrenheit, part of his heroic efforts to change Singapore into a temperate climate country in thought and deed). Lee gave the vice-president a smooth rendition of his earlier remarks to me, and then the two went off to the prime minister's office for a private chat. This bothered me, as it would any professional, because it gave Lee a future chance to discount things I might say about Singapore's actions or policies—or on the flip side, fail to follow up on points the vice-president might have made. I could tell that Agnew had been mightily impressed by Lee, and as this was the usual American reaction, I realized that egos were involved and didn't press the vice-president on what transpired.

The two got along even better the next day at golf. A round at the beautiful Island Club course had been on the schedule from the first. I had been dismayed that Singapore protocol had ruled out my suggestion that one of the low-handicap military officers at the embassy take my place in a foursome with Lee, Agnew, and Dr. Goh Keng Swee, the alert low-handicap deputy prime minister and minister for defense. The go-between in the matter quoted the prime minister as saying, "He isn't that bad." True, the first time I had played with him in the company of Frank Galbraith, my predecessor, I had performed way over my head, but I had never reached that standard again. My anxiety rose sharply after the embassy's public affairs officer proudly told me that he had arranged for American TV coverage of the tee-off. It peaked when the vice-president and I arrived in our Rolls Royce and saw the cameras mounted beside the tee.

It was decreed that the prime minister and vice-president would be partners, facing the defense minister and the American ambassador. We teed off closely surrounded by the Secret Services and press pools of both countries, the best caddies in Singapore, the chosen members of the vice-president's staff, and, somewhat in danger to the left, the cars and drivers for the group. Lee, as the host ("show you the way") drove straight into the deep rough 150 yards on the right; Agnew hit a high irretrievable pop-up into a clump of jungle 120 yards even further over; Goh, a formidable, determined golfer sent a screaming long shot over the trees out of sight to the left. Momentarily encouraged by the thought that I had usually done better than anything I had seen thus far, I took some easy professional-looking practice swings, and weakly confident, addressed the ball. Then, as the cameras whirred on my back swing, I topped my intended ferocious drive; the ball bounced erratically down the path and stopped in the foot-high weeds by the parking lot five feet from a half-dozen politely unsmiling Malay chauffeurs lounging against Singapore's expensive cars. The cameras, having no other victim, moved with me focusing on the ball, recording for evening TV in Singapore my three frantic flailings to reach the fairway and a desperate wood shot out of danger—and sight.

As we progressed less traumatically, the crowd was winnowed to the unobtrusive Secret Services of both countries, experts in golf security. The PM kept score. Goh had kept us even but we lost the match because last to putt, I missed a 2½ footer on the final hole. Lee, adding pressure, had termed it "a little character builder"; and Goh, who like most Singaporeans played everything for keeps, groaned, "It's not our day," as the ball rolled slowly to rest an inch short. The VP obviously had a good time, and this miserable experience for me may have helped him with the PM. At the time, I thought this would be good for the United States as well.

THE *SINGAPORE HERALD*

The official atmosphere changed rather abruptly in the late spring of 1971 (of course, there are no seasons on the equator) when, for reasons of his own, Lee took on three sacred American institutions at once: the *New York*

Times, whose stringer had written some mildly critical phrases about Singapore, the Chase Manhattan Bank, and the CIA, which Lee accused of collusion in a far-fetched "black operation" involving a local newspaper he wanted closed. We were partially able to quiet the furor over the *New York Times* by arranging for the stringer to leave town rather than face some trumped-up charges. This was not a diplomatic triumph and I was unhappy over Lee's unfairness to a young reporter, but nothing more could be done for the latter at that moment. As it happened, my simultaneous efforts to clear Chase and the United States government from Lee's accelerating attacks ultimately resulted in the Crosses leaving Singapore.

Lee's behavior in this case, although repeated in the years since, remains a mystery to me. He was at the height of his success in 1971, having totally crushed the real and imaginary communists on his island. The noncommunist opposition was rather a joke, sincere but ineffective against Lee's well-organized and disciplined People's Action Party (PAP). His stature in the non-Asian world was so high that he was talked about as a possible secretary general of the United Nations. Why did he react hysterically to his own hunch that foreign governments would subsidize criticism of him, including, illogically, the United States, which was heartily investing in Singapore at the time?

My journal covering this period does not say what Lee objected to in the *Singapore Herald*. The paper was just getting started, but it did carry livelier stories than the dominant *Straits Times*, whose British owners and editors had learned during colonial days not to stray from the acceptable. It is possible that the *Herald* had printed gossip about some preferences given to PAP adherents in Singapore's national service system. Such inferences would have been false, because the draft procedures were fair, and would have been extremely sensitive to the Singapore government, which was using the National Army in its multiracial unifying programs. They would also have provided an adequate basis to close the paper outright under Singapore laws. I think that it was Lee's imagined American penetration into the Singapore press world that set him off, launching his lifetime battles with such journals as *Newsweek*, the *Asian Wall Street Journal*, the *Far Eastern Economic Review*, and others that have appeared critical of him or Singapore (same thing in his eyes).

In short order, Lee:

1. Badgered a Hong Kong member of a prominent Overseas Chinese family, Miss Sally Aw Sian, into withdrawing her monthly support payments to the *Singapore Herald,* which she was making in partnership with the Singapore publishers. The embassy had reports that this took a whole day of nonstop haranguing by Lee himself at his beach hideaway and left Aw Sian in tears.

2. On May 19, 1971, called in the Singaporean Chase Bank officer who handled the *Herald* account and questioned him roughly in the prime minister's own office on how the bank would react to Aw Sian's withdrawal of funds. The officer finally agreed that if the facts were as Lee had stated them, the bank would probably have to foreclose on the $200,000 loan it had made to the *Herald* for printing presses. He pointed out, however, that he was not the boss. Lee then summoned Henry Kwant, the bright, fortyish, hard-working Dutch manager of Chase's Singapore branch, and put the same questions to him. Kwant also replied that he guessed they would have to foreclose, but such a drastic action would have to be considered carefully in accordance with Chase's standard procedures.

3. Brought Kwant back the next day and grilled him unmercifully about the bank's practices in the company of two of the *Herald's* managers and Foreign Minister Rajaratnam. After they had finished to his satisfaction, Lee opened a drawer in his desk and announced that everything said was on tape and that "since we don't do things by half in Singapore," threw open the big doors to his office and invited the bankers to repeat their answers to an immediate televised press conference. Kwant, sad and ashamed of his unbanker-like role, was forced to admit that lending $200,000 to the *Singapore Herald* was "probably not" a good business decision because Aw Sian had dropped out. Lee then went on to infer that there was more to such an error in judgment—a sinister American scheme to subvert the country.

It was all childish behavior for a national leader of Lee's reputation, but because he had embarrassingly caught the State Department twice during the previous few years in denials of attempted CIA operations, I checked with Washington. Formally reassured from there, I devoted the next few days to trying to help Chase extricate itself from a miserable position. Its chairman, David Rockefeller, who was somewhere in Latin America at the time, had been immediately barraged by news organizations from all over the world asking him in the name of press freedom to hold off foreclosing on the *Herald*. After much searching, I was able to exchange thoughts on his dilemma over the well-monitored phone connections. Speaking as much to Lee as I was to him, I advised Rockefeller to hold to the line that the bank would follow its regular procedures and that he would send a high bank officer to discuss this "misunderstanding" with the Singapore authorities. My twofold purpose in suggesting this was to relieve the pressure on Kwant and allow Lee time to find a way out—if he wanted one.

My tactics for damage control of Lee's attacks on the United States were simple enough: respond privately to Lee's allegations or not at all and wait for Lee to cool off. This commonsense approach appeared to be working, but sadly, Washington did not leave things alone.

First, over my objections and without discussing it in depth with the State Department, the CIA sent a high-ranking officer to tell Lee something he knew all along—that, in this case, CIA was not involved. Predictably, this encouraged Lee to elevate the excitement. The CIA representative, a good friend of ours for many years, and I sat directly under the roaring air-conditioner in the palace reception house, Sri Tamasek, and mostly listened while the prime minister laboriously ran through his suspicions of American involvement: Singapore had not heard from the British, with whom they had close intelligence liaison arrangements, and that meant that no communist power was involved but, equally, that a friend of theirs must have been; Australia and New Zealand "weren't up to this kind of thing"; Japan was unlikely; West Germany had no reason; the British themselves were possible but they knew that Lee would react strongly and wouldn't dare; that left only the United States. I asked why Lee thought the United States would be interested in such a project. He replied that we would want to have an influence here in the more distant future and, since it took a long time to establish a newspaper, we would get started on this one. I commented only that this might appear superficially to be a good idea for us but the United States was not involved.

Lee then waded in on Chase and set a deadline for it "to prove that it really is a bank," in other words, foreclose on the poor *Singapore Herald*. I talked him out of that, and we parted calmly—nothing settled. It is worth noting at this point in the story that even during the height of the *Herald* affair, Lee and I maintained good personal relations. I realized that his behavior was due to temporary defects of his personality rather than motivated by deep policy considerations and that an unflustered approach to him would eventually calm him down.

Then, as things began to cool and Lee dropped his public attacks on the United States, Vice-President Spiro Agnew suddenly desired to visit Singapore again—the kind of stopover he had enjoyed before—minus much of the formality, but including golf. I opposed the visit in personal "Eyes Only" cables to the secretary of state on the grounds that it was not the time for "a gesture of esteem on our part"—which it wasn't. Agnew came anyway. He did take my advice and told Lee that he had checked carefully and found there was nothing to the *Herald* story. He wobbled by saying that the United States government was very big and that we would appreciate being told by our friends where we were wrong. Despite this lead, Lee dropped the subject temporarily and shortly afterwards closed the *Herald* using the authority he had had all along.

A couple of months later, in September 1971, we were curtly informed that we were being transferred. The reason given to me informally was that Lee had told Agnew that he "would prefer" another American ambassador. This may have been Lee's true feeling while I was trying to tone down his anti-American tirades, but a member of the vice-president's staff told one of the junior officers at the embassy that Agnew had taken my earlier opposition to his visit personally, fearing that President Nixon would question his ability to deal with even minor international issues. Equally as telling to the staff member was that I was known to admire Averell Harriman, whom Agnew had been attacking publicly for his part in the Vietnam peace process.

We were disappointed by what happened to us, but the whole affair was of small significance to U.S. relations with Singapore. I have described it in some detail as instructive about occasional perils in the career American Foreign Service.

AFTER AGNEW

After Singapore, Shirley and I hoped finally to focus our career on China. The timing seemed right. The secret Kissinger trip to Beijing in July 1971 had upset the Southeast Asian countries' reliance on America's heretofore publicly unswerving opposition to the PRC, on which their own policies had been based. The skillfully executed "opening to China" directed by President Nixon and controlled by Henry Kissinger had actually begun in 1969, the first year of the Nixon administration. But no reliable hints of such a spectacular change in policy had found their way to our corner of the field—although some of us earlier speculated that that hard-headed duo might carry off some less dramatic move. (I had noticed that the Nixon Doctrine, publicized the same year, emphasized no permanent American animosity to China—previously a basic ingredient of Nixon's political career.) Much of my time in the final months of our stay in Singapore was given over to trying to convince people of all kinds—Singapore leaders, Indonesian and Thai diplomats, Japan's ambassador to Singapore (Japan was the country most shocked by this development), and well-known American newsmen drifting through—that this wide swing of the pendulum did not mean that the United States was abandoning the area or dividing up Asia with the Chinese.

Oddly, I was also barraged by instructions from the State Department to lobby the Singapore government to retain the Republic of China on Taiwan's seat in the United Nations while admitting the PRC. This ploy had no realistic chance anyway, but it was simultaneously being undermined by behind-the-scenes advice given to Asian representatives in Washington from the Kissinger region in the bureaucracy not to take it seriously—temporarily increasing Asian uneasiness about all aspects of

United States policies. Privately though, I was excited by the prospects of a new era and the possibilities that Shirley and I might share in.

Our assignment to the University of Michigan as a diplomat-in-residence fit these aspirations. There, I was introduced and guided by Roger Hackett, my friend from Carleton and the Marines. I taught a class on modern diplomacy and guest lectured in several other courses dealing with Southeast Asia. But mostly I concentrated on reading extensively on Chinese subjects, advised by Alan Whiting, who had been briefly a Foreign Service colleague, the economist Alexander Eckstein, and others of the superb faculty that has made Michigan a national leader in Asian studies. The year passed profitably for us.

We returned to Washington in 1973, and I joined the Policy Planning Staff (SP) in the State Department. The atmosphere was self-consciously intellectual and much was made of our detachment from operations. We were expected to service the so-called principals on the seventh floor: the secretary of state, the deputy secretary, and the under secretary for political affairs.

Our methods were collegial. Several members of the staff were genuine scholars, experts in the fields of economic development, or writers on East Africa and the Middle East (serious discussion of the policy implications of Islamic fundamentalism began in SP at that time). The Foreign Service officers were experienced in the areas they covered: mine were Indo-China and China/Taiwan; Richard B. Finn, a star classmate at the Navy Japanese Language School at Boulder, Colorado, did the work on Japan.

The Policy Planning Staff has been valuable to policymakers, but it all depends on whether the "front office" is willing or able to use it—willing to listen to its advice above the clamor of the department's geographical bureaus, able to take the time to think ahead. Thus, during much of 1973 I felt that my own efforts were inconsequential, mainly because the estrangement between Secretary William Roger's State Department and Henry Kissinger's National Security Council apparatus discouraged discussion—in the State Department anyway—of policies for either of my two areas of supposed expertise. Once more our minds ran to going to the field.

That happened sooner than we had expected. In the early evening of October 10, 1973, the telecast of the National League playoffs between the Cincinnati Reds and the New York Mets, which I was watching on an airport television in Omaha, suddenly was interrupted by the announcement that Vice-President Agnew had resigned, having been caught accepting bribes. This was good news, because I had been hearing for months that Agnew's people had been intently blocking us from any new appointment. It was a surprising turn, however. Standing there in the silent crowd, I remembered a rare easy moment during one of his visits to Singapore when Agnew had gently spoken proudly of his Greek ancestry and what the rise to his high position had meant to Greece and Greek-Americans. I thought I understood him in that. In the weeks before his actual fall when rumors about him were discussed, I had refused to believe that he would have almost casually thrown away his reputation.

I was slightly sorry that I had been wrong but glad that the State Department personnel would undoubtedly change directions as far as we were concerned. Sure enough, a couple of days after I had returned from that speaking trip to my office in Policy Planning, I received a call from a previously stiff high-ranking personnel officer asking me in a comradely way whether I would like to go to Hong Kong as consul general. This time we were there for three and a half years.

Chapter 18

Hong Kong Again

Prejudiced in a way, I do not use the words "recovered" or "returned" favored by Chinese commentators for the peaceful transfer of Hong Kong to Chinese control in 1997, because they are inaccurate to describe the vastly transformed rocky island colony the British seized in 1840. I understand the pride all Chinese take in the formal departure of the last foreign rulers over Chinese territory; but no Chinese government in the previous 157 years could have brought about the Hong Kong of 1997. Nor could the British have done so without the extraordinary Chinese people of Hong Kong and the special cosmopolitan breed of other foreigners who have made Hong Kong their home and place of business. This mix of ruler and ruled always existed, and it might be useful to look back at Hong Kong as it was in the mid-'70s when we served there.

Then the State Department treated the glamorous British colony as a country in its own right, important to the United States. Nowhere else was there such free-wheeling enterprise, as mighty fortunes were made from scratch by shrewd hard-driving refugees from China and then lost overnight. Even before computers made possible the wink-of-an-eye transfers of vast sums, Hong Kong had become one of the top four banking centers of the world, the multinational capital of Asia, where hundreds of American companies maintained regional headquarters in the skyscrapers leaping up everywhere. Ships using its constantly modernizing container port had the fastest unloading/loading time in the world. All of this spectacular achievement had been far from assured when we left the first time in 1954.

But there it was—our much-missed Hong Kong—when we came back exactly twenty years later. Surely it was one of the political anachronisms of the twentieth century: a militarily indefensible place administered by a far-removed metropolis, which had long since dismantled the rest of its empire and which, at home, had only a pallid interest in its last major colony, and a free-swinging economy right up against, and essential to, the most tightly controlled communist state of all. In the mid-'70s Hong Kong was a living triumph of practice over ideology. How this was done relates to how Hong Kong will adjust to Chinese rule in the future and vice versa.

It was a break for Shirley and me that Her Majesty's governor of Hong Kong was Sir Murray MacLehose during our entire tour in Hong Kong. In London he had been the cooperative and helpful private secretary to George Brown, the British foreign secretary, and in Danang had been my guest for several days. He and Lady MacLehose, known as "Squeak" to her friends (British nicknames are incomprehensible), immediately welcomed us with a family dinner at Government House when we arrived in Hong Kong in February 1974.

Murray was particularly qualified for his responsibilities. A tall man very much in command, he was the first British Diplomatic Service officer to be inserted into the long line of Colonial Office appointees. He had had much China experience, including service as a Royal Navy "Coast Watcher" on the Fujian Coast of China in World War II, and walked with a slight limp from injuries suffered during that duty. Already honored for his diplomatic career, Murray was knighted again in 1975 for his achievements in Hong Kong (someone congratulated him, "Twice a (k)night at your age!") and given a life peerage by Queen Elizabeth after he had left Hong Kong. I picked up some of the special qualities of the British Hong Kong/Communist PRC relationship from private talks with him in his office or on the governor's old-fashioned yacht, *Lady Maurine*, one of the several nice perks of his job. I believe that even now some of the same subtleties will still be required as the Chinese of Hong Kong try to preserve the former colony's world position under its Chinese rulers.

By the mid-'70s British officials were claiming that the colony and China were getting along better than at any time in Hong Kong's history. The Chinese reacted quickly to the recurring crises over water and food and for several years had avoided provocation along the heavily guarded borders. This forthcoming attitude was ascribed to the value of Hong Kong's contribution to China's economy—then almost 40 percent of China's foreign exchange receipts, for example. Nevertheless, I often added in my briefings on Hong Kong that some of the improvement came from the skillful British handling of the relations with their Chinese neighbors—or, put another way, how smoothly sometimes practicalities can fall into place after a Chinese principle has been acknowledged, even though not formally recorded.

One example I used came from far away, at the United Nations. In 1972, the British simply kept silent after the PRC, which had just supplanted the Republic of China on the Security Council, called on the

United Nations to remove Hong Kong and Macau from the list of colonies to be regularly reviewed by the Trusteeship Council. By not challenging the PRC on the issue, the British indirectly conceded—without practical effect on their control—that Hong Kong was Chinese territory "temporarily administered" by Britain. By tacitly accepting the principle, the British de-emphasized the colonial treaties and resulting legalistic arguments, thereby producing a basic understanding.

Complex issues such as the return of illegal immigrants were successfully negotiated at the local level. The British accepted the Chinese principles that all Chinese citizens permitted by the PRC authorities must be allowed to go "from one part of China to another" and those "illegals" not authorized by the Chinese must be "returned" to PRC control. The British got an informal but carefully enforced limit on the "legals" and a quiet promise that the returned "illegals" would not be harshly punished. On occasion, the British would apprehend PRC agents in Hong Kong who they felt were overactive. The agents were not brought to trial, and eventually the British quietly notified the Chinese that one of their citizens would be delivered at the border crossing at Lowu on a certain date. The PRC accepted the detainee without any question.

THE NEW CHINA NEWS AGENCY

The colony's busy equivalent to a foreign minister was its political advisor, Alan Donald, also a British Diplomatic Service officer, later Her Majesty's ambassador to China. Alan not only talked freely and candidly about Hong Kong's own relations with the PRC—always tricky, but not invariably unfriendly—but also about China itself. He had served at the British embassy in Beijing during an unpleasant phase of the Cultural Revolution but was able to assess events in China coolly in the light of the British position in Hong Kong. His political dealings with the PRC were through the New China News Agency, which became the representative office of the PRC's in the colony after 1949. He was also responsible for the British side of the several other ad hoc arrangements that kept the Hong Kong/China border peaceful.

The reasoning on both Chinese and British sides for this arrangement was clear enough: The Chinese would not maintain a consulate because that would imply that Hong Kong was a foreign territory; the British would not allow the stationing of a Chinese commissioner or special representative there because that would imply that the PRC had some legalized relationship with the Chinese living in the colony. Like so much of diplomacy with China, the informal NCNA machinery worked well for the very reason it did not officially exist—but everyone knew it did.

Consulate general officers met with NCNA on several levels, starting very slowly but becoming quite extensive by the time Shirley and I left toward the end of 1977. Chinese attention to hierarchy meant that I dealt only with Li Zhusheng, their top man, at Hong Kong's interminable receptions. We never met by appointment because we couldn't admit to having official business to conduct, but he or I would let someone on the other's staff know if we wished to ask for a comment on something that was happening in either of our countries. We usually talked through his worried young interpreter if he had something significant sounding to ask; but when the Gang of Four were arrested, Li expressed his satisfaction to me in Chinese. It was the beginning of the end of Maoism, although neither of us hinted at it.

Almost thirty years of the ups and downs of their leaders had bred caution into all Chinese, but we almost immediately sensed a lifting of spirits at NCNA after the four power-crazy cultural revolutionaries were abruptly removed in September 1976. A corresponding willingness to begin approaching the borders of frankness followed. This relaxation extended to Fei I-min, the talkative editor of *Ta Kung Pao*, one of the two major PRC-controlled papers; to the officers of China Resources, China's state trading organization; to the tall Harvard-educated head of the Bank of China; and to others of the growing PRC establishment in Hong Kong. By late 1976 these and others began to accept invitations to our official-looking residence on the Peak—after checking on who else was coming to avoid being singled out as having a special relationship with Americans. These modest "get acquainted" receptions for American businessmen and traveling academics along with consulate general officers occasionally led to productive contacts—a slow loosening up.

AND THE UNITED STATES

At an early meeting, MacLehose stressed that the United States and the People's Republic of China were the two basic facts of life for Hong Kong. He meant no hint of United States responsibility for the political future of Hong Kong, because the United States did not have a strategic interest in Hong Kong nor had we ever been involved in the internal affairs of the colony and its relations with China. However, even though the British ran the place, the United States was the predominant foreign influence. We were Hong Kong's biggest customer and its largest foreign investor. Already sixty American banks were represented there and taking a larger and larger share of Hong Kong's burgeoning financial activities. Visits by the U.S. Seventh Fleet were the only appearance of real military power visible to the colony because the British had drastically run down their forces. Clothing styles of the young, television features, and even the food consumed by large sections of the population were increasingly Americanized; 12,000 Hong Kong students studied in the United States. These ties increased in the next decades, beyond our most optimistic estimates. Thus, while it was possible for policymakers to say that there was no vital U.S. interest in Hong Kong, that was not the assumption of a growing number of Americans who had reasons to worry about the absorption of Hong Kong into the PRC.

The Chinese takeover was to happen in a hurrying twenty years. How Hong Kong would survive the interim with no natural resources and without defenses would depend—as it always had—on the energy and initiative of the Chinese and foreigners who came to live and work there. Hong Kong would thrive only if its people felt that the termination of the lease on the New Territories in 1997 would not bring the essentially independently operating Hong Kong to an end. As Lee Kuan Yew had warned earlier, that confidence could only come from American steadiness and constancy throughout East Asia. The nervous, intense, local Chinese would not be impressed by rhetoric and propaganda but would react to what the Americans actually said and did. In this respect, the United States was fortunate in the sophisticated and energetic American presence in Hong Kong.

We listened to President Nixon announce his resignation on the morning of August 9, 1974, in the consulate's crowded conference room. Immediately, we were made aware from sources around the colony that Hong Kong Chinese were watching the reactions of Americans to what they regarded as a disturbing development. Nixon had set Sino-American relations on a new path of great potentialities for Hong Kong. What did his fall really mean? Moreover, his misdeeds, as publicized, were incomprehensibly trivial to Chinese eyes; there must be hidden motives, naturally concerning China.

I issued a statement for the local press in Hong Kong, copied from one by Secretary of State Kissinger, stressing the continuity of the presidency. This was augmented, without any prompting on the consulate's part, by similar statements carrying the same message from Hong Kong's vigorous American Chamber of Commerce and several visiting American scholars and journalists who were invited to talk on television. What came through was that constitutional procedures were followed without fuss and fanfare. The image of continuity conveyed by the American presence was that China policy would not regress.

Another example of steadiness came from Vietnam. Saigon fell to the North Vietnamese on April 28, 1975. Along with many others, we in Hong Kong had felt for several weeks that this was inevitable. An Army major in the consulate had briefed the American Chamber Board of Governors three weeks before the fall, accurately foretelling how the battles would develop. For weeks, at the requests of companies and organizations, we had been forwarding to the embassy in Saigon lists of Vietnamese employees for possible evacuation. Several consulate wives served as nurses on planes from Saigon taking orphaned babies to the United States. Nevertheless, the final fall came as a shock, and I suspect that most Americans, particularly those in Asia, reacted in highly personal ways.

The consulate had people who had served in Vietnam, including me. Many businesses and relief enterprises involved with Vietnam were also headquartered in Hong Kong. Among us there was concern for the Vietnamese themselves—derided by some, patronized by others, appreciated and respected by those who had stayed with them the longest. It was impossible for us to be indifferent to their fate. The American community made an immediate, highly sustained, and highly organized effort to assist the overburdened Hong Kong authorities in handling thousands of Vietnamese refugees plucked from the South China Sea. Shirley and I went out to the airport at midnight for several nights in a row to say good-bye to Hong Kong and welcome to America to hundreds of calm Vietnamese bound for Guam—little speeches heavy on the immigrant tradition, translated into Vietnamese by the beautiful wife of one of the consulate's officers.

The humanitarian effort was to be expected, but more important politically was the general American response to the changed situation. Our long involvement, the treasure, and above all the lives expended required the United States to take another look. Nowhere would the process be more acute than in this area where Americans who knew the most about Vietnam lived. Vietnam ran deep in our country then, and the effort could be abortive and turn accusative. Or we could do things in ways that would appear to the people of East Asia as the result of fatigue or loss of interest. The United States followed neither road. We consciously forced ourselves to look to the future. Commitments were reaffirmed; long-range economic programs in Asia were deliberately shown to be unaffected; and above all, the American presence remained.

From a parochial State Department viewpoint, Hong Kong was a magnet adding enthusiastically to the American presence. Its glitter drew floods of congressional visitors, active and retired military brass, American politicians of all kinds, religious leaders like Billy Graham, university presidents, major American CEOs, hundreds of thousands of tourists, and thousands of other well-connected, influential citizens. We didn't see them all, of course, but how these visitors were briefed on developments in China—especially the state of Sino-American relations—or were assisted in their journeys or their business, or received by the consul general, had a bearing on the style of the whole American presence. Our guest book shows that we "entertained" officially 2,432 people in the nine months after we arrived in 1974.

WATCHING THE PRC II

The PRC, Hong Kong's other fact of life, filled the other half of our working days.

By 1974 the consulate general in Hong Kong had been the main American China Watching post for twenty-five years. Its function had not qualitatively changed with the creation of the United States Liaison Office in Beijing the year before, although the United States now had much needed representation in the capital. However, USLO, the precursor to a regular embassy and soon to be headed by George Bush, was still restricted in staff, access to Chinese, and ability to travel freely. The Hong Kong consulate's greatest advantage was its staff of experienced Chinese, who provided institutional memory and canny insights for the regular reports sent in by its trained American officers.

Much information was elaborately extracted from Chinese provincial newspapers, at that time officially unavailable in Beijing to foreigners but obtainable secretly in Hong Kong. American journalists covering China were based in Hong Kong, had their own sources, and were eager to exchange guesses about what was going on. American scholars, fresh from visits to China, came in for long discussions of developments in their fields. All China Watchers had access to the facilities of the University Services Center, a descendent of the Union Research Center that started during our first tour in Hong Kong twenty years before.

There were the usual calls for recarving the bureaucratic turf, but the key career officers in Beijing had all served in Hong Kong; the reporting officers in Hong Kong hoped to be assigned to China eventually. Except for occasional flashes of professional irritation over the interpretation of events—and some scorekeeping by both posts on successful guesses—the two posts worked well together.

The consulate general "watched" China from numerous angles, through mazes of often grossly cooked statistics, trying valiantly to reflect the United States government's interest in what was going on— namely everything: wheat production by province; China's oil reserves; new policies for the communes (now gone but then the essence of communism); the prospects for China's multiyear economic plans; possible joint ventures with the PRC in Hong Kong; China's expanding population (once we thought we had discovered the population of Guangdong Province by noting a story in a Guangzhou paper boasting about a provincial swimming program, which claimed that 20 percent of the province, or so many million people, knew how to swim); comprehensive analyses of China's foreign exchange reserves and moves into international banking; nuances of differences between the "party line" in Beijing and the communist press in Hong Kong. As it had for twenty-five years, the political section edited material to be translated for the *Survey of the China Mainland Press*. The service attachés and the CIA added information and leads derived from their special sources and methods.

The entire post worked on assembling biographic information on Chinese at all levels—who is on top?—who is going down?—what happened to so-and-so in the Cultural Revolution?—what did the publicized shifts in a high military command mean?—building up background files on hundreds of individuals, some going back to Howard Boorman's original files of the early '50s (chapter 8).

This list touches on only a fraction of the subjects covered by the consulate general's officers who represented fourteen U.S. government departments and agencies plus the State Department. USLO in Beijing, steadily expanding the scope of its coverage during the years Shirley and I served in Hong Kong, worked with information it had obtained in China itself, commented on our reports based on their own observations, and reported on all aspects of Sino-American relations and on conversations with friendly ambassadors in Beijing.

Our embassy in Taipei occasionally learned of developments on the mainland. Foreign Service officers at posts all over the world added local insights on Chinese affairs and traded information (as I had done in London [see chapter 12]). All the products of this mighty, fairly well-coordinated labor ended up in Washington where they were reanalyzed, cross-referenced among the numerous interested agencies, discussed in detail with scholars, argued back and forth between the State Department and CIA, and eventually synthesized into short reports and studies. It might not be saying much, and is an unverifiable claim, but the United States was then possibly the best, certainly the most, informed nation in the world on China—including China itself. I often wondered whether all this knowledge was valuable to policymakers in Washington—as against storing it up for the whole country's general background.

Furthermore, as we saw it in Hong Kong, there was little the United States could do about developments in China. Chinese internal politics lacked logic, bound up as they were in bundles of ruthlessly competing personalities under a Mao Zedong who retained power even while his consciousness was fading. China had only just begun stumbling from the insanity of the Cultural Revolution by the mid-'70s. Her great leaders were dying: Zhou Enlai, possibly the only loved one, survivor of purges over the decades of revolution and communist power, symbol of stability, went first in December 1975; Zhu De, the founder of the Chinese Red

Army a few months later; and the senile Mao himself finally succumbed at eighty-three in September 1976, a few weeks after one of the century's most devastating earthquakes struck North China.

During our tour, Deng Xiaoping was almost fully rehabilitated from his place as Mao's leading "capitalist roader" target, then kicked out again shortly after Zhou's death by the Gang of Four—leftist extremists including Mao's wife left over from the Cultural Revolution. The ups and downs of this small, tough, Long March veteran who eventually turned the PRC away from Maoist foolishness—but not from Communist Party control—gave us clues but no final answers to what was happening in China. We watched him disappear from public view in April 1976 only to surface in January 1977, living comfortably in South China, reported by a Chinese source to us as bowing to a group of smiling and clapping officials at whom he sardonically shouted *pi Deng; pi Deng* ("Criticise Deng; Criticise Deng")—a slogan officially still in use at the time. He returned to Beijing in the summer.

The French consul general, François Geoffroy Dechaume, followed Deng closely. I tried to see François once a month, not so much to hear the French interpretation of events but to learn about China. He spoke beautiful, colloquial, well-educated Mandarin and could describe conversations with Chinese by emphasizing key points in their own accents. One story provided a Sino/Gallic turn to the famous statement Deng used in the stormy initial attacks on him for defaming Maoist revolutionary spirit. Deng had enraged his Maoist enemies with a colorful argument for pragmatism: "It doesn't matter whether the cat is white or black as long as it catches mice." Disregarding the obligatory quality of "Redness" had led to Deng's painful, although temporary, downfall. François joked to his Chinese friends, "What the fanatics meant to say was 'It doesn't matter whether the mouse is black or white as long as the cat is Red.'"—actually a good description of China then. François and his Irish-born wife, Nellita, were posted to Rangoon after Hong Kong. There this refined diplomat, deeply at home in three languages and cultures, was killed in a car crash, a loss to China Watching and to us as a friend.

CHINA TRIP

In May 1975 Shirley and I made our first trip to the PRC. With commendable reserve for a consul general, I had properly waited my turn in the State Department–decreed slow rotation of the consulate general's China Watchers to experience a bit of the real China and improve our skills. The obstacles to more frequent travel were not all American. All travel by foreigners in China was closely controlled by Beijing, and permission was granted only after a capricious application process. Because the State Department under Henry Kissinger hoped to avoid the tit-for-tat diplomatic travel battles that occupied the time of numerous American and Soviet officers in Moscow and Washington, it was reluctant to press too often for trips from the consulate general. However, the patience and firmness of the United States Liaison Office in Beijing enabled us to establish a routine of sending an officer every few weeks. All those eligible when we arrived in Hong Kong in March 1974 had already gone. Their colorful accounts inspired envy.

We went by a comfortable, clean, on-time train from Guangzhou (Canton) to Beijing, where we stayed ten days as guests of Martha and John Holdridge, the DCM, conducting business with the United States Liaison Office headed by George Bush, visiting historic places in and near the city not damaged by the Cultural Revolution, and hoping to be allowed to see more of the country. As it was, all requests to go to Xian (Qin Shihuangdi's clay soldiers then being unearthed) and even to look for my old house and school in Tongzhou, already incorporated into Beijing, were refused as being *bu fang bien,* "inconvenient." We managed to extract several days in Shanghai on the way back, as well as a more-than-enough two nights in Guangzhou's disintegrating Dong Fang Hotel, the resting place for foreigners visiting the annual international trade fair, then the starting point for almost all commercial relations with China.

The brief little incidents described here portray an exhausted society forced into monumental hypocrisies, sustaining fakery on a national level about the incessantly praised Cultural Revolution and concealing miseries we could only guess at. It was the last year of Mao's life, and the differences in China then and now have had to be seen to be believed. I remind myself of these extraordinary changes when I look at today's China and realize that, despite the Tiananmen Massacres and the daily denial of certain human rights everywhere, it is a better China for its people.

It took almost a day to leave Hong Kong. We crossed the border at the Lowu Bridge, where as an engrossing part of my work over twenty years before, I had met family friends and other foreigners emerging to freedom from communist prisons and house arrests. I felt the same indefinable tension of those more dangerous days as I watched the smartly turned out Hong Kong Chinese policeman silently eyeing the Peoples' Liberation Army soldier in his loose mustard-colored uniform, a bright red star on his cap and cradling an AK-47 automatic rifle, who stood sentry just beyond the midpoint of the bridge. The two Chinese did not speak to each other.

On the Chinese side we were received impassively, without noticeable interest, although the China Travel Service moved us quickly to the special waiting room for foreigners, where we filled out forms and stood by ourselves for hours. Like Intourist in the Soviet Union, the *Liuxingshe* had made all the arrangements, produced personnel to keep us from straying from the paths assigned to us, and solved with dispatch any big problems, like changing reservations. Usually distantly cheerful, they were really the only Chinese we were able to talk to aside from those officials we met in Beijing. We tried throughout the journey to get at the personalities behind the smiling masks. Two flickering moments stand out.

The officious young man meeting the train at Guangzhou was obviously a type. His sharp commands in the Mandarin of Northern China to the porters handling our bags and his slow but eager English marked him as a person who, unlike most Chinese then, did not seem to worry about being noticed. I responded coolly to his immediate personal questions about us, our ages, our family, where we lived in Hong Kong. However, trained from childhood to expect these intrusions into people's lives and even to regard them as polite interest, I let him practice his English. Abruptly, though, he switched to Chinese and asked about the consulate general. I didn't tell him anything that wasn't known to the man in the street in Hong Kong, but I sensed that I could learn something about the Chinese attitude toward our establishment and let him go on. He soon came to his point and inquired about the number of our employees: "How many people do you *guan?*" using a word with several meanings but which I chose to interpret as "boss." I gave him a figure that had appeared in the English-language press in Hong Kong of "around 400" but went on to scold, "In democracies like America we do not use words like '*guan*' because that puts one person over others."

That concept, so expressed, surprisingly loosened him up, perhaps as an indication Americans were as given to ritual cant as Chinese. Uncharacteristically for the times, he began to chatter about himself. He was indeed from the North, near Tianjin, and had been "sent down to the countryside" during the Cultural Revolution, when former Red Guards were deported to rural areas "to learn from the people." He apparently didn't spend too much time with the peasants, because after a stop in the big city of Wuhan, he came to Guangzhou. He learned English "from a friend," passed an exam, and got his job with the China Tourist Bureau. In answer to my question, he said that he hoped to rise to the top of the China Travel Service in Guangzhou (and presumably "*guan*" other Chinese). We were fascinated because we were hearing naked ordinary ambition of the kind normally concealed by young Chinese, who invariably replied in the words of the communist catechism when asked about their plans: "To serve the people" or "Serve Chairman Mao." We were tasting the future in China but didn't know it.

In Shanghai the required China Travel Service guide was a dignified, but sad, fiftyish man who, after introducing himself at planeside, announced in excellent English that his best foreign language was really French. He then spoke to us in Chinese. He was evidently a sort of overseer. Unlike the younger guides, he was unperturbed that the American consul general in Hong Kong and his wife had the bad habit of wandering about on their own between the formal sightseeing. Having met us, he saw us off. We chatted during the long wait at the airport while seated on a wooden bench outside the terminal—to separate us from the other passengers—slowly working around to his own experience, about which he revealed little. He said that he had been "sent down to the countryside" for several years but didn't elaborate on how long or where, adding unconvincingly, the usual, that he had "learned from the people." However, he must have sensed that we would be sympathetic to more than the routine and disclosed quietly that his only son had also been sent away at the same time, to the far north in Heilongjiang on the Soviet border. Phrasing my question carefully, I asked when he expected the son to return. He looked at his hands resting spread out on his knees and after a long moment said only, "We never received letters."

XUEXI ON THE TRAIN

Meals on the train from Guangzhou were not convivial affairs. Although the dining car was just ahead of us and seemed unoccupied most of the day, diners were summoned separately by status and nationality so that Chinese and foreigners would not be burdened by each other or, most disappointing to us, talk to each other. First to sway slowly past our door was an old—probably very important—People's Liberation Army general, supported, as was reported to be Mao's habit also, by two not unattractive female soldiers. His jacket had the two extra pockets of an officer, but he wore no other badges of rank. A comrade general sharing his end of the car, and who may have suffered a stroke, had to be carried onto the train in an ancient wheelchair and never left his compartment. The latter's medical staff sat in the aisle during the whole trip and joined the military entourage at the first sitting for meals. Then followed in short order groups of civilian cadres wearing good quality, dark blue Mao jackets. No real ostentation; the atmosphere of power was conveyed by subtleties.

After the Chinese had all returned forty-five minutes later, the first of the foreigners were summoned: she, the spectacular wife of a Scandinavian diplomat in Beijing, blonder than blond; he, not her husband, who had seen the pair off at the Guangzhou station—foreign goings-on, which fascinated the otherwise surly car attendant. Next asked was Mr. Seti, an Indian diplomat on his way back to his post in Ulan Bator. He had begun the trip assigned to our compartment, but he had stocked up so heavily on records, tapes, books, and other bulky material to get through another couple of years of his "horribly isolated" life in Mongolia that there was not enough room for him, his baggage, and ours on the two top berths. A move to another compartment for our fellow diplomat and part of his baggage was accomplished without grace by the "car worker," although, it is necessary to add, without a bribe or a tip either. Mr. Seti shared the compartment with a silent Chinese high official and spent much time talking to us in ours.

We were invited last; and when we arrived for our breakfast, only the Indian remained. The waiter curtly refused our mutual request to be allowed to join him, "*bu xing*, out of the question" and no explanation. Chastened, we looked out the window and ate our scrambled eggs at the other end of the car. Personnel from other parts of the train strolled in for snacks or a second breakfast. They were assembling for their daily *xuexi*, or study session, based everywhere in China those days on a passage from Chairman Mao's "Little Red Book," which each Chinese always seemed to have with him.

By 1975 the Chinese had practiced Maoist methods of indoctrination for over twenty-five years, and I had never gotten over my uneasy amazement at their totality. The mighty campaigns had marched one after the other to stir and exhaust the Chinese people: land reform in the earliest years of the regime, wrenching the countryside, violent on purpose, killing hundreds of thousands; the "3-Antis," officially against corruption, waste, and "bureaucratism" but really attacks on the "national capitalists" (those businessmen who had stayed in China to help the new regime); followed by "Oppose America/Help Korea," which had featured silly attempts to prove by concocted physical evidence that the United States was conducting germ warfare against the Chinese peasantry. In 1956 a colorful slogan drawn from the classics, "Let a Hundred Flowers Bloom; Let a Hundred Schools of Thought Contend," became an official invitation to sincere criticism, which cruelly turned against the critics from the intellectual elite in the immediately following "Anti-Rightist Movement," heartily participated in by Deng Xiaoping. The catchy sentiments of the "Great Leap Forward," Mao's disastrous whim to transform China by channeling the strengths of its people into massive nontechnological cooperative efforts at production, resulted in the commune system throughout the country, experiments with small steel furnaces, and public lying on such a scale that for years realistic estimates of deaths by starvation—actually in the tens of millions—were not fully accepted by the outer world. Then came the "Great Proletarian Cultural Revolution," a nearly ten-year disaster by 1975 whose deep scarring of relationships between Chinese were still being felt. The two major campaigns of the mid-'70s were "Criticize Lin (*Biao*); Criticize Confucius"—pointed indirectly at Zhou Enlai by Mao's wife and the Gang of Four—and "Water Margins," which turned one of the classic stories of Chinese literature upside down by attacking one of its heroes—also aimed at Zhou, but more noticeably.

Campaigns were preceded by often hard to discern hints in key party publications that provided much of the stuff of China Watching. These led to editorials and slogans in the mass media, followed by larger meetings in different parts of the country, then huge gatherings everywhere, then "study" in small groups at work until, frighteningly, everyone was saying the same thing at the same time. Before we discovered how to lower—but not turn off—the speaker in our compartment, we listened for long hours to continuous "inspirational" revolutionary music interspersed with impassioned lectures on the dictatorship of the proletariat, self-satisfied descriptions of the defeat of American imperialism in Indo-China, reminders on brushing teeth and on not letting children urinate on the car floors—none differing in emphasis and all delivered in the excited high-pitched tones of used car commercials at home.

As we observed it, *xuexi* on the train was short and to the point: The leader quickly read the entire text for the day from "The Little Red Book"—perhaps two paragraphs—to the group, most of whom were smoking and gazing out the window. He spoke to the man sitting next to him, "*Li tongjr* (Comrade Li), please explain about this subject." Comrade Li read the first sentence of the text in an assured voice. "Comrade Wang, do you have any thoughts to express to us?" After a few seconds Comrade Wang then read the last sentence of the text. The leader thanked him and turned to working matters: "Today the stop at Changsha will be ten minutes."

Other consulate and USLO travelers had observed the same casual treatment of the sacred texts elsewhere. I now think that we may have been reluctant to personalize our China Watching and perhaps underemphasized in our reports these small cracks in the Maoist façade. We were, after all, trying to follow the battles among the leadership at the top of China and cautious about injecting mere atmospherics into our analyses.

A SCHOOL

Shirley and I requested to see a secondary school in Shanghai, giving as our reasons that Shirley was a teacher and that we were particularly interested in the examination system, which was said to be based on "combining learning with practice." The visit was easily arranged. We were taken to a former Catholic girls school in the old French Concession area, turning into a narrow opening in the high, thick wall that surrounded the compound and drove straight onto a basketball court, interrupting a game like an imperialist of old or a modern party functionary. A group of twenty-five or thirty greeted us with applause, and we perfunctorily clapped back.

Shirley described the school as "incredibly dark, dingy, dirty, rusty." She couldn't believe that it had 2,600 students, both boys and girls. Her journal description: "We were met by the principal, a singularly ugly woman about fifty wearing a rumpled gray Mao jacket and pants and faded army green, very big tennis shoes, the kind issued to soldiers. Chuck made the mistake of asking her if she were the principal and was informed crossly that such terms were not used, that she was the vice-chairman of the Revolutionary Committee." I had forgotten that after the Great Proletarian Cultural Revolution all institutions were supposed to be run by Revolutionary Committees, and that in the whole country there was only one chairman of anything in 1975—Chairman Mao.

Joining a small throng, we hurried through the decaying halls to a clean and orderly conference room with two long tables, a covered tea mug at each place, and the Revolutionary Committee of the school seated in a row. The vice-chairman announced that because Shirley was a teacher, this meeting would be "an exchange of experiences" and described the school as one where "all groups" learned from each other. By contributing to joint efforts, the whole would "advance as one in the service of the people." She then called on members of the Revolutionary Committee to describe their roles.

A janitor, probably was the only genuine "worker" on the ground, was chosen to speak first. It was clear from his hesitant tone and his frequent glances at the vice-chairman that having to perform most of the productive labor in the school himself, he wasn't sure what he should say he was learning from the rest. He ended up by claiming with a small smile that he had learned to work with others, translated quickly by the well-versed interpreter to "he learned the strength of unity." A young male math teacher, obviously suffering from advanced boredom (the school was constantly being visited by foreigners), described how all the problems he gave his students dealt with "concrete and practical matters." A self-confident sixteen-year-old boy representing the students explained that there were no academic examinations because admission, promotion, and status in the school depended on class background and recommendations from work units rather than academic qualifications as they did in "the old society." Pompously, he gave an example of a recent examination at a nearby commune where the students "worked with the peasants" several weeks each year. There they were tested on the repair, maintenance, and operation of the commune's tractors, which they had learned from "direct experience." He maintained this was different from student experience in other societies.

There was no discussion and no "exchange of experiences." We were asked if we had any questions. When Shirley asked one and we had waited for a reply, we were told to ask all our questions at once and they would be answered in order. Because there would be no way to follow up, we produced only a couple of queries on schedules and daily routines. They asked us no questions and made no comments on our few polite expressions of interest. Both we and they were relieved when we gave up and accepted a tour of the three workshops the school conducted: to put the students in touch with the people, to teach them how to serve the people, and, less ideologically, to bring some money into the school.

We saw an anti-communist caricature. We were led down black, oily, worn stairs, past broken and rusted security mesh in the stairwells, to cluttered, unsafe work areas in the remnants of the old classrooms. In the electricity workshop, which made small transformers, the only persons really working were a couple of the "people," a pair of old ladies, "hoping to learn to help in their retirement." There was slightly more student activity in the carpentry shop, which was making and repairing primitive table-desks for the school. The machinery workshop had some antique lathes, and the youngsters assigned there were sanding and repairing old electric fans for use by the people. Nonchalant indolence was evident everywhere.

As a final treat, we were invited to sit in on a rehearsal for the school's celebration of the thirty-third anniversary of something Chairman Mao had said or done. A good orchestra of Chinese instruments played an ear-splitting number; then a girl with an accordion accompanied a girl singer in the song that had caused the cancellation of a group's performance in the United States, "We must Liberate Taiwan." We listened impassively and did not applaud with the others.

The sixteen-year-old walked out with us to the car still parked in the middle of a furious basketball game. Trying to be friendly, I spoke in Chinese for the first time: "It must have been interesting to drive a tractor at your age, coming from the city." "We didn't drive the tractor." "Still it must have been difficult to repair one because they are big machines." "The commune Revolutionary Committee did not want us to work on them." "Anyway you could watch them being repaired." Sheepishly now, "We did several times." I didn't feel sorry for catching him out so completely. He might even have thought that he did learn something (that real Chinese farmers worked really hard and that it would be best not to get too mixed up with them). In the meeting he had said exactly what was expected, and it was beside the point if the foreigners were not fooled by his blatant nonsense. No one was really supposed to believe it; it was just required to speak it well. Everyone in the country acted, especially the radical leadership of the Cultural Revolution then in charge in Beijing. The boy was just an ambitious sycophant like everyone else we met in the school, especially the vice-chairman, who aggressively showed the right stuff of the Cultural Revolution—excepting, of course, the good old janitor.

Our experiences on this brief return to China after thirty years were not unusual for Chinese-speaking American travelers at that time. In themselves they had little connection to U.S. relations with China, which, under Secretary of State Henry Kissinger, featured the systematic search for overlapping national interests between the two countries, stressing opposition to the Soviet Union. What they did for me was to put a more familiar Chinese face to reports from the consulate general and USLO on reactions of the Chinese people to political events in China and our guesses on the stability of the Mao regime. The introspection resulting from this intense observation of China at first hand bolstered my already strong belief that, although lessening the long estrangement between the United States and the People's Republic of China was good for both countries, the United States should not put too high a premium on expanding the relationship merely for Cold War reasons. China seemed too backward, too self-centered, its people too embittered and tired, privately motivated differently from the slogans they professed, its leaders too uncertain for consistent policies or to be reliable partners.

Lucian Pye wrote a historically valuable account of a December 1972–January 1973 journey to China by a delegation from the National Committee on U.S.-China Relations.[1] Although always guided closely, the group was able to see much more of China, talk to more Chinese, and certainly wander about more than Shirley and I could two years later. Lucian rightly warns against claiming insights about a "real" China, as I have just done. It is better to call such impressions "tentative generalizations" as he did. But thoughts like these affected my approach to American policy on Taiwan as the United States and the PRC sparred over the only substantive issue between them to the late 1977 end of our tour in Hong Kong. They remained in my mind when Shirley and I returned to Taipei to help carry out a new United States relationship with both the PRC and Taiwan a year and a half later.

NOTES

1. Lucian W. Pye, *China Revisited* (Center for International Studies—MIT, 1973).

Chapter 19

Return to Taiwan

American missionaries of my father's generation often claimed that Chinese and Americans were much alike. To me, growing up in China, this platitude defied objective observation most of the time, although I enjoyed the thought of common threads running through the two cultures. When challenged, my father simply drew on behavior of both groups within their own societies. For him both peoples had a strong irreverence for pomposity, admired cheerfulness, expected friendliness, had a rough and ready attitude toward others, worked hard, and believed in moral foundations for society, to mention a few of his favorites. My mother didn't buy all of this—on either side—and she early made me realize that these were his own attributes, which he affectionately gave to the Chinese, assumed in Americans, and happily continued to find in individuals of both groups throughout his long life.

More skeptical about human nature than my father was, I nevertheless find his lifetime conclusions useful when I try to account for the reality that Americans and Chinese generally seem to like each other without either one understanding the other very well. During our posting to Taipei in 1979–81 as the first director of the American Institute in Taiwan (AIT), the sharp edges of mutual misunderstandings and irritations cut at the new "unofficial" relationship between the United States and Taiwan; yet I like to think that the reasonable success of the difficult diplomacy came from the cautious respect the Chinese and American operators of the new arrangements had for each other.

My father would have agreed because he linked respect and liking. He had been proud of all our Foreign Service assignments, giving to each a significance that was apparent only to him, but AIT particularly intrigued him because he could see that the relationship would have to be conducted pretty much the Chinese way, with great attention to appearances and symbolism. The last time I ever talked to him was when Shirley and

I were to depart on this final Foreign Service adventure. Sitting up in his rest home hospital bed, he advised at my request for help: "If you show respect for them as you learned as a boy, they will respect you; as always in China, *Yo banfa*" (there is a way/can be done).

"*Jin cheng suo zhi jin shi wei kai*"(Absolute sincerity can influence even metal and stone). "Absolute sincerity" is hard to come by in diplomacy, but I used this saying often in Taipei to show that we could solve all problems by the right attitudes toward each other. Everyone understood that it was the thought that counted.

On December 15, 1978, the State Department called a meeting in its largest auditorium, commanding the presence of most of its senior and middle-grade officers and briefly freeing hundreds from other work to attend. The purpose of this uncharacteristic touch of drama was to announce the final act in the long process of the normalization of relations with the People's Republic of China (PRC): the shifting of the American embassy from Taipei to Beijing and the abrupt slashing of diplomatic ties with the Republic of China (ROC), henceforth simply to be called "Taiwan" with whose "people" the American "people" would "unofficially" pursue "trade, cultural, and other relations." None of the briefers could say how this would be done, but in later statements the Carter administration promised that sales of "carefully selected defensive arms" to Taiwan could continue despite the termination of the twenty-five-year-old Mutual Defense Treaty with the ROC. Taiwan would not be "abandoned."

After the meeting I was asked by the Office of the People's Republic of China and Mongolian Affairs to change gears from writing my report on the inspection of our embassies in India, Sri Lanka, and Nepal and go south as part of a nationwide PR effort by the Carter administration to create optimism about the new formal Sino-American relationship. My audiences were the editors of the *Atlanta Constitution* and the members of a Rotary Club in Tampa, Florida. I was equipped with the texts of the joint announcement in Beijing and Washington and a dull canned speech that I didn't use. In short, I winged it, as I suspect other State Department speakers must have done elsewhere in the country.

Both groups seemed to share my own hopeful interpretations of the future but were politely unconvinced that Taiwan would not be harmed by the sudden symbolic downgrading it had been given by the United States. Their skepticism affected me. I flew back to Washington already sure in my mind that if the Taiwan parts of the equation were harshly psychologically damaging to the people on the island, our overall China policy would fail, because it would lack support from the American people—a formulation that I would use over and over again during the next few years. The full implications of this deceptively simple thought were unclear to me. I had no good picture then of the subtleties, the agreed hypocrisies, and the degree of un-American reticence that would henceforth be needed to keep Sino-American relations in balance. Nor did I anticipate the intensity of clashing political pressures by the American supporters of Taiwan against the then-ascendant enthusiasts in the State Department and elsewhere for the PRC as counterweight to the Soviet Union—or the widespread bureaucratic warfare and unusual working flexibility involved in conducting a new kind of relationship with Taiwan.

Obvious, to me anyway, some knowledge of China and the Chinese would be valuable, and I let it be known that I was interested in the job as head of whatever would replace the American embassy in Taipei. I was fortunate that both Roger Sullivan, deputy assistant secretary of state in the East Asian Bureau and in charge of organizing the unprecedented setup, and David Dean, who became the first Washington director of the AIT, the carefully concocted nongovernmental name for the new entity, had been my deputies in Hong Kong and intervened on my behalf—as did Averell Harriman.

In effect, Sullivan and Dean became my bosses and did all the hard preparations in Washington: breaking new ground every day, fending off criticism from pro-Taiwan elements in Congress that AIT was too hard on our former ally, goading an uncomprehending State Department bureaucracy into providing facilities and support for AIT in an "unofficial" way, even to finding, renting, and furnishing a modest office for it in Rosslyn, Virginia, across the Potomac from Georgetown and Foggy Bottom.

In Taipei, William Brown, retitled from chargé d'affaires at the American embassy to deputy director of AIT/Taipei, carried the psychologically painful load of finding new space for a nonembassy/embassy, reducing the American staff, reassuring the retiring Chinese employees about their pensions, and moving the State Department's (now AIT's) Chinese Language School from Taichung in the central part of Taiwan to Yang Ming Shan, the hills above Taipei.

Some of the decreed changes worked out for the better. We moved out of the dilapidated embassy chancery building and into the old Military Assistance Advisory Group compound in another part of town and slowly transformed it into a functional and self-contained office complex. We substituted Quarters "A," the American admiral's house up in Yang Ming Shan with its swimming pool, for the beat-up ambassador's residence in polluted downtown and then sold off both the chancery and the residence at an enormous profit for the United States government.

Jack Connolly, surely one of the Foreign Service's most skilled and experienced administrative officers of the time, was indispensable to

AIT's future in both Washington and Taipei. Jack, an old friend from our Kuala Lumpur days, traveled several times across the Pacific setting up new "unofficial" machinery and procedures and smoothing the way at both ends. I came along to take charge in Taipei after others had done most of the work.

One requirement for the job was that I had to retire from the Foreign Service. The idea was to present to the Chinese on both sides of the Taiwan Strait an individual to head the Taipei office of the AIT with no formal connection with the United States government. David Dean and Jack Connolly had also retired. This scrupulous attention to niceties was to impress the PRC with the sincerity of our aims and Taiwan with the firmness with which we would pursue the changes.

So, on April 19, 1979, I walked down the first floor, southeast corridor of the State Department to the Retirement Office, reflecting sadly on how easy it was. Once my rank and previous titles had appeared on the computer, I was unhurriedly guided through the forms, but there was no disguising the fact that the Retirement Division was primed to work efficiently to reduce numbers. Even though my retirement was rather a charade and I was really just moving to a new and exciting post, there was a heavy letdown: "You wanna retire?" "OK, please sit here and sign where indicated." "Checks in six weeks"—a feeling that thirty years had passed too quickly and more attention should be paid. Others less lucky than I might have been hurt.

Shirley and I, on the other hand, enjoyed two years of action-crammed real diplomacy from that moment.

THE TAIWAN RELATIONS ACT

President Carter had signed the Taiwan Relations Act (TRA) into law on April 10, 1979, a bipartisan example of the American urge to legalize the complicated. Despite regular, logical objections by the PRC to its very existence, in that the TRA openly defined how the United States would deal with territory that we had accepted—along with both sets of Chinese—as a part of China, and despite the limitations that this put on the State Department's negotiating flexibility with the PRC over Taiwan, the TRA has been a practical framework for U.S. relations with the island, and thus in many ways also with the PRC, ever since. It clearly defined the three key operational areas for AIT: the unofficial relationship, the sales of defensive arms, and human rights on Taiwan.

The State Department's original draft of this act had been developed with the understandable aim of allowing the widest scope to the department in shaping U.S. actions toward Taiwan, so that it could take into account the state of relations between the United States and the People's Republic of China. Although the draft had provided for the establishment of the AIT as an unofficial entity, it dealt imprecisely with the continuity of treaties and agreements between the Republic of China and the United States and with the legal status of future agreements between the United States and Taiwan. It also avoided explicit statements on the importance of Taiwan's security to American interests in East Asia and of formal arrangements for the sale of arms to our former longtime ally, both of these being especially provocative to the PRC. There was strong bipartisan concern expressed during the three months of hearings in the Senate over these aspects.[1]

The TRA took care of the worries of American business over the durability of long-standing agreements by legislating that all treaties and agreements with the ROC would remain in force and new ones negotiated by AIT would have full validity under United States law. More controversially in the end, and despite opposition by President Carter himself, China scholars such as A. Doak Barnett of the Johns Hopkins School of Advanced International Studies, and Senator Frank Church of Idaho, "Declarations of Policy" were included in the final version. These clearly stated that the decision to establish diplomatic relations with the PRC "rested upon the expectation that the future of Taiwan would be determined by peaceful means"; that nonpeaceful means, including efforts by boycotts or embargoes, would be a "threat to the peace and security of the Western Pacific area and of grave concern to the United States"; that the United States would provide Taiwan with "arms of a defensive character; to maintain the capacity of the United States to resist any resort to force or other forms of coercion that would jeopardize the security or the social or economic system of the people on Taiwan."[2] From the PRC point of view, the Taiwan Relations Act was a direct and unequivocal denial by the American government of the principles of China's right to "recover" Taiwan by any means it chose.

Nevertheless, as I saw it, the TRA provided the only politically practical means for carrying out the three general short-range objectives of AIT: (1) To avoid letting the unofficial arrangement with Taiwan obstruct the U.S./PRC relationship while making it possible, with care, to preserve the confidence of Taiwan's leadership in the future. I would return often to this political theme in policy proposals to the department. (2) To maintain, and where possible, to expand trade, cultural, and "other" relations with Taiwan in line with the TRA, adding a sub-objective of providing services and care needed by U.S. citizens, formerly performed by the embassy. (3) To keep an eye on developments in Taiwan, particularly those that might affect the continued stability and security of the island, including, especially, human rights. I think that after some start-up difficulties, AIT did rather well in all these areas.

However, the extreme political sensitivity of the subject, the strong feelings about China and Taiwan in America, and the certainty of leaks precluded any genuine policy discussion at this early stage about the future of Taiwan—at least with those of us in charge of carrying out relations with it. This was a serious, if unavoidable, defect in an otherwise sophisticated foreign policy endeavor. It led to incoherence in our treatment of Taiwan and failed to take into full account the importance to the United States of the de facto independent island.

OFFICIALLY UNOFFICIAL

The tactics and symbols of "unofficiality" dominated my briefings in the State Department, which feared that the de-recognized Republic of China would damage the enhanced relationship the United States hoped to have with the PRC, if the AIT and the multitude of its Washington superintendents were not alert. This suspicion of the ROC's motives, especially in the American embassy in Beijing and the East Asian Bureau, was, however, not unfounded. We knew from the start that we would encounter determined efforts by the ruling Kuomintang leadership—indeed everyone on Taiwan—to demonstrate to the world that AIT was "just an embassy by another name" and that its officers were conducting what amounted to official business between governments while pretending they didn't. Therefore, AIT's operating style would determine how well the United States could politely, but firmly, maintain the unofficial look of the working arrangements, thereby observing our agreements with the PRC.

An extensive exchange of messages between the rump embassy and the State Department's task force on Taiwan before we arrived in Taipei produced a set of ground rules preserving "unofficiality" but permitting all essential business. AIT's contacts with the ROC would be through Taiwan's counterpart organization, the Coordinating Council for North American Affairs (CCNAA), staffed by officers of the foreign ministry. The behavior code centered on the restrictions (with some exceptions for emergencies) against calling on Taiwan officials (other than those in CCNAA) in their offices and avoiding publicity on the few occasions when it might be necessary. Naturally, the more the ground rules on "office calls" irritated the Taiwan officials, the more they tried to test them; the more the rules were noticed, the fewer opportunities there were to change them.

Shirley's and my positions required constant alertness in sorting out the ordinary courtesies of Chinese social life from efforts to trick us from our unofficial roles. For example, at a concert we had to insist on being

moved from the diplomatic section, where we had been formally ushered, to the equally nice seats actually reserved for us a few rows over.
This was accomplished under bright television lights after we noticed
that suddenly we were surrounded by well-dressed foreigners speaking
Spanish, the Latin American last remnants of Taipei's once large diplomatic corps. For the first few weeks I had to discourage the politely prof-
fered title of "ambassador" fearing that it would find its way into print,
and finding myself stymied by the polished American-educated, "once
one, always one" kind of response. Americans living in Taiwan, presum-
ing that I resented my unofficial status as much as they did, would say,
"We know THEY (the American government in Washington) don't want
us to call you our ambassador but we will anyway!" These harmless
good-humored remarks almost died out over time but were occasionally
given added impetus by members of the legislative branch throughout
our tour. My journal entry for August 20, 1981, almost at the end of it
records:

> *A relatively quiet day until the end when we went to the airport to meet Codel
> Zablocki.*[3] *Lots of disorder with reporters and an unprepared press conference by
> Zablocki, plus the American and ROC flags on the cars* [an absolute no-no for any
> other kind of American official unofficial] *sort of dulled the theme. Nevertheless,
> Zablocki, who is suffering from a bad back, gave me a very friendly greeting, calling
> me "Chuck" and then with a big wink saying loudly, "Hello, Mr. Ambassador."
> Chinese standing near thought this was hilarious.*

We had to be careful always that the Taiwan press didn't invent political inferences from these little sallies and set off some reaction from Beijing. We in AIT followed the rules, and in the end all of us became the
accomplished "unofficial" professionals of the Foreign Service—unsung,
but proud. We understood that while it would be uncomfortable (or silly)
at times for us personally, once we established a working system it would
lose its exotic, contentious aspects and the relationship would be productive, as indeed it was from the beginning. After some initial sparring—and
no final decision—AIT and the foreign affairs establishment in Taipei went
back to the methods of an earlier diplomacy. We most often discussed
problems in restaurants, which was no hardship in superbly fed Taipei,
but the heavy emphasis on entertaining, even beyond the usual at a Chinese post, eventually proved quite wearing. Much depended on the Chinese we dealt with, a collection of strong and competent individuals. I
shall mention only two who had the most influence on our overall success.

Frederick F. Chien, the vice-minister of foreign affairs, was near the top
of the hierarchy on the Taiwan side and seemed to have the final say
under President Chiang Ching-kuo on Taiwan's United States policies. We

usually made contact with him through the CCNAA. The studiedly informal business meetings at restaurants, at our homes, at golf, and in the huge rooms of the Government Guest House across the wide street from the Foreign Ministry, were on matters that particularly interested Chiang.

In 1983, Fred became the CCNNA representative in Washington where for five years he was very effective in keeping Taiwan's interests up front in the United States. He became foreign minister in 1990 and has remained at the top of KMT officialdom.

Chien is a Yale PhD. (A Chinese once claimed that there were more American PhDs in the cabinet in Taipei at that time than in the one in Washington.) He came from an intellectual family. His father was head of the Academica Sinica, the most prestigious scholarly institution in China, and made sure that Fred was given a thorough Chinese education before sending him off to New Haven. He was thus a cultivated individual in two cultures. I gathered that Fred had been rather lonely, as so often happens with Chinese graduate students in America. He told me once that he had never been invited to an American home during his time at Yale, and I suppose that experience could have accounted for a certain prickliness some Americans found in him.

I grew to understand the tensions of Chien's job by watching him host dinners with prominent Americans. On the one hand, he was expected by his colleagues to show hurt pride over how the United States was treating Taiwan; on the other, he needed to underline Taiwan's friendship with the United States and its hopes for the future without attacking any American politicians—or AIT—personally. We saw him masterfully walk this thin line many times, introducing twenty or more guests by name, without notes, saying something kind and pertinent about each one. I remember Republican Senator Orrin Hatch of Utah being characterized as a friend and who promised in his return remarks to remain one; Bill Clinton, the young, enthusiastic Democratic governor of Arkansas in 1981, being encouraged to seek Taiwan investment in his state—and who in turn outlined several possibilities. Still, polished as he was, Fred's position made him a leader in what seemed to AIT as an incessant effort by the Taiwan authorities to reverse the form of the unofficial relationship while quietly accepting the substance.

Enforced unofficiality allowed Chien to express himself to me with a degree of irritation not common among official representatives of foreign countries. One night, after a furious argument at his house over a problem Northwest Airlines was having remitting its Taiwan earnings, he alleged several recent perfidious acts by the United States unconnected with the problem at hand. I slowed his tirade a bit by remarking, "It's a good thing I'm not an ambassador, Fred, because no *real* American ambassador would sit through this kind of thing." But that night, as always, we parted amicably to resume skirmishes and efficient collaboration on other matters in a few days. Northwest eventually won out, as Fred probably knew it would.

Admiral Ma Chi-chuang, the personal advisor to President Chiang Ching-kuo, was a thoughtful, reliable person who carefully conveyed messages directly to and from the president. Not being in the chain of command but known to be influential, he occupied a traditional place in Chinese politics as the "smoother-over" of rough spots in disputes. We were introduced early by Paul Tso, Ma's son-in-law and the deputy director in the Taipei CCNNA. A few months later we began to meet for lunch at our house in Yang Ming Shan.

These meetings were helpful to me because we were able to discuss privately, and without rancor, critical matters such as Taiwan's nuclear energy research, about which the United States had nonproliferation concerns, and the whole area of human rights where the KMT-controlled security services were displaying brutal behavior toward elements of the Taiwanese population. In these cases and others I could lay out the U.S. positions in terms I thought would be the most effective with President Chiang. It wasn't that Ma hadn't heard our views, because others in AIT were batting on these subjects all the time, but I could emphasize how seriously they were regarded by the American government without moralistic preaching. I never learned much about Admiral Ma's naval career. He was not a bluff seaman, but he earned my professional respect as a diplomat—and as a friend.

By 1979 golf rapidly supplanted anti-communism as a way of life for many of the older Kuomintang politicians and had already become a passion for the younger ones and the modern businessmen. Thus, several of us in AIT had genuine excuses for playing regularly. Fortunately for the United States, I am a good-natured bad golfer, easy to beat and to compare oneself to favorably. Even mediocre golf often enabled me to use one of the key techniques of diplomacy with Chinese—to find go-betweens to carry messages to the highest officials, whom we were precluded by the ground rules from calling on personally, including President Chiang Ching-kuo. This allowed us to raise matters without raising them; to receive answers without receiving them—indirect, subtle, courteous—as the unofficial game required.

Chinese are naturals for these old-fashioned diplomatic ways. Despite the pain it caused them, Taiwan officials usually played ball because they had to, even while they complained about AIT to their many friends in Congress. They distinguished between individuals in AIT with whom they had to deal and the State Department, which everyone knew gave us our orders. For example, General Wang Sheng, a hard core, doctrinaire

KMT political general, would tell American visitors, "We know Cross and Dean are our friends but they are under the control of the pro-Communist China elements in the State Department," stuff he knew would cause trouble in Washington, especially for those on the China desk, who would hear it from opponents of the expanding United States relationship with the PRC.

Occasionally, the strict application of the ground rules in Washington had rude consequences for prominent Chinese and affected personal relations critical to the success of "unofficiality." Dr. K. T. Li, a British-trained, internationally known scientist and cabinet officer in Taiwan, visited Washington in the late spring of 1979. Some of his professional contacts in the American government were forbidden by the State Department to receive him in their government offices as they had for decades. Their public complaints and the ensuing publicity in Taiwan made it impossible for AIT to deal productively with this sophisticated gentleman for months.

The PRC monitored both American political parties. On January 16, 1981, a few days before the inauguration of President Reagan, we reported that fifty-three "Taiwan personalities" had been invited by Republican groups to attend the festivities. The list included President Chiang Ching-kuo's son, a former ROC ambassador to the United States, the CCNAA Washington representative and members of the Legislative Yuan (Taiwan's parliament). The most controversial were Y. S. Tsiang, the secretary general of the Kuomintang and a former ROC foreign minister, and the governor of Taiwan, Lin Yang-kang, both of whom had been invited by Anna Chennault, the Chinese-born widow of famous World War II "Flying Tiger" General Claire Chennault and a prominent Republican. AIT/Taipei was ordered to disinvite Tsiang when the PRC ambassador in Washington let it be known that he would not attend any ceremony where Tsiang would appear.

The flap lasted through a weekend. High-priority messages ordered me to call on Admiral Ma and seek assurances that Tsiang would not attend the inaugural ceremony. The request was to be from "a very high official in the incoming administration," who I learned later was actually my friend John Holdridge, the newly appointed assistant secretary for East Asian affairs in the State Department. He was under heavy pressure from the PRC embassy and Secretary of State–designate Alexander Haig not to allow any Taiwan presence at the inauguration.[4]

It took two unsuccessful office calls at the department's instructions to convey this message. I was asked to go back again; but just before my meeting I read in the Taipei press that Tsiang had the flu. This meant that I could hold back on the exceedingly rude demarche I had been ordered to make, and I was able to assure Washington "mission accomplished."

Tsiang might really have been ill; but if he had been allowed to attend, he certainly would have recovered enough to show the world that Taiwan would be treated more respectfully by the Reagan administration than it had been under President Carter. The Taiwan Chinese did not blame the new administration for this face-losing blow, which they assigned to the State Department's "fear of Communist China." Unfortunately for them, they didn't learn from this sorry episode that they shouldn't rely on Republican big shots who couldn't deliver to upset a national policy, and they continued to try.

The most publicized complaints from the American side were about State Department bans on travel to Taiwan by federal government officials—not, of course, on Congress or its staffs, who poured into Taiwan, but even there expensive complications arose. The United States Air Force planes bearing groups of congressmen had to leave the airport immediately for Okinawa after depositing their passengers. Their crews were required to wear civilian clothes for their brief period on the ground in order to carry out literally our promise to the PRC that all American military forces had been withdrawn from the island. This attention to "unofficiality" actually produced extra television footage in Taiwan of the planes' arrivals, which focused on the "United States Air Force" proudly displayed on the sides of the aircraft and possibly negating the effort.

The root cause of these practical difficulties was that the American government was expected to act as if Taiwan were part of China—which we had agreed it was—but had to live with the reality that it was not part of the PRC. The latter was sensitively alert to references by any U.S. government source implying the existence of a functioning government on Taiwan. The PRC insisted that would indicate the United States was still sticking to a "One China; Two Governments" policy, meaning that, although the United States had agreed to recognize only one government for China of which Taiwan was a part, it was acting as if there were a separate, independent government on the island. The State Department had a hard time with this, because there *was* a fully functioning government on Taiwan with which the U.S. government had had myriad relationships, most of which would continue though in publicly altered form. And the English language can be stretched only so far.

My Japanese colleague—or counterpart, because colleague is very much a term of diplomacy as in the salutation *cher collègue*—found these American contortions of unofficiality amusing, although revealing of national character differences. I asked him how he avoided charges of "officiality," given that the Japanese Interchange Association officers made routine business calls on Taiwan officials and issued visas directly in Taipei (ours ostensibly came from the consulate general in Hong Kong). He was surprised at the question.

"Who says the Interchange Association is official?"

"Oh, maybe Taipei newspapermen, businessmen . . . ?"

"No, no, never journalists; we say we are not official; same with businessmen."

"Do they believe you?"

"Oh, yes, because we always declare we are unofficial! Easy for Japan; we say we are not official so we are not official—no question."—a slight smile.

ARMS SALES

The issue of arms sales to Taiwan, having been the chief obstacle to normalization with the PRC, figured heavily in the drafting of the TRA by Congress. It stayed the most persistently contentious issue between our two countries (and between AIT/Taipei and Washington in general) the entire time Shirley and I served in Taipei. I disagreed with the treatment of this issue by the Carter and Reagan administrations because they both worsened the situation by dithering in the face of the PRC's public opposition to the sale of an advanced fighter aircraft to Taiwan.

Arms sales exemplify the permanent political strains on each of the three parties in the triangle. For the Chinese in Beijing, arms sales have been a recurring symbolic reminder that the United States stands against their ruling Taiwan. For the Chinese in Taipei, the arms have been symbols of moral support, and their value has been judged not by the qualities and quantities of the weapons, but by the United States' responses to PRC opposition to specific sales. To the United States, providing arms to Taiwan has been symbolic of our fiat that the Chinese must settle Taiwan's status peacefully.

Taiwan's dogged determination to acquire a replacement fighter for their nearly out-of-date Northrup F-5 Es was based on these symbolisms more than on the easily demonstrated "need" for a newer plane. The sale of an advanced defensive aircraft, the most visible, expensive, and realistically available long-term weapon, would constitute unquestionable evidence of U.S. support of Taiwan's defense through the mid-1990s. But PRC leaders could not easily accept such a visible arms sale and its long-run implications without raising doubts in Chinese and American minds about their stated priority national objective of "recovering" Taiwan. The symbolism was so obvious to all Chinese that the issue of advanced aircraft for Taiwan remained up front in U.S.-PRC-Taiwan triangular relations throughout the Carter, Reagan, and Bush administrations. During those years PRC officials often were able to make the whole U.S.-PRC relationship look dependent on American arms sales decisions, and

American policymakers felt they were forced to adjust to PRC complaints. The more the PRC fussed, the more Taiwan and its American supporters pressed for reassurances that Taiwan's interests were not being
sacrificed, the more difficulty for U.S. administrations in meeting Beijing's demands. The situation has changed, but it is still instructive of the
hazards of entering a long-running Chinese game with Chinese about
China without firm plans of your own on how to face the certain political and public relations counterpressures from both Chinese sides.

However, President Carter was correct in discouraging Taiwan from
hoping that his administration would abandon the Nixon-Ford policy of
not selling Taiwan what were then front-line aircraft such as the F-16,
which would be too upsetting to the PRC. Instead, he came out with a
radical change in fighter export policy whereby aircraft companies could
develop, competitively and on their own, lower-capability military jets
for sale to countries that could not afford—or, like Taiwan—were being
denied the more advanced product. This came to be called the FX
scheme, and although it had worldwide implications, the Chinese in
Taipei and the aircraft companies believed that the FX program had special applicability to Taiwan. Consequently, from January 1980 when the
scheme was announced until January 1982, when the Reagan administration denied the FX to Taiwan, there was constant publicity, vigorous
lobbying in Washington by Taiwan supporters and the fiercely battling
manufacturers' agents; and, naturally, ever closer attention by the PRC.
The FX scheme also had the unintended result of preventing Northrup
from passing off its still-to-be-built F-5G as a mere upgrading of its F-5E
already in Taiwan's inventory and, therefore, not a new class of plane.

Once the FX was put forth as a possibility for Taiwan the Carter administration was powerless to stop publicity about it. Some kind of PRC reaction was inevitable. In the end, the Carter administration was excused
from making a decision one way or another on the FX for Taiwan by the
Reagan victory in November 1980.

Taiwan's leaders were elated at Reagan's election. Here, finally, they
saw a Republican of the old breed—not like Nixon and Ford, who had
changed Taiwan's place in the world—a hard-liner against communism
everywhere, like the Kuomintang itself. Taipei was inundated by American visitors purporting to represent a whole new U.S. approach to the
island. To be fair, no one I talked to (Richard "Dixie" Walker, later ambassador to Korea and friend from Yale days, Jim Lilley, whose older brothers had been my friends in summers at Beidaihe, or Edward Luttwak, a
sharp, conservative mind on defense matters) held that Reagan would
reverse overall China policy. As far as I could tell, their still not formulated slant was that the new administration would be kinder and gentler
to Taiwan, mostly in the treatment of Taiwan's officials and in arms sales.

These expressions of warmth were good for Kuomintang morale, and I thought at first they would ease AIT's burdens in Taipei. However, because the Reagan administration showed no signs that it had really thought about its China policy, I soon began to fear a Taiwan overreaction, leading to a letdown.

I was spurred to warning Washington by observing the gleeful response by Taiwan officials to another American visitor. Ray Cline, a former CIA station chief in Taipei and a skilled operator close to President Chiang, seemed to be speaking for the new administration, promising big changes in the way the United States would be conducting business with Taiwan. In Washington, Republicans claiming to be in the know hinted publicly that Taiwan might be allowed to buy the F-16. Unless carefully handled and warned, the Taiwan leadership, which had been cautious on my advice during the transition period, might go beyond requesting the dropping of minor irritants in its initial approaches to the Reagan administration. It could agitate for the kind of gesture that could only cause the PRC to question the reliability of U.S. undertakings in the joint normalization communiqué, thus throwing off our relationships with both Chinese parties. I settled on two lines of action for AIT in Taipei.

First I talked to Fred Chien and Admiral Ma Chi-Chuang about the dangers of moving too fast. I said, "Reagan has shown publicly and privately that he is well disposed towards you; he will do for you what he is going to do; what that will turn out to be I don't know; but he will not be able to do much if Taiwan talks in advance about possible favorable moves he might make." Both of these eminently intelligent officials had already seen the common sense of this advice and later—after obviously checking—intimated that President Chiang Ching-kuo agreed.

More difficult would be my second approach—to get across to the incoming administration that the United States was severely restricted in flexibility by its agreements with the PRC, the TRA, and the psychological attitudes of Taiwan's leaders.

Actually, I had already made these points earlier. Notes in my journal say that in the summer of 1980—a year after we had arrived in Taipei—I sent off a long think-piece that I had prepared with Mark Pratt, the indefatigable head of our small political reporting section (called for purposes of unofficiality the General Affairs Section), entitled enigmatically, "The Iron Framework."

The situation has changed since our time there, but I believe that the "Iron Framework" still applies in large part. I said in that 1980 message (according to my notes) that Taiwan would not peacefully join the Chinese Mainland in a "One-China" ruled by the communists nor, in the short run, respond positively to PRC offers to "negotiate"; that the United States did not have the capability to intervene in this Chinese affair and, it was hoped, would not be misguided enough to try—a real fear on my part because of the activist attitudes of those who found it tough to live with constant PRC complaining or who had genuine doubts about Beijing's patience. Although the status quo was advantageous to the United States, our analysis continued, we could not indicate this formally or even stress this fact in publications, congressional testimony, and the like without risking our developing relationship with the PRC. Finally, we could not upgrade the form and style of the United States-Taiwan relationship to nearly the level Taiwan would like (and American supporters of Taiwan had led them to hope) without antagonizing the PRC and forcing the United States into some very difficult either/or choices on substance, particularly on arms sales.

I did, however, suggest to the department, very early in the Reagan administration, that several minor changes in the form of the United States-Taiwan relationship were possible within the "Iron Framework"and recommended that sooner or later Taiwan be allowed to purchase the F-X. My immediate purpose was to blunt the inevitable drive by Taiwan on arms in general and the F-X in particular—perhaps before the administration had even faced these issues. Such an effort would certainly draw fire from the PRC. The department was not interested in such ideas at that early time, and I was asked to desist.

In May 1981 I flew to Washington for consultations at my request. My purpose in making the long trip was to urge Secretary of State Alexander Haig to disconnect the issue of the F-X for Taiwan from any U.S. arms sales gestures to the PRC, which were expected to be the chief items of business in his forthcoming visit to China.

Nothing was accomplished. I did not see Haig, and I certainly heard nothing about what was going to be done or said in Beijing. It became quite clear from several long talks with Assistant Secretary John Holdridge that what he called the "Soviet imperative" dominated the thinking at the State Department and that nothing was going to be allowed to interfere with the creation of ever stronger U.S. ties with the PRC—or the appearance of that to the Soviet Union— particularly any suggestion traceable to the administration that Taiwan would eventually get the F-X. Jim Lilley, then at the NSC, had basically the same negative approach (Lilley later succeeded me in Taipei and went on to become the American ambassador to South Korea and to the PRC). John Holdridge's instructions were to continue doing what we had been doing all along, counseling patience and quiet to Taiwan without offering it any incentives to do so. I returned to Taipei, more worried and less wise than when I left.

However, a month later a breakthrough came. Shirley and I spent the weekend of July 18–19, 1981, as guests of the Fred Chien and James Soong families. (Soong was the government spokesman at that time.) We played golf at a nine-hole course I had never heard of and then went to Paisawan (White Sands Bay) Country Club, a modern place with motel-type rooms, squash court, indoor tennis courts, a huge swimming pool, several restaurants, library, and game rooms.

Naturally, the purpose of the gathering was business. Both Chien and Soong had been given permission by President Chiang to miss a special reception in Taipei because Chiang wanted to get across to me certain new aspects of Taiwan's approach to the Reagan administration.

Its main point was that President Chiang Ching-kuo's speech of July 15 to the Kuomintang Standing Committee (KMT's politburo) was, as AIT had immediately reported, a most authoritative and important policy statement[5]—important because it emphasized that the United States government faced many problems and that Taiwan was certainly not one of them. Chiang had said that Taiwan must therefore be patient and move ahead "little by little, with maximum patience and total perseverance."

In response to my direct question, Chien said that this was a signal that Taiwan was not concerned over the lack of forward movement by the Reagan administration on things Chiang thought were important. They were responding to my advice not to get publicly nervous or to push such matters as the F-X in public lest this lead to more difficulties for Reagan. Chiang had pointed out in his speech that Reagan, as a confirmed anticommunist, would do what he could for them anyway.

I took with a grain of salt Chien's claim that the speech itself was the result of a long debate within the KMT hierarchy because there were many who thought that by acting patiently Taiwan would lose out. Fred had been making the same argument to me weekly for months, especially when he could quote reports from CCNAA—and the aircraft companies—in Washington that the PRC embassy was actively lobbying against Taiwan's receiving the F-X. However, we did know that Chiang had always held to the line that with patience, the Americans would come around, but he had not enforced it in public. He now feared an appearance of confrontation or disagreement between President Reagan and himself and he wished to avoid that.

Elated, I went to the office the next morning, passing the good news of a big mission accomplished only to the deputy Stan Brooks, political chief Mark Pratt, and Larry Ropka, who was in charge of military sales. I told these solid officers that we had successfully carried out our instructions and that Taiwan at the highest level had agreed that it would not, for awhile anyway, push openly for a decision on the F-X. Arms sales to Taiwan would not have to be publicly disputed with the PRC unless Washington brought it about by indicating that the issue of the F-X was closed against Taiwan. There might even be care in raising questions of form.

Therefore, I felt that we in AIT had made a substantial contribution to overall China policy and that I could leave Taipei on an upbeat, which we did a couple of months later.

President Chiang would not have taken the cautious line the Reagan administration wanted if he had not been reassured by the president himself that Taiwan would get some sort of advanced aircraft "in terms concrete enough to be acceptable," as Fred Chien said to me in the private dining room at Paisawan. Fred implied that Chiang expected the "advanced aircraft" to be the F-X at least. What the American president actually said may never be known. Reagan was often imprecise. The message was not conveyed through American channels but most probably through Singapore's Prime Minister Lee Kuan Yew, who had maintained unpublicized relations with President Chiang on Taiwan and continued those he had formed with Governor Reagan of California during the latter's 1971 visit to us in Singapore.

My feeling of a successful mission dissipated later as I watched from outside. The Reagan administration ultimately responded to public PRC pressure. In January 1982, six months after my weekend with Fred Chien and after we had left Taipei, the State Department denied the F-X to Taiwan. When the PRC, playing immediately on its success with the F-X, adopted a hard line linking all arms sales to the future of the entire U.S.-PRC relationship, the United States agreed to the August 1982 Taiwan Communiqué, in which the United States promised not to increase qualitatively or quantitatively the arms it would sell Taiwan. The Taiwan Communiqué was later skipped by the United States when President Bush, in a search for Texas votes during the campaign of 1992, allowed the sale of the F-16 to Taiwan. However, it lies there to be brought up by the PRC, whenever it chooses, ever since.

The American insistence on a "peaceful settlement between the Chinese themselves" is the key symbolism for all three sides to the triangle. The Chinese Communist leaders know that the weapons the United States and others provide to Taiwan are not the real reasons the island has not joined up with the mainland. Even under the earlier authoritative rule of the Kuomintang, which enforced an absurdly unrealistic "One China" policy of its own based on overcoming the communists, the young, modern-minded Chinese on Taiwan were looking for a wider role for themselves and their island than being merely another province of China—although they had to pay lip service to that concept. The paradox has always been that the only sure way to peaceful unification would be through a deal between two unrepresentative regimes. Now, as democracy expands on Taiwan and contempt (based on knowledge rather than propaganda) grows for politics as practiced on the mainland, there is even some sentiment, especially in the largely Taiwanese opposition

Democratic Progressive Party, pulling toward a formal declaration of independence. It is hard to see the Beijing government actually ruling Taiwan short of invading it.

At the same time, Taiwan does not suffer actual hardships from its anomalous situation except for memberships in some international organizations and the personal inconveniences to its citizens from a not always accepted passport when traveling. The Chinese of Taiwan have succeeded through their own skills and efforts in establishing Taiwan as a world pilot in unofficial diplomacy and as a major economic power— as we in AIT had assured them they would from the start. They are in an excellent bargaining position with the PRC to continue working out peaceful arrangements. These could result, over time, in a more widely recognized—and PRC-accepted—international role for Taiwan while reinforcing Taiwan's influence on the mainland itself, perhaps as a partner in a Chinese federation. Spectacular changes in China's economy and society have made anything possible. Like everything else concerning the island, Taiwan's pains are in appearances—honest success unrewarded.

The majority of Taiwan's electorate seems to understand that a drastic change in the accepted "One China" myth by a formal declaration of independence would threaten Taiwan's security. It would set off the PRC, and so needlessly test the American "peaceful settlement" informal guarantees. It will be the task of quiet, unflustered American diplomacy to reinforce these realities on Taiwan.

The Taiwan situation has always looked reasonable for United States interests and not damaging to either Chinese party. Neither our adherence to the One China principle, which we have consistently reaffirmed whenever challenged, nor the bureaucratic complications of the unofficial relationship with Taipei have been burdensome to us. Despite arguments with Beijing, we have sold only defensive armaments to Taipei, fully in keeping with a peaceful Strait of Taiwan. Meanwhile, for both sets of Chinese, trade and investment with us and with each other have expanded beyond our wildest guesses in 1981, when Shirley and I left Taiwan.

American difficulties in maintaining this useful status quo lie in the habits of our politicians. Congress has a sporadic tendency to enter the Taiwan scene by trying to push the pace of changes in the *forms* of the unofficial relationship. Both Republican and Democratic administrations have failed to pay enough attention to attitudes on Taiwan—or faced them only in relation to the PRC—until it is too late and Taiwan's American supporters have created an issue, which then causes the ever-nervous PRC to take a public stand. This happened, for example, over the F-X in 1981–82, when his own administration reversed President Reagan's assurances to President Chiang Ching-kuo that Taiwan would get a follow-on fighter. It happened again over the unofficial visit of Taiwan President

Lee Teng-hui to a Cornell University reunion in 1995, when the Clinton administration first turned the visit down in response to advance complaints by the PRC and signs from Taipei that the visit would be portrayed there as evidence of a significant relaxation of the ground rules, and then under congressional pressure was forced to grant it. The United States did not earn useful credit from either Chinese party in either case. Both mistakes were due to lack of forethought and the mental discipline needed for our leaders to resist promising something until they are sure of delivering. They won't be able to do that until the United States fits an actually independent—if not internationally recognized—Taiwan into a coherent, overall China policy sustainable against political influence in the United States by all Chinese parties. It is a matter of making up our collective minds, and that calls for national self-control until we do.

CHANGES

I mention last the happiest and most significant developments on Taiwan itself since 1979. These fit my long view of China and lie in human rights and the evolution toward democracy. Although the results were not readily apparent when we left Taiwan in 1981, AIT's efforts in both these areas occupied more of its time during those first years than anything else. The entire staff was involved in the tasks of comprehensive reporting on the arrests and trials of dissident Taiwanese, assisting American citizens who were in serious trouble with the Kuomintang authorities for relationships with oppositionists, flagging false statements by the security services to the American press, meeting publicly with non-Kuomintang politicians and journalists to display our interest in their futures. We arranged for prominent Americans such as Senator and Mrs. John Glenn to meet the families of jailed Presbyterians at our house. (The Glenns' sincere sympathy was noted and, I believe, contributed shortly after to an easing of the treatment of this particularly persecuted group.) All this pressure on the Kuomintang was conducted by the original AIT officers and our successors steadily, quietly, and without threats.

Things changed slowly and certainly not just because of American urging. Taiwan's emerging democracy comes from the Chinese living there. However, Taiwan's solid modern economy is due in part to enlightened American assistance and the inspired land-reform programs already underway in the dark days of 1949, when Shirley and I served there the first time, and major American investment and strong trade ties since then. Taiwan's bright and questing young people have become more conscious of the rest of the world through American cultural exchange programs. Its technocratic leadership have mostly received their advanced education at American institutions. Above all, though, it was the confidence, sustained by United States diplomacy and a vigorous American presence in many forms, that Taiwan was not going to be forced to accept dictation from the PRC after 1979 that convinced the Kuomintang to follow a more democratic path.

Our service ended, as it had begun, in Taipei. It was there that we received a full-circle lesson in the vital connection between Asian leaders' confidence in the future to the progress of their countries. I see the greatest American achievements in East Asia since World War II in terms of Asian morale. Japan, South Korea, Taiwan, the postwar independent Philippines, Indonesia, Malaysia, Singapore, a once-threatened Thailand, and perhaps even the fought-over Indo-China countries in time, all owe America more than they will ever acknowledge for creating an optimistic and safer international atmosphere for their development—and the freedom to make their own mistakes. I'm not stretching out that already wide generalization too far when I say that the inspiration for our national approach goes back to the early decades of the century—to Americans like my parents—and to the continuous American presence in its multitude of forms ever since.

I am a charter member of the American presence by birth, and so my personal China is the end of this long story.

From my earliest memories as a Peking boy—cherished and protected by Wang Nai Nai, Ma Erh, Xu Shi-fu, Pastor Zhang, the voluble front gateman, the quiet back-gateman and his children (my Chinese playmates), my mother's persistent piano lovers, my Aunt Laura's eager English students inspired to learn English to join their country to the modern world—I was much a part of China and not conscious of it.

Through my emotional high-school years—the Japanese cruelties, my lively Chinese-American girlfriend at the rival Peking American School, the solemn young men standing nervously in the hallway of our Tongzhou house saying good-bye to my mother before slipping into the night on their dangerous way to West (Free) China—I was a passionate partisan of China but not a participant.

Later, inspired that my country was also saving China, I fought in the same Pacific War, comforted in my conscience that killing Japanese would serve that end. When the train slid slowly into the Peking station beside the city walls in the early fall of 1945, I experienced a silent moment of supreme pride that it was the American Marines who were taking the Japanese out of China.

I have watched China more dispassionately in the over fifty years since, while her rulers led her on strenuous paths, encouraging then dashing, re-igniting and then dampening the hopes of the Chinese people in cycles common to Chinese history. I have adjusted without rancor to the on-again, off-again official enmity of the PRC toward the United States and professionally, without emotion, to my country's duplicating moods of hostility and friendship to China. And I've accepted as natural the superior achievements of Chinese people in Singapore, Hong Kong, Taiwan—and on the mainland itself.

In the American Board Compound in Tongzhou on July 3, 1940, the day before I was to leave China forever really, I had finished all my packing, closely supervised by my mother. Nobody else my age remained on the compound; all had gone to Beidaihe. Melancholy by myself, I climbed up to the peaked roof of the school building by secret ways I had learned seven years earlier. There I sat for an hour, my back against a chimney.

To my left through the trees were the gray two-story school buildings and high towers of the Luhe Boys School, the pond for skating and hockey already green with summer slime, the hill that the Japanese had attacked three summers before, and, farther on, a convoy of Japanese Army trucks between the rows of willows on the Tianjin Road, towing dust behind them.

To my right was the brown, tight little village of Fuxingzhuang, with the mission's Rural Reconstruction office and the stable for our ponies in the middle; and five or six miles beyond it across the summer green plains, stood the tall skeletons of the German-built radio towers, climbed by Lucian and other brave North China American School girls and boys, but not by me—a shame three years old by then.

Directly in front was the old Sunken Road, worn down to a ravine by centuries of donkey carts, which ran between the American School and Luhe and from the village to the South Gate of Tongzhou just beyond the mission hospital. That day two bicycles approached each other in the unhurried way of those who ride for transportation and not for exercise; close, the riders dismounted without really stopping, bowed, and after a couple of steps pedaled easily away. The American School was silent, but around me rose the sounds of China outdoors: dogs yelping in the village, noisy cry-baby little children running in a flock tended by a shrill big sister, roosters boasting loudly, the back-crawling squeaking of a water wheelbarrow, and behind me in Tongzhou city, the swelling and falling of the flute-like pigeon whistles of my childhood.

I stared at my sneakers pressed on the slate roof, "How can I give it up?" I thought. All is changed. But probably, in some ways, I never have—though still, always, a foreigner.

NOTES

1. *TAIWAN: Hearings before the Committee on Foreign Relations* (Washington, D.C.: Government Printing Office, 1979).

2. *Taiwan Relations Act*, Public Law 96-8, 96th Cong. (10 April 1979), Sec 2(b), 6.

3. The late Clement Zablocki, Democratic chairman of the House Foreign Affairs Committee, who was leading another congressional delegation (CODEL in bureaucratese) to "inspect" the workings of the Taiwan Relations Act.

4. John H. Holdridge, *Crossing the Divide* (Lanham, Md.: Rowman and Littlefield, 1997), 199–200.

5. We could hardly have missed the significance of the unusual publicity for a normally routine speech, and several of us were telephoned the next morning to draw our attention to it. There were offers to send us a "good translation" if we needed one, even bald suggestions that it was worth reporting to Washington.

Index

Frankland, Mark, 145
French Annamites, 154
Fuerwerker, Albert, 216
FX scheme, 264–68

Galbraith, Francis X., 88, 93, 223
Galbraith, Martha, 91
Gang of Four, 243
Geneva Conference on Laos
    1961–1962, 129–33
George, Scott, 81
Gilman, First Lieutenant Michael, 188
Glenn, John, 270
Goh Keng Swee, Dr., 227
Golden Fleece, 167–68
golf, 227–28
Goodpastor, General Andrew, 194
Goulding, Philip, 191
Graham, Billy, 240
Great Leap Forward, 15, 247
Great Proletarian Cultural Revolution,
    247
Green's Farm, 44–45, 71p
Guangdong Province, 241
Guthrie, John, 140

Hackett, Roger, 42
Haig, Alexander M., 261–66
Han Hsu, 132–33
Hanna, Willard, 92–93
Hanoi Hilton, 183
Harbin, China, 2
Harriman, W. Averell, 133–34, 137–42;
    drafting for, 140–42; Fourteen
    Nations Conference on Neutrality
    of Laos, 131; initial meeting,
    133–34; as negotiator, 137–40;
    President Kennedy and Laos,
    134–37; Vietnam, 200
Harris, Richard, 108
Hatch, Senator Orrin, 259
Heidemann, John, 108
Hepburn, Rolfe, 48
Hindmarsh, Commander, 42
Hiroshima, Japan, 60

Ho Chi Minh, 148, 155
Hodge, Captain William, 47
Hoi Chanh, 193
Holbrooke, Richard, 160
Holdridge, John, 108, 261, 266
Honey, Patrick, 145
Hong Kong, 80, 97–105, 235–43
Horse Marines, 41
House of Commons, 144–46
Hummel, Arthur, 107
Hu Shih, 6

I Corps, 162, 186
Indonesian Women's Association, 91
International Control Commission
    (ICC), 130, 138–39
Iwo Jima, 46, 54–58, 66–70, 73p

Jakarta, Indonesia, 88–94
Japanese Defense Agency, 66
Japanese Occupation of Tongzhou,
    24
Japanese surrender, 59
Jardine Matheson, 80
Jenner, Senator William, 110
Johnson, President Lyndon B., 145,
    156, 176, 184, 200
Johnson, U. Alexis, 135
Joint Intelligence Center Pacific Ocean
    Area (JICPOA), 59
Jones, Louis R., 47, 50, 62, 74

Kennedy, President John F., 112,
    128–29, 134–36, 154, 173
Kennedy, Senator Edward, 176
Khesanh, Vietnam, 183–84, 213
Khrushchev, Nikita, 129
Kissinger, Henry, 226, 232
Kit Carson Scouts, 193
Komer, Robert, 158, 160
Korean War, 98
Koren, Henry L. T. "Barney," 158–62,
    179, 183
Koster, Major General Samuel, 212
Kuala Lampur, Malasia, 115–26

About the Author

Charles T. Cross was born in Beijing, experienced the Japanese occupation of North China in the late 1930s, and served in the Marines during World War II. During his thirty-two-year diplomatic career, he was stationed in posts throughout the world, including Indonesia, Malaysia, Egypt, Cyprus, London, and Vietnam (1967–1969), where he was the chief of pacification efforts in I Corps. He was also ambassador to Singapore (1969–1972), consul general in Hong Kong (1974–1977), and the first director of the American Institute in Taiwan (1979–1981). After his retirement in 1981, Cross was a distinguished lecturer in international studies and history at the University of Washington, a member of the faculty of the Semester at Sea Program of the University of Pittsburgh, and a Benedict Distinguished Professor at Carleton College. He continues to serve on foundation boards connected with Chinese universities and Asian language studies. He lives in Seattle with his wife, Shirley.